WebPlus X2 User Guide

How to Contact Us

Our main office
(UK, Europe):

The Software Centre
PO Box 2000, Nottingham, NG11 7GW, UK

Main: (0115) 914 2000

Registration (UK only): (0800) 376 1989

Sales (UK only): (0800) 376 7070

Customer Service/
Technical Support: http://www.serif.com/support

General Fax: (0115) 914 2020

North American office
(USA, Canada):

The Software Center
13 Columbia Drive, Suite 5, Amherst NH 03031, USA

Main: (603) 889-8650

Registration: (800) 794-6876

Sales: (800) 55-SERIF or 557-3743

Customer Service/
Technical Support: http://www.serif.com/support

General Fax: (603) 889-1127

Online

Visit us on the Web at: http://www.serif.com/

International

Please contact your local distributor/dealer. For further details please contact us at one of our phone numbers above.

Contents

5. Formatting Characters and Paragraphs 113

6. Working with Tables 125

12. Adding Dynamic Content 245

Contents

Welcome to
WebPlus X2!

Welcome to WebPlus X2 from **Serif**— still the easiest way ever to get your business, organization, or household on the Web!

If you've used WebPlus in the past, you'll know that WebPlus offers a powerful and easy way to design and publish your Web site from scratch or by using design templates. Equipped with an operational Internet Service Provider (ISP) account and WebPlus X2, you can get online in the least time and at a low cost— no experience required.

WebPlus X2 builds upon the award winning history of previous versions to bring a vast range of features that help you make exceptional Web sites quickly and easily.

Ease of Use

- Context sensitive toolbars ensure the most common options always fall easily to hand. The flexible layout of the studio tabs allows you to create custom workspaces to ensure that you can work most efficiently. Check out some of the pre-defined workspace profiles available from the Startup Wizard for some ideas.

Text Support

- Have complete control over your text with WebPlus's DTP style text control. HTML text frames allow you to remain HTML compliant whereas Artistic Text can be used to give your web sites high impact. All with editing capabilities compatible with top of the range word processors!

Graphic Flair

- Give your Web site graphics a whole new dimension with the easy to use Instant 3D tool great for creating 3D logos, banners and buttons. Easily add stunning lighting effects, increase the depth of your objects creating outstanding 3D graphics to make your Web site stand out from the crowd. Enhance your text, photos, graphics and shapes with striking Filter Effects, including bevels, embossing, shadows and glows.

WebPlus makes it easy to apply multiple effects in one go and adjust the settings to get the exact look you require. Each object remains editable once Filter Effects have been applied and they're easy to turn off for complete flexibility. There's no need to use a separate design program with all these graphical effects and enhancements quickly to hand in WebPlus.

Image Control

- Correct and enhance your images directly in WebPlus with the simple to use Image Adjustments dialog, which allows you to combine multiple adjustments and preview changes as they're made. You can even remove the dreaded red eye effect on subjects in your photos with a single click of the Red Eye tool. Easily make corrective adjustments with tools such as Brightness & Contrast, Dust & Scratch Remover, Channel Mixer and Hue/Saturation/Lightness controls, or enhance images with WebPlus' range of stunning Effects including Diffuse Glow, Motion Blur and Add Noise. Quickly transform your photos into professional-looking images with powerful and easy-to-use image adjustments.

Easy Navigation

- Choose from the full selection of WebPlus' Themed Graphics, which offer pre-designed sets of buttons, headers, banners, bullets and navigation bars that you can easily add, to your Web sites with just a single mouse click. With a fantastic selection of different styles to choose from, you'll find one to suit your needs. WebPlus's Themed Graphics will also save you design time and help you achieve a consistent and cohesive look throughout your Web site. The hierarchical page site structure tab makes it easy to see the overall layout of your Web site plus complete control over standard hyperlinks, anchors and hotspots makes for a comprehensive web editing package that can grow with your needs.

What's New in WebPlus X2...

- **Database Merge** (see p. 287)
  Present database content on your Web page from Serif databases (.SDB), Microsoft Access (.MDB), dBASE, ODBC server data, and other well known database formats, as well as Microsoft Excel, HTML, and delimited text files. Product lists, mailing lists, inventories, in fact any database information can be served to your web audience. Place text or pictures into **repeating areas**, repeating **Buy Now** or **Add to Shopping Cart e-commerce forms**, or even **HTML fragments**. Create your own **photo database** (with EXIF fields) for subsequent merging.

- **Site Tools** (see p. 68)
  Manage all your **Page/Master Page Properties**, **resources**, **fonts**, **text**, **hyperlinks**, and **anchors**—all from within WebPlus's **Site Manager**. Powerfully manage Web pages individually, by selection, or apply to all pages. The new Resource Manager shows images, media, links, HTML code resources, and so much more... even resample or link/embed images. Site Checker detects Site Navigation, Text Formatting, and Form/e-commerce problems and carries out automatic fixes where possible.

- **New Smart Objects** (see p. 306)
  Serif Web Resources, Serif's Smart Object hosting service, now offers a series of exciting new Smart objects:

  - **Forum**—Stimulates lively thread-based discussions in a full-sized window. Create multiple forums and manage independently (moderate discussions and set up user login access).

  - **Access Control**—offers page or site access control by management of simple **user lists** or "zonal" **user groups** (e.g., Personnel). Web visitors can self-register via a site's user login (with optional email activation).

  - **Analytics**—collects and presents Web page statistics related to site visits, browser details, referrers, and search terms.

- **News**—For simple news announcements such as Web site updates or next club meeting dates.

  All Smart objects now support **multiple languages**!

  For a Blog Smart Object, now add personal **profiles**, **social bookmarking links** and use **trackbacks** for inter-blog cross-referencing. Change blog appearance with different pre-defined **Visual Styles** (or use your own!) Use **Editor groups** for multi-author article publishing. Last but not least... users now edit articles in RTF!

- **Picture power with Media Bar and Photo Gallery!** (p. 185 and p. 205)
  No more repetitive photo importing! Keep photo content to hand in the new **Media Bar**—drag and drop from the Media Bar onto pictures to replace! Search for pictures by their meta data. Control picture sizing and alignment within its frame. Import multiple images and paste one by one!
  Wow your friends, family and colleagues with stunning **Flash-based photo galleries**. Various gallery styles offer photo navigation by selection from thumbnails, thumbnail rollovers, photo grid or photo stack. Use the Autoplay feature for looping photo slideshows.

- **Multipage DesignTemplates** (see p. 21)
  Make "tailored" Web sites of a chosen scheme and theme in an instant—choose design templates from Business, E-Commerce, Personal, Entertainment, Email, and Interests categories. Simply cherry pick template pages with the option of adding additional pages from the same or different template at a later date.

- **Search Engine Optimization** (see p. 81)
  Control how search engines index your Web site! Include or exclude pages from indexing by using search engine sitemap or robot files—protect confidentiality while offering potential Web visitors accurate search results from your site.

- **Site Search Tool** (see p. 87)
  Perform **text searches** throughout the entire Web site with the powerful **Site Search Tool**.

- **Navbar extras** (see p. 238)
  WebPlus now supports Breadcrumb and Anchor **navbars**—great for e-commerce database merging. A new Combo theme set offers drop-down "combo box" page navigation. Enable anchors in any navbar type.

- **Navigation Site Maps**
  Add a **navigation site map** to visualize the layout of your Web site.

- **Active Document Frames** (see p. 41)
  Hyperlinks can open a page in a document frame on another page. Set an **Absolute URL** for more accurate inter-frame navigation.

- **YouTube® Videos** (see p. 202)
  Pick your favourite YouTube® videos and include them on your Web page!

- **Podcasts** (see p. 270)
  Create your own **podcast** feeds and broadcast your own audio and video episodes frequently and easily. Web visitors can subscribe with all the most popular Web browsers and via on-click subscription to Google Reader®, My Yahoo!®, and Apple iTunes®.

- **Popup Rollovers** (see p. 235)
  Create your own simple photo gallery—show a larger version of a picture on thumbnail hover over.

- **New 2D/3D Filter Effects** (see p. 167)
  Add stunning reflections of an object—great for Web page titles and pictures! **Blur** any object or stroke a coloured solid or gradient border around object edges (stroke with a new **Contour** fill which applies gradient fill from the inner to outer outline width). 3D effects are boosted with realistic glass-like **Transparency** control of non-reflective/reflective surfaces and multiple separately coloured lights for dramatic lighting effects. All filter effects can be applied in preview mode or to the object on the page. Use the new **Shadow Tool** for on-the-page shadow control.

- **Instant 3D with On-screen Transforms** (see p. 174)
  Transform 3D objects **in-situ** with 3D editing from a context toolbar.
  Apply awesome multi-coloured **lighting effects** (with directional
  control), along with custom **bevel** and **lathe** effect profiles to create your
  very own unique contours. **Hardware-accelerated rendering** boosts
  redraw performance (hardware dependent).

- **Year update for Calendars plus inline events** (see p. 135)
  Update your calendar's year and add named personal events, plus
  country- or region-specific public holidays, all with powerful event
  control.

- **Text and Style Formatting!** (see p. 91)
  Apply gradient colour fills and transparency to creative table and frame
  text; apply to selected characters, whole words or even entire paragraphs!
  Ctrl-select multiple words or paragraphs (frame or artistic text alike) to
  apply common formatting. Change text style assignment simultaneously
  with the new Text Styles tab. View your currently installed font set in the
  Fonts tab, including recently used and Websafe fonts. Search for fonts
  and preview your fonts on selected text.

- **Enhanced Tables** (see p. 129)
  Add/remove columns/rows by dragging end headers. In-context drop-
  down menus on row/column headers manipulate individual rows or
  columns. Distribute or autofit selected rows, columns, or your entire
  table—even set absolute row/column sizes! Sort single- or multi-
  column/row contents. Now benefit from resizing of table columns
  without affecting overall table width. New functions (including logical
  and trigonometric) are added for more comprehensive "spreadsheet"
  functionality.

- **Tab view controls**
  WebPlus now features auto show/hide tab controls, with supporting
  slide, fade, or roll animation effects. Favourite user-defined workspace
  profiles can be loaded from the Startup Wizard (or use a preset
  workspace profile).

- **Layout aids** (see p. 49)

  Take advantage of labour-saving "sticky" guides, a great way of moving (in bulk) all objects snapped to your ruler guides—move the guide and objects will follow!

- **New How To tab**

  The How To tab provides quick access to step-by-step, illustrated topics that introduce you to key WebPlus features, and help you plan, design, and create your Web site projects.

..and some very useful additions you've been asking for!

Take advantage of customizable keyboard shortcuts! **Default ALT text** offers better accessibility for exported images. More user-friendly toolbar customization. **CAPTCHA spam protection** for Serif Web Resources (forms and blogs). Now Publish to Web with **automatic upload**, then view your live Web site with View site online. Smart Object Preview shows Smart Object contents directly on the page. Use **Select All** in the Find and Replace feature to view all matching text instances. Sort paragraphs or lists either alphabetically or numerically. Line styles now let you scale line ends (e.g., arrows) and control line end placement. Also include author name, copyright notice, and publication date in page headers. Colour schemes offer an off-page browser window **Background Colour** and **On-page colour** settings. The re-designed Transform tab now resizes, repositions, scales or rotates objects from a set anchor position. Alternatively, rotate objects about a moveable on-the-page origin point. Lock QuickShape geometry to preserve original arrows shapes and curved corners. Swap the User Interface look-and-feel—choose Silver, Blue, Aqua, Silver-Blue, or Classic (WebPlus 10 look).

Don't forget to register your new copy, using the Serif Registration Wizard. That way, we can keep you informed of new developments and future upgrades.

Installation

System Requirements

Minimum:

- Pentium PC with DVD/CD drive and mouse

- Microsoft Windows® 2000, XP or Vista operating system

- 256MB RAM

- 389MB free hard disk space (Program CD only)

- SVGA display (800x600 resolution, 16-bit colour or higher)

- Internet Explorer 5.5 (6.0 or above for Smart Object use)

Additional disk resources and memory are required when editing large and/or complex images.

Optional:

- Windows-compatible printer

- TWAIN-compatible scanner and/or digital camera

- Internet account and connection required for Publishing to Web and accessing online resources

First-time install

To install Serif WebPlus X2, simply insert the Program CD into your DVD/CD drive. If AutoPlay is enabled on the drive, this automatically starts the Setup Wizard. If you are installing WebPlus on Microsoft Windows® Vista, you may need to click on **Run autorun.exe** from within the **Autoplay** dialog. If AutoPlay is not enabled (or doesn't start the install automatically), use the Manual install method described below.

The Setup Wizard begins with a Welcome dialog, click **Next** to proceed. Follow the steps of the wizard, clicking **Next** each time to proceed. At this point, you may be informed that there is a Reboot Pending. If this happens, we recommend rebooting your PC. Remember to remove the Program CD from the drive and to close all other applications before you restart. The Setup

Wizard should now run successfully when the CD is replaced in the DVD/CD drive.

Please read through the license agreement. Click **Next** to proceed.

Enter your User Name, Organization (if applicable) and the software **Product Key** that came with your software. For more information, click ⍰. Click **Next**.

Choose the language that you want the program to use. Click **Next**. Select the Default Dictionary Language. Click **Next**.

At the **Setup Options** dialog, you have the opportunity to customize your installation.

To install the recommended options, simply click **Next**. However, if you are concerned about disk space, you may choose to run some of the features from the DVD/CD. The drop-down boxes display the available options for each feature:

- ⊟ **Will be installed on the local hard drive.** If this option is selected, it will install the feature to your hard disk but will not automatically install any subfeatures that may be available.

- ⊟ᴴ **Entire feature will be installed on the local hard drive.** By selecting this option, all of the subfeatures relating to this feature will also be installed. Some subfeatures can require a substantial amount of hard disk space.

- ⊕ **Will be installed to run from [Media Type].** If this option is selected, you will save space on your hard disk but you will need to have the installation media at hand to access the features.

- ⊕ᴴ **Entire feature will be installed to run from [Media Type].** This option this option will allow you to access the content and all of its subfeatures from the installation media, saving you disk space.

- 🖳 **Will be installed to run from network.** If you are installing the software from a network, this option will allow you to access the content from the network storage, saving you disk space.

-     **Entire feature will be installed to run from network.** If you are installing the software from a network, this option will allow you to access the features and all related subfeatures from the network storage, saving you disk space.

-     **Entire feature will be unavailable.** By choosing this option, you will not be able to use the selected feature. However, if you later decide that you want to use the feature, you will be able to install it by modifying your installation.

When you select a feature installation option, the information pane on the right of the list will inform you of the amount of hard disk space that the feature needs. Not all installation options are available for all features.

> If disk space is not an issue, you may decide to install the entire program to your hard disk. This can improve performance and you will be able to use all of the features without the need to keep the program disk in your DVD/CD drive.

If you do not want to install the program to its default location, click the **Change** button. Browse to the folder that you want to install WebPlus in and click **OK**. Caution should be taken here as changing the default settings may affect subsequent installs of later versions of the software.

> ⚠ Changing the installation defaults may result in some options of the program being unavailable. It is only recommended for advanced users.

At the Shortcut Options screen, you can choose to automatically create shortcuts by checking the option boxes. Click **Next.**

Click **Install** to accept your settings and install the program. The dialog will display a progress bar as the program installs. Once installation is complete, click **Finish** to exit the Setup Wizard.

[Optional] If you've also obtained the WebPlus X2 Resource CD, install it now following the same procedure you used for the Program CD.

Your installation is now complete and you can begin using Serif WebPlus X2!

Manual install

For manual installation, use My Computer (Windows® XP), or Computer (Windows® Vista), to navigate to the DVD/CD drive in which your WebPlus Program CD is located. Double-click the DVD/CD drive, double-click setup.exe in the displayed folder, choose Serif WebPlus X2 from the menu, then follow the on-screen installation instructions.

Modifying, Repairing or Removing WebPlus

To modify, repair or remove the installation:

Microsoft Windows® XP:

1. Click the **start** button and select **Control Panel** from the Windows Start menu.

2. Double-click on the **Add/Remove Programs** icon.

3. Locate Serif WebPlus X2 in the list of installed programs, then select it.

4. Click the **Change** button to make changes to the install via the Setup Wizard.

Microsoft Windows® Vista:

1. Click the **Start** button and click **Computer**.

2. Click the **Uninstall or change a program** button.

3. Locate Serif WebPlus X2 in the list of installed programs, then select it.

4. Click the **Change** button to make changes to the install via the Setup Wizard.

You can also access this via Programs and Features by clicking **Control Panel** from the Windows **Start** menu (or **Settings>Control Panel** from the "Classic" Windows **Start** menu), clicking **Programs** and then clicking **Programs and Features**.

To change the installed features:

Open the Setup Wizard as described in the previous steps. To change the installation, select the **Modify** option and then click **Next**. From here, you will be able to change the program language or add/remove some of the program features. Adding additional content may prompt you to insert your original WebPlus X2 Program CD; removing content does not require this CD. See the steps in **First-time install** if you are unsure about any of the options.

> Some features, such as fonts, cannot be removed by the Setup Wizard once they have been installed. This is due to the way they are used by other applications. Modifying the installation settings in this case will never free up disk space. Fonts in particular, will even remain if the program is completely uninstalled.

Removing WebPlus X2

Open the Setup Wizard. Select the **Remove** option and click **Next**. Click **Remove** to completely remove WebPlus X2 from your computer.

Repairing WebPlus X2

On occasion, it may be necessary to repair your installation of WebPlus X2. Open the Setup Wizard and select the Repair option and click Next. Click Repair. Once the repair has completed, open WebPlus X2. Any problems should now be resolved.

Getting Started

Understanding Web sites

What's involved in creating a Web site?

It can be as simple as choosing and customizing a Web template... or you can start from scratch—it's up to you. Either way, you'll appreciate the ease with which WebPlus lets you revise text, graphics and adjust the design of each page. WebPlus gives you the freedom to lay out page elements in any composition that suits you. It's a bit like putting together a newsletter—so if you're already comfortable with the basics of DTP, you'll find it easy going. If you're just beginning, you can learn to use WebPlus tools as you go.

WebPlus lets you assemble all the elements of your site-in-progress into one convenient, multi-page document that can be saved in a single step as a WebPlus **project file**. At any time—again with just one step—you can **publish** the project as a separate set of pages that comprise your **Web site**.

What exactly is a Web site?

The **Internet** is a global network that interconnects computers around the world. The **Web** began as a way of using the Internet to access information stored in a file format known as **HTML**, or Hypertext Markup Language. Broadly defined, a **Web site** is a collection of (mostly) HTML files stored on a **file server** that someone with a **Web browser** can get to. Actually, Web sites don't depend on the Internet at all—they can be (and often are) accessed just as well over a local area network or private intranet. Remember, a Web site is just a collection of files.

The HTML format is a way of describing the layout of a page. An HTML file uses plain text with various embedded codes to describe a page that somebody has designed, consisting of text and clickable hypertext links. Besides HTML files, a Web site generally includes other files (pictures, for example) that the designer has seen fit to incorporate. A Web browser such as Microsoft Internet Explorer or Mozilla Firefox is a program that can read an HTML file and display the page (one hopes) the way the designer intended it to look

Typically, a Web site has a single **Home Page** using a standard file name like INDEX.HTML. The Home Page is the first page a visitor sees. It usually will contain links to other pages on the site, which in turn have links to others.

To the person using a Web browser to access the site, the information appears seamlessly linked—navigable with a click of the mouse.

WebPlus takes the pages you've laid out and converts them to HTML.

What will I need to preview or publish my Web site?

You can **preview** one or more pages at any time, either within WebPlus (using a special window based on the Internet Explorer browser) or separately using any browser installed on your system.

Publishing a site with WebPlus is a one-step operation that both: (1) converts your project to separate files for the Web, and (2) copies the Web files to a location you specify, either to a local folder or to a Web host.

- To publish to a **local folder**, you don't even need a connection to the Internet.

- To publish to the **Web**, you'll need a **host** for your Web site—that is, disk space on a server connected to the Internet—so that others can access your site. This usually means opening an account with an online service provider: either a large entity such as America Online or a specialized Internet service provider (ISP). The big subscription networks typically allocate to each user several megabytes of server space for a "personal Web site," and many plans are available from smaller ISPs. Once you've set up your account and can connect your computer to the host, publishing to the Web is simply a matter of transferring your files. The Publish to Web feature included with WebPlus takes care of this.

What about HTML?

One advantage WebPlus has over a dedicated Web-page creation program is that you can take your newsletter layout, or a print ad with a wild mix of multicolour graphics and fancy typography, and publish them intact to the Web. In fact, your page can look as great on the Web as it did on your screen!

While you don't have to know HTML (the description language for Web pages) to use WebPlus, you should understand that:

1. The time it takes a visitor to load your page is directly related to the size of the HTML file <u>plus</u> any accompanying graphic or multimedia files. These other files take up considerably more space and slow down loading time.

2. Those parts of your layout that WebPlus cannot translate to HTML will be output as graphics. The more of your layout that WebPlus can translate into HTML, the better.

If you're used to working in a Desktop Publishing environment, you may have to scale back your typographic expectations somewhat when designing for the Web. However, WebPlus gives you a lot of design latitude. In laying out text, you can specify any point size, use variable leading and letter spacing, and even justify paragraphs! The result is a nearly WYSIWYG match between what you see on-screen in WebPlus and what ends up in the Web browser; HTML positions elements using absolute co-ordinates, overlapping elements are allowed, and file sizes are reduced.

In theory, you can use any font you like. However, if a specified font isn't present on a visitor's computer, an available font will be substituted, with unpredictable results for your beautifully designed layout! As a rule, stick with the WebSafe fonts available within WebPlus. They are shown by default in the Fonts tab and can applied to any currently selected text.

> WebPlus's Site Checker will warn you if your site uses unsafe fonts (non-WebSafe), has navigation problems, or if Form or E-Commerce problems exist.

Startup Wizard

Once WebPlus has been installed, you'll be ready to start. Setup adds a **Serif WebPlus X2** item to the Windows **Start** menu.

- Use the Windows **Start** button to pop up the Start Menu, click on **All Programs** and then click the WebPlus item.

The Startup Wizard presents several choices:

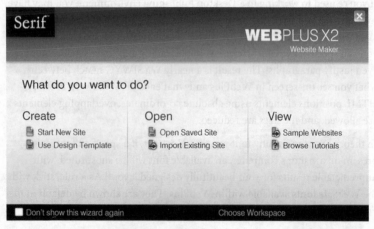

The options are self explanatory, where site creation can be made from scratch or from a pre-supplied **design template**. Previously saved sites can be opened or non-WebPlus Web pages can be imported into your project from file or URL.

> The Startup Wizard is displayed by default when you launch WebPlus. You can switch it off via the **Don't show this wizard again** check box on the Startup Wizard screen, or on again via the **Use Startup Wizard** check box in **Tools>Options...** (use General menu option).

Creating a Web site using a design template

The first time you launch WebPlus, you'll see the **Startup Wizard**, with a menu of six choices. The first of these is **Create>Use Design Template**. Using a design template speeds you through the process of creating a professional site. Whether you're just beginning to work with WebPlus—or an old hand exploring new design possibilities—put WebPlus templates to work for you!

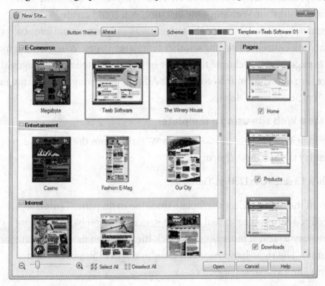

Categorized WebPlus design templates provide a range of selectable options such as:

- **Button Themes**—pick a named theme (e.g., Ahead) for your buttons, bullets, dividers and navigation bars.

- **Schemes**—choose a named colour scheme to apply a specific look and feel (e.g., Atlantis).

- **Page selection**—select some or all template pages (e.g., Home, Products, Downloads, etc.) to base your new Web site on.

Template categories range from Business and E-Commerce, to the more leisure-focused Personal, Entertainment, and Interests.

Some templates contain Smart objects (see p. 306) such as newsletter sign ups and polls. As Smart objects are stored in Serif Web Resources they have to be associated with a valid Serif customer account. If you want to make use of the Smart Object (if unwanted just delete them), double-click it and login to Serif Web Resources; this will associate the object to your account.

WebPlus doesn't stop at just offering pages from a single template. You can easily adopt additional pages from a different template to add some style variation within your Web site—for instance, you could create Web pages with a set look and feel, but a separate members-only area could adopt a different look entirely by adding another templates' pages. When adding more template pages you can choose to copy or ignore associated master pages as the pages are added to your Web site. See Adding, removing, and rearranging pages on p. 36 for more details.

To create a Web site using a template:

1. Launch WebPlus, or choose **Startup Wizard...** from the File menu, to display the Startup Wizard.

2. Click **Create>Use Design Template**.

3. From the dialog, select a template from the main pane. Templates are grouped into subject-based categories; use the scroll bar or collapse a category to reveal more options (click the ⊟ button next to the category name). The right-hand pane refreshes to display thumbnails of that template's available pages.

4. From the right-hand pane, decide which pages you wish to be part of your Web site. Check or uncheck under each page as appropriate, or use **Select All** or **Deselect All** buttons for all or no pages.

5. Pick a **Button Theme** and **Scheme** from the drop-down lists. The page thumbnails refresh to reflect the new page's appearance. For a closer look, use the Zoom In/Zoom Out buttons or Zoom slider at the bottom of the dialog.

6. Click **Open**.

The site opens to the first (Home) page, with the Studio's Site tab displayed on the right, showing the various pages that comprise the site in its Site Structure tree.

Opening an existing Web site

You can open an existing WebPlus site from the Startup Wizard, via the File menu or Standard toolbar. A range of other file formats, including WebPlus templates and Serif PagePlus files can also be opened.

It is also possible to **Import Web Pages** from existing HTML Web sites via the Startup Wizard. (See WebPlus help or more details.)

To open an existing WebPlus site (Startup Wizard):

1. Select the **Open>Open Saved Site** option. In the Documents pane of the **Open Saved Work** dialog, you'll see either your computer's folder structure for navigation to your Web sites (Folders tab) or a list of most recently used Web sites (History tab). Preview thumbnails or Web site details can be shown in the adjacent pane depending on your current view.

2. Click a file name, then click **Open**. The site opens to the first (Home) page.

To open an existing WebPlus site (during WebPlus session):

1. Click the 📂 **Open** button on the Standard toolbar.

2. In the Open dialog, select the folder and file name and click the **Open** button.

To revert to the saved version of an open site:

- Choose **Revert** from the File menu.

Font substitution

WebPlus supports automatic font substitution as you open a WebPlus site which has fonts which are not stored on your computer. The dialog that shows also lets you manually substitute a missing font if necessary. See WebPlus help for more details.

Starting a Web site from scratch

Although design templates can simplify your design choices, you can just as easily start out from scratch with a new, blank Web site.

To start a new site from scratch using the Startup Wizard:

- Launch WebPlus, and select **Create>Start New Site**.

The new site opens with a blank page using default page properties.

To start a new site during your WebPlus session:

- Choose **New** from the File menu.

Working with more than one site

WebPlus lets you open more than one site at a time. Each new site you open appears in a separate window with its own settings. Convenient tabs let you switch quickly between windows, and with windows reduced or tiled you can drag and drop objects between windows. You can also preview the current site in a separate window (see Previewing your Web site on p. 321).

To close the current window:

- Choose **Close** from the File menu or click the window's [X] **Close** button at the upper right. If it's the only window open for the site, the command closes the project and you'll be prompted to save changes.

Saving your WebPlus project

To save your work:

- Click the [disk icon] **Save** button on the Standard toolbar (or **Ctrl+S**).
  OR
  To save under a different name, choose **Save As...** from the File menu.

Developing Sites and Pages

Developing Sites and Pages

Understanding site structure and navigation

Unlike a printed publication, a Web site doesn't depend on a linear page sequence. When designing a site, it makes more sense to think of the site in spatial terms, with a **structure** like that of a museum which people will explore. You can generally assume that your visitors will come in through the "front door" (the Home page)—but where they go after that depends on the links you've provided. These **navigation** pathways are like corridors that connect the various rooms of the museum. It's up to you as the "architect" to develop a sensible arrangement of pages and links so that visitors can find their way around easily, without getting lost

In WebPlus, you can use the **Site Structure tree** to visually map out the structure of your site and then add navigation elements—special **theme graphics** that dynamically adapt to the structure you've defined. You'll encounter the Site Structure tree as you learn about working with pages.

Site structure

Unlike the museum in our analogy, the "structure" of a Web site has nothing to do with its physical layout, or where pages are stored. Rather, it's a way of logically arranging the content on the site so that visitors have an easier time navigating through it. One of the most useful organizing principles—which WebPlus strongly reinforces—is an "inverted tree" structure that starts with the Home page and then branches out to other pages. To the visitor navigating your site, this arrangement presents your content in a familiar, hierarchical way, structured into **sections** and **levels**.

A **section** is a content category, for example "Who's Who?," "Products," or "Links." The various major sections are typically listed on the site's Home page in a navigation bar. Ideally, each page on the site belongs to a particular section. And unless there's only one page in a given section, the section will have its own main page, which usually serves as a menu for subsidiary pages.

The **level** is the number of steps (i.e. jumps) a given page is removed from the Home page. The Home page will always reside at Level 1, normally along with main section menu pages. This allows navigation bars to work easily and automatically. Pages one step "below" the section menu pages reside at Level 2, and so on.

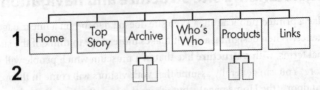

In WebPlus, the Site Structure tree (in the **Site tab**) provides a visual aid that lets you organize the content on your site into sections and levels—in other words as a hierarchy of parent pages branching to child pages. Here's how a similar structure might appear in the WebPlus Site Structure tree:

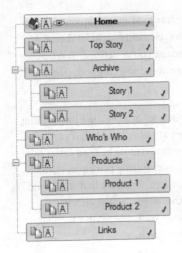

The Site Structure tree makes it easy to visualize relationships between pages and lay out your site in a way that makes sense for the content you have to offer. Of course, a Web site is truly an interconnected web of pages, and the tree structure doesn't prevent you from installing links between any two pages. But it does expose the major pathways within your site—up, down, and sideways. Logical section/level design makes your site easier to navigate, and WebPlus makes it simple to create **navigation bars** (or "navbars" for short) that mirror your site structure and help guide your visitors along those "main roads."

Click the .html ↻ button above the Site tab's Site Structure to view pages by their file name rather than their titles.

Incidentally, WebPlus also
supports HTML pages and offsite
links which can be inserted into the
Site Structure as for any other page.
Either page entry is slightly
different in design to a standard
web page to indicate that it is based
only on HTML code (see Creating
HTML pages on p. 247) or that it
points to a location outside of the
Web site.

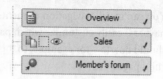

As an example, compare the
HTML page "Overview", the
standard Web page "Sales", and the
offsite link "Member's forum".

Navigation

In WebPlus, certain types of **theme graphic** we'll call "navigation elements"—
such as Previous/Next buttons and navbars are pre-programmed to
understand your site structure, making it easy to design a site that's simple to
navigate. You simply select one from the Studio's **Theme Graphics tab** and
WebPlus does the rest! Previous/Next buttons automatically link laterally, to
adjacent pages on the same level. Navbars combine buttons with popup
menus to facilitate movement between the various sections and levels of a site.

For example, here's a navbar we selected for the site shown in the main tree
above. The buttons provide links to the Home and section menu pages (all at
Level 1) and popup menus that link to child pages (Level 2 in this case).

Here's a brief summary of the advantages of incorporating navigation
elements in your site design:

- You can install navigation elements at any level of your site, and (for navbars) easily customize which part(s) of the site structure each navbar should link to—for example, to top-level pages, pages on the same level, child pages, etc.

- Because navigation elements are theme graphics, you can use the Theme Graphics tab to select co-ordinated design elements (buttons, etc.) for a consistent look, and change the overall appearance with a single click.

- By default, all pages in the tree are "included in navigation"—that is, they can be linked to by navigation elements. You can **exclude** certain pages so they'll be ignored by navigation elements. Included pages show a ✓ mark in their page entry, while an excluded page lacks the mark. For example, suppose you had a section of reference pages that you didn't want visitors to explore top-down. Excluding the parent page for that section would remove it from the navbar. Of course, you can still create hyperlinks to the page—it just won't appear in navigation elements.

- Best of all, a WebPlus navigation element updates dynamically if you subsequently alter page names or relationships, or cut/paste the navbar to another page. For example, "Story 1" above is just a placeholder for an actual title—common practice when designing a site before all the intended content is in place. Once we have the actual story, suppose we rename that page to "Smith Appointed to Board of Directors"... the navbar would instantly reflect the change!

Understanding pages and master pages

Pages are the basic unit of Web design. WebPlus lets you structure your site's content by arranging pages into a branching "tree," which in turn helps visitors navigate through the site. Looking at individual pages from a design standpoint, each WebPlus page has a "foreground" **page layer** and a "background" **master page layer**.

Master pages are part of the structure of your WebPlus project, and provide a flexible way to store background elements that you would like to appear on more than one page—for example a logo, background, border design, or even a navigation element. The key concept here is that a particular master page is typically shared by multiple pages, as illustrated below. By placing a design element on a master page and then assigning several pages to use that master page, you ensure that all the pages incorporate that element. Of course, each individual page can have its own elements.

The Studio's **Site** tab includes an upper Master Pages section with icons for each master page, and a lower Site Structure in the Pages window that provides feedback indicating which master page is being used by each of your Web pages:

Viewing Pages

The WebPlus workspace consists of a "page" area and a surrounding "pasteboard" area.

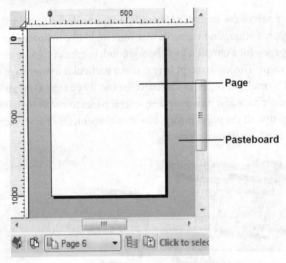

The **page** area is where you put the text, graphics, and other elements that you want to appear on your final Web page. The **pasteboard** is where you generally keep elements that are being prepared or waiting to be positioned on the page area. When you publish your Web site from the WebPlus project, anything which overlaps the page area appears, while anything entirely on the pasteboard does not. The pasteboard is shared by all pages and master pages, and it's useful for copying or moving objects between pages.

To move or copy an object between pages via the pasteboard:

1. Drag the object from the source page onto the pasteboard (hold down the **Ctrl** key to copy).

2. Display the target page (see Switching between pages on p. 33).

3. Drag (or **Ctrl**-drag to copy) the object from the pasteboard onto the target page.

WebPlus makes it easy to see exactly what you're working on—from a wide view of a whole page to a close up view of a small region. For example, you can use the **scroll bars** at the right and bottom of the main window to move the page and pasteboard with respect to the main window. The view automatically re-centres itself as you drag objects to the edge of the screen.

The **View toolbar** at the top of the screen provides the 🖐 **Pan Tool** as an alternative way of moving around, plus a number of buttons that let you zoom in and out so you can inspect and/or edit the page at different levels of detail.

> 💡 If you're using a wheel mouse, spinning the wheel scrolls vertically. **Shift**-spin to scroll horizontally and **Ctrl**-spin to zoom in or out!

Switching between pages

WebPlus provides a variety of ways of getting quickly to the part of your site you need to work on. The Studio's Site tab provides a central "control panel" including both the **Site Structure tree**, which depicts the hierarchy of pages in your site (see Understanding site structure and navigation on p. 27), and icons for each of the site's **master pages**.

.html ↻ The pages will show either their page titles (by default) or file names according to the **Toggle between Page Title and Filename** button setting. The Site tab lets you switch between pages, and view or set page properties.

The Site Structure dialog (click the 🗐 **Site Structure** button) affords similar tree-based functionality showing pages by their titles or file names, and the Hintline's **Page Locator** offers yet another convenient method of jumping to a particular page.

Selecting vs. viewing a page: <u>Single-clicking</u> a page/master page entry merely **selects** the page, which you might do for example if you were about to delete it from the right-click menu. To actually **view** the associated page/master page you need to **double-click** an entry or use one of the methods noted below. Feedback from the entry tells you whether it's currently viewed and/or selected, i.e.

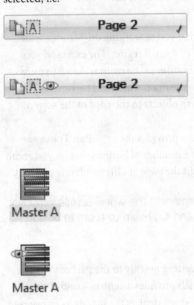

An orange entry (with bolded page name) denotes the selected page.

The eye icon denotes the currently viewed page—which you're able to edit in the workspace. This example shows a viewed (but unselected) page.

A highlighted master page icon in the Site tab's upper window denotes the selected master page.

An eye icon in the master page icon (Site tab's upper window) denotes the currently viewed page—which you're able to edit in the workspace. This example shows a viewed (but unselected) master page.

To view a specific page/master page:

Several methods can be used to view a page:

- On the Hintline, use the Hintline's ◀ ▶ page navigation buttons.
  OR
  Click the entry for the page or master page in the **Page Locator** list.

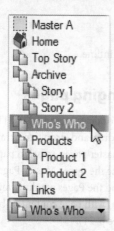

- On the Studio's **Site** tab, double-click the entry for the page (or master page) you want to view. The Site Structure window of the tab includes a tree with entries for pages in the site, while the Master Pages window shows only master pages as thumbnails. You may need to click the **Master Pages** button to display the master pages window.

- Click the **Site Structure** button on the Hintline or on the Site tab's Page window. Select the page entry in the dialog's tree (double-click tree entries if necessary to expand each branch). Then click the **View Page** button.

For master pages:

- On the Studio's **Site** tab, click the Master Pages ▼ button to reveal a master page window. One or more master page icons will be displayed.

- Double-click the icon for the master page you want to view.

To switch between the master page and page layer (for the current page):

- Click the **Page/Master Page** button on the Hintline.
  OR

- Choose **Master Page** from the View menu (or **Page** to switch back).

As a shortcut to view the site's Home page:

- Click the   **Home Page** button on the Hintline.

Adding, removing, and rearranging pages

Using the Studio's **Site tab**, you can quickly add or delete standard or HTML pages at any level of your site structure, and use drag-and-drop to rearrange pages within the structure as needed, add new master pages, reassign pages to particular master pages, and add offsite links. Use the upper Master Pages window of the Site tab to access master pages, and the Pages window (tab's central Site Structure tree) to access pages. Pages (with page content or blank) can also be added from multi-page templates (see p. 21).

Besides the Site tab, WebPlus offers a variety of other ways to manipulate pages: the **Site Structure** dialog, the **Master Page Manager**, and both standard and right-click (context) menus.

To add a new blank page:

1. Click the down arrow on the   **Add** button directly above the Site tab's Pages window. From the drop-down menu, choose **New Blank Page**.

2. In the dialog, specify options for the new page:
   - Type an optional **Page name**. (If you don't type a name, WebPlus will apply a default name.)
   - Specify which **Master page** the new page should use, i.e. your project's master page (e.g., Master A) or if using templates, the blank page's master page (i.e., Template Default).
   - To duplicate the design elements from a particular page, check **Copy objects from page** and select the source page in the activated list.
   - In the Placement section, specify the page in the site structure from which you can insert a page Before, After, or make it a Child of the named page.

3. Click **OK**.

A new page appears at the specified location in the site structure.

When clicked, the Site tab's 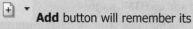 **Add** button will remember its last chosen menu item.

While adding standard pages lets you start page design from scratch, you can make life a little easier by adopting "ready to go"pages from supplied WebPlus templates. To maintain the page's original design, any master page associated with the added page can optionally be "imported" with the page.

To add a new page from a template:

1. In the Pages Window (Site Structure tree) of the Studio's Site tab, select a page after which you want to add the new page.

2. Click the down arrow on the 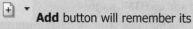 **Add** button directly above the Pages window. From the drop-down menu choose **New Template Page...**.

3. From the **Add New Page from Template...** dialog, select a template from the left-hand pane, and check the page for addition (check further pages for inclusion if needed). If necessary, use the Zoom controls at the bottom of the dialog for a closer look at the page thumbnails.

4. WebPlus lets you control if an associated master page is copied with the page. Pick from the top-left drop-down menu choosing one of:

    - **Copy Master Page**. To always copy the master page into your project.

    - **Compare and Copy Master Page**. Checks if the master page already exists in your project then copies it if not present.

    - **No Master Page**. The page's master page is never copied to the project.

5. Click the **Open** button. The pages are added to the Site tab.

As an alternative to blank or template Web pages, HTML pages can be added to any Site tab's Site Structure. Such pages can be included in navigation as for standard pages.

To add an HTML page:

1. In the Pages Window (Site Structure tree) of the Studio's Site tab, select a page after which you want to add the new page.

2. Click the down arrow on the ⊞ ▾ **Add** button directly above the Pages window. From the drop-down menu choose **New HTML Page**.

A new HTML page is added to the Site tab. See Creating HTML pages (p. 247) for more information.

You can also add an **offsite link** to your site structure. Typically, this would be a page or resource separate from your site that you wanted to include in your site's navigation structure (for example, a forum or blog that you manage via Serif Web Resources). The offsite link appears in the Site Structure tree and in navigation elements, so you can manipulate it just as if it were a page in your site.

To add an offsite link:

1. In the Pages Window (Site Structure tree) of the Studio's Site tab, select a page after which you want to add the new page.

2. Click the down arrow on the ⊞ ▾ **Add** button directly above the Pages window. From the drop-down menu, choose **New Offsite Link...**.

3. In the dialog, click to select the link destination type, and enter the specific offsite hyperlink target, and the window in which you want the target to appear (the **Default** option will adopt a Navigation bar's target frame setting, other settings will override it).

4. Type a **Menu name** to identify the offsite link in the Site Structure tree (the equivalent of its page name).

5. Click **OK**.

To add a new master page:

1. On the Studio's Site tab, ensure the 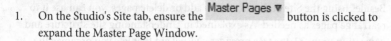 button is clicked to expand the Master Page Window.

2. Click the ⊞ **Add** button above the Master Pages window.
   OR

3. Click the ⊞ **Master Page Manager** button above the Master Pages window.

4. Select the dialog's **Add...** button. Enter Width and/or Height settings if different from the defaults.

5. (Optional) From the Background tab, opt to use scheme manager settings, i.e. set a schemed off-page background colour (or picture) and/or an on-page colour.

6. (Optional) From the Page Transitions tab, select an entry and/or exit transition (after checking Override master page setting) when navigating between pages using the master page.

7. Click **OK**.

A new master page appears in the Site tab's Master Pages window.

To clone a page:

- In the Studio's Site tab, right-click on a selected page and choose **Clone Page**. An identical copy is inserted below the selected page.

To delete a page or master page:

1. On the Studio's Site tab, select the page (or master page) to delete by clicking its entry.

2. Click the ⊟ **Remove** button above the window to delete the page.

> When you delete a page, you'll have the option to **remove** any hyperlinks in your site that point to it, or **redirect** the hyperlinks to another specified page (hyperlinks to anchors on the deleted page can optionally be deleted).

Rearranging pages

Besides using the Site Structure tree to add or delete pages, you can use it to rearrange pages as needed. As explained in Understanding site structure and navigation on p. 27, the tree provides a visual aid that lets you organize the content on your site into "sections" and "levels"—that is, as a hierarchy of **parent** pages branching to **child pages**. Not only does the tree help you keep track of your content, but WebPlus translates your logical page arrangement into a site that's easy to navigate. Special theme graphics called navigation elements like Previous/Next buttons and navigation bars (navbars) are pre-programmed to understand your site structure and will update dynamically if you rearrange pages!

Using the parent/child structure, rearranging pages is an intuitive process whether you use drag-and-drop or convenient buttons. You can move a page:

- To a different sequential position (up or down) at the same level of the structure

- To a higher (parent) level

- To a lower (child) level

To move a page:

1. Display the Studio's Site tab.

2. Single-click to select the page in the Site Structure tree.

3. (Using drag-and-drop) Drag the page entry up or down and drop it at a new position in the tree. Watch the cursor for feedback on the new position relative to that of the page just below the cursor:

   ⌐▭ moves the page to the same level as, and following, the page below the cursor;

   ⌐▭ makes the page a child of the page below the cursor.

Assigning master pages

If you've defined more than one master page for your site, you can use a variety of methods to reassign a specific master page to individual pages, one page at a time. You can also set a page to use no master page—for example, if you import an HTML page you may want to see only its original design elements without adding others from a master page. The key thing to remember is that each page can use only one master page. (For an overview, see Understanding pages and master pages on p. 30.)

To assign a master page to a page:

- On the Studio's **Site** tab, click on the master page thumbnail (in the Master Pages section) and drag onto the page entry (in the Site Structure section).

Working in frames

WebPlus allows one or more frames, also known as **Iframes**, to be placed on a single page, each accessing another page within your Web site. Just like an image, a frame can be placed anywhere on the page and can be drawn to any size. While it's typical to link to a page, you can also link to a range of other link destinations (an Internet page, local file, Smart object, or stored user data) as well.

A great way of always showing the same page (e.g., showing a product list) within every page in your site is to apply a frame to the site's master page. Taking the idea further, you can add selection buttons (or menu options) to change what the frame displays. In more detail, if each button links to a different page (but always to the same frame) the framed document's contents change when clicking different buttons—this takes advantage of the automatically generated HTML ID (see p. 254) which should be referenced as the Target Frame name (type Document Frame) in each button's hyperlink.

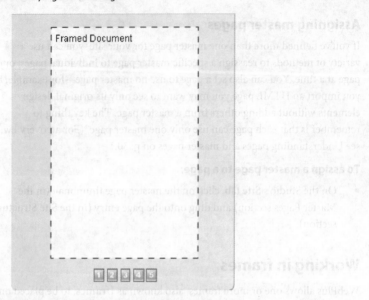

> ⚆ If adding a frame to a master page ensure that the frame's destination page does not use that same master page (this avoids an unwanted page-in-page effect).

Frames are applied via a **Framed Document Tool**. The term "Framed Document" is used in WebPlus to keep the concept of Iframes distinct from that of HTML or Creative text frames (used for controlling the placement of text on the page)—both very different features within WebPlus.

WebPlus also supports **Active document frames**. These are useful when you have a framed Web site and want to open a particular page in a frame. The name of the active document frame is identified by a combination of page and frame name. For example, Home: ifrm_6 represents the "Home" home page and "ifrm_6" an automatically generated frame. Pages can redirect to the frame that should contain them—useful when found by search engine. To activate this for each page that will appear within a frame go to **Edit > Page Properties > Open in active document frame** and **Redirect to this frame if necessary**.

To create a framed document:

1. Select the page on which you would like to add a frame.

2. From the Web Objects toolbar, select the ▢ **Framed Document Tool**.
   You'll see the mouse pointer change to a cursor. What you do next
   determines the initial size and placement of the frame.

3. To insert the frame at a default size, simply click the mouse.
   OR
   To set the size of the inserted frame, drag out a region and release the
   mouse button.

4. A dialog is displayed immediately into which you can specify a link
   destination. Choose an icon representing a page in your site, an Internet
   page, Smart object, a file on your hard disk, an anchor, or User Data.

5. Set the Frame Contents Information (the page name, internet page, etc.)
   which will differ depending on the link destination.

6. For any framed document you can apply various frame content settings.
   Choose from:

   - **Active Document Frame**: check to allow hyperlinks to open a page
     in a frame on another page.

   - **Show Border**: displays a thin border around the frame to indicate
     its position.

   - **Transparent Background**: if the page that appears within the frame
     has a transparent background, checking this option allows it to pick
     up the background of the site. If unchecked, a transparent page
     background will default to white when it appears within the frame.

   - **Scroll Bars**: Choose to automatically use scroll bars when needed
     (**Auto**), or force them on (**Yes**) or off (**No**) always.

7. Click **OK**.

Absolute URLs

Since frames divide a web page into panes which each display their own HTML document, you need to make sure that each part of the frame is referenced using absolute URLs. This means that when a visitor bookmarks the page on your site, the page within the frame will also be bookmarked. To use Absolute URLs, you will need to set a **Site Base URL**—the part of the URL common to all pages, e.g. https://www.serif.co.uk/URL/example/. WebPlus will use this to create the rest of the URL.

Using layout aids

Layout guides are visual guide lines that help you position layout elements, either "by eye" or with snapping turned on. When the snapping feature is turned on, objects you create, move, or resize will jump to align with nearby, visible layout guides. WebPlus provides a variety of layout guides to assist you: page margins, row/column guides and ruler guides.

- **Page margin** settings are fundamental to your layout, and usually are among the first choices you'll make after starting a site from scratch. Narrow margins around the perimeter are a good starting point for clean page design. The page margins are shown as a blue box which is actually four guide lines—for top, bottom, left, and right—indicating the underlying page margin settings. If you like, you can set the margins to match your current printer settings.

- **Row** and **column guides** act as an underlying layout aid, separating your page into multiple rows or columns shown with dashed blue guide lines.

- **Ruler guides** are free-floating "sticky" red guide lines that are great for aligning objects vertically or horizontally.

> Unlike frame margins and columns, these layout guides don't control where frame text flows. Rather, they serve as visual aids that help you match your frame layout to the desired column layout. Usually the frame column width matches the underlying page column guides, but sometimes (for example in multiple-column layouts) the frame column will take up two, or even three, of the page columns.

To define layout guides:

- Click the 🔲 Layout Guides button on the Page context toolbar.

The **Margins** tab lets you set guide lines for page margins, rows, and columns. You can set the left, right, top, and bottom margins individually. The dialog also provides options for **balanced margins** (left matching right, top matching bottom).

Use the **Row and Column Guides** section to define guides for rows and columns with an optional in-between gutter (gap). If you want rows or columns of uneven width, first place them at fixed intervals, then later drag on the guides to reposition them as required.

The **Guides** tab lets you fine-position ruler guides by specifying absolute pixel positioning (guides can also be dragged onto the page from WebPlus rulers; see Creating ruler guides on p. 47).

To show or hide layout guides you've defined:

- Click or unclick **Guide Lines** on the View menu.

This setting also affects any ruler guides you've placed on the page area.

Rulers

The WebPlus **rulers** mimic the paste-up artist's T-square, and serve several purposes:

- To act as a measuring tool.

- To create ruler guides for aligning and snapping.

- To define the dot grid, and (indirectly) the snapping grid.

The actual interval size of the ruler marks depends on the current zoom percentage. In zoomed-out view, for example at 50%, there's less distance between ruler marks than when zoomed-in to 150%. To handle work where you want finer control or smaller snapping increments, click a zoom button to magnify the page.

Adjusting rulers

By default, the horizontal ruler lies along the top of the WebPlus window and the vertical ruler along the left edge. The default **ruler intersection** is the top-left corner of the pasteboard area. The default **zero point** is the top-left corner of the page area, but this can be changed.

Ruler intersection

Drag tab marker to set new zero point

To define a new zero point:

- Drag the tab marker on the ruler intersection to the new zero point on the page or pasteboard. (Be sure to drag only the triangular marker!)
  OR

1. Choose **Options...** from the Tools menu and select Rulers.

2. Enter a new origin value (expressed in pixels) for your horizontal ruler, vertical ruler or both.

To move the rulers:

- With the **Shift** key down, drag the tab marker on the ruler intersection. Both horizontal and vertical rulers become free-floating and can then be positioned at an area on the page. The zero point remains unchanged.
  OR
  Double-click on the ruler intersection to make the rulers and zero point jump to the top left-hand corner of the page or, if selected, an object. This comes in handy for measuring objects on the page.

To restore the original ruler position and zero point:

- Double-click the tab marker on the ruler intersection.

To lock the rulers and prevent them from being moved:

- Choose **Tools>Options...** and select the **Rulers** page, then check **Lock Rulers**.

Rulers as a measuring tool

The most obvious role for rulers is as a measuring tool. As you move the mouse pointer, small lines along each ruler display the current horizontal and vertical cursor position. When you click to select an object, blue ruler regions indicate the object's left, right, top, and bottom edges. Each region has a zero point relative to the object's upper left corner, so you can see the object's dimensions at a glance.

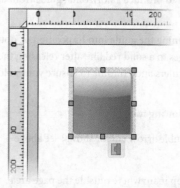

Creating ruler guides

WebPlus lets you to set up horizontal and vertical **ruler guides**—non-printing red lines you can use to align headlines, pictures, and other layout elements.

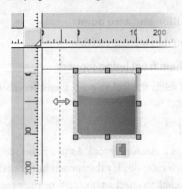

1. For a horizontal or vertical guide, click on the horizontal or vertical ruler, respectively, at the position you want your guide to appear. Hold down the **Alt** key before guide creation to produce a horizontal guide from a vertical ruler and vice versa.

2. Drag onto the page while fine-tuning the guide into its position. A dotted red line will appear which changes to a solid red line after releasing the mouse button. You can use the rulers and Hintline to ensure your guide is positioned accurately.

Guides can be manipulated in the following ways:

- To move a guide, drag it (the double arrow cursor shows; see above example).

- To remove a guide, drag and drop it anywhere outside the page area.

- To lock ruler guides, choose **Tools>Options...** and select the **Layout** option, then check **Lock guide lines**.

- To fine-position ruler guides, Click the ⊞ Layout Guides button on the Page context toolbar and select the **Guides** tab. You can use the tab to create or delete individual guides. To delete all ruler guides at once, click the **Remove All** button.

Sticky guides

Guides are normally "sticky" in that objects snapped to them will be moved when the guide is moved across/down the page. Objects stuck to guides can be unstuck individually at any time or the whole feature can be switched off if necessary.

To make individual objects "non-sticky":

1. Select the object.

2. Click one of two small red triangular markers shown at the point where the object is attached to the guide. You'll see a link cursor (⊖) as you hover over the sticky guide marker.

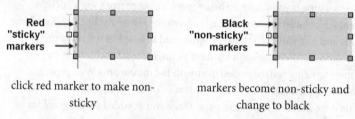

Red "sticky" markers	Black "non-sticky" markers
click red marker to make non-sticky	markers become non-sticky and change to black

3. If you then drag the red guide away the object will not follow.

> ☞ You can make the object stick to a guide again by offering it up to the guide line.

To turn sticky guides on and off:

• Check/uncheck **Sticky guide lines** from **Tools>Options>Layout**.

Previously stuck objects will remain sticky even after sticky guides are switched off—you'll have to make them non-sticky manually.

Using the dot grid

The dot grid is a matrix of dots or lines based on ruler units, covering the page and pasteboard areas. Like ruler guides, it's handy for both visual alignment and snapping.

To turn the dot grid on and off:

- Enable (or disable) the **Dot Grid** button on the View menu.

  OR

  Choose **Options...** from the Tools menu and select **Snapping**. Check or uncheck **Dot Grid**.

You can also set the grid spacing, style, and colour via the Options dialog.

Incorporating theme graphics

The Studio's **Theme Graphics** tab provides a wide selection of ready-made themed objects, which you can add to your pages with a single click. (Or you can use a dialog if you prefer.) Theme graphics range from static "design elements" like bullets to hyperlinked "navigation elements" like Previous/Next buttons and navigation bars pre-programmed to adapt to the site structure you've defined. Theme graphics behave as single objects, with built-in responses to being resized, rolled over with the mouse on a Web page, and so on. Where applicable, you can edit the text or other properties of a theme graphic once it's been added to a page. Once you've added theme graphics to your site, you can instantly update any or all of them to use a different theme.

Using the Theme Graphics tab, you can view and select theme graphics in two ways: by **type** or by **set**. A "type" is a particular category of design element— for example, bullets and buttons are two different types. A "set" is a collection of elements using the same visual theme, with one element of each type and a descriptive name for the visual theme—such as Bright, Candy, Clean, etc. For example:

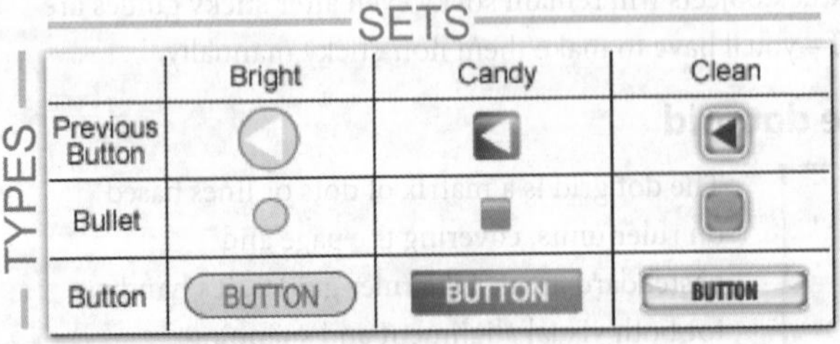

SETS	Bright	Candy	Clean
Previous Button	◁	◀	◀
Bullet	○	■	■
Button	BUTTON	BUTTON	BUTTON

(left axis label: TYPES)

For a consistent appearance throughout your site, choose theme graphics from a single set. Then if you decide to go for a different "look" later on,

simply click a different set on the Theme Graphics tab to instantly update all
your theme graphics.

To add a theme graphic to a page:

1. Display the Studio's **Theme Graphics tab**.

2. In the Categories tree, select a category to browse.
    Click **Current Site** to view theme graphics already in use, for example if
    you want to add an element again.
    OR
    Expand the **Sets** or **Types** list, and then select a category to view its
    gallery.
    OR
    With "Theme Graphics" selected as a category, click the **Current Site**,
    View Sets, or **View Types** thumbnail in the lower Theme Graphics
    section. Then click the thumbnail for the type or set you want to browse.

3. Browse the gallery of available elements and click a particular theme
    graphic to add it at the centre of your page. You can also drag from the
    gallery thumbnail and drop an element at a specific location.
    OR

1. Click the ▄▄ **Insert Theme Graphic** button on the Tools toolbar's
    Navigation flyout.

2. Select a theme **type** from the drop-down list at the top of the dialog, and
    choose a theme **set** by clicking a thumbnail in the lower gallery.

3. Click **OK**.

> In the Theme Graphics gallery, clicking a thumbnail triggers the
> default action. You can right-click the thumbnail or click its down
> arrow to view a popup menu with other actions Insert, Replace in
> Selection, or Replace in Site.

Once you've added theme graphics to your site, you can update any or all of
them to use a different theme.

To update theme graphics to use a different theme:

1. Display the Studio's **Theme Graphics** tab.

2. Expand the **Sets** list in the Categories tree, then select the theme you want to apply.
   OR
   With "Theme Graphics" selected as a category, click the **View Sets** thumbnail in the lower Theme Graphics section. Then click the thumbnail for the theme you want to apply.

3. You can perform several functions:

   - To update a **specific theme graphic**: Select it and note its type on the Hintline, then right-click the thumbnail of the *same element type* in the gallery. Choose **Replace in Selection** from the popup menu.

   - To update **all elements** of a particular type: Select a representative theme graphic of that type, then right-click the thumbnail of the *same element type* in the gallery. Choose **Replace in Site** from the popup menu.

   - To update **all theme graphics in your site**: Click the **Apply <Theme>** thumbnail in the lower Theme Graphics section (see note below). This action updates all theme graphics, regardless of type.

Each chosen theme will adopt the currently set colour scheme for your WebPlus project. You can change your colour scheme at any time, which will alter the appearance of your themed graphics.

To move or resize a theme graphic:

- Drag the object to move it, or drag by its edge or corner handles to resize.

You can edit the text of individual theme graphics, and set various properties for a single theme graphic, or for all theme graphics of a particular type or set.

To edit one or more theme graphics:

1. Double-click the object. (If you're updating a type or set, choose a representative object.)
   OR
   Select the object and click its ⌐T⌐ **Edit** button.

2. Use the dialog to change theme graphic settings for both normal and hover over states. The actual properties you can edit depend on the type of theme graphic, but may include text, subtext, text fill colour(s), and font. Most tabs (other than for Text) let you specify separate settings for the selected theme graphic, theme graphics **of this type**, and/or **in this set**. The updated settings will apply only to theme graphics in the current site.

3. Click **OK** to apply changes.

Using the Gallery

The **Gallery** tab serves as a container for storing your own design objects (such as Flash banners, text blocks, tables, unlinked text frames or HTML fragments) you'd like to reuse in the same or different Web sites. Once you've copied a design to the Gallery, it becomes available to any Web site—simply open the Gallery!

Additionally, the tab includes categorized pre-designed elements that you can customize and use as a starting point for your own designs (you'll get even more design categories and elements if you purchase and install the *WebPlus X2 Resource CD*).

To view the Gallery tab:

- The **Gallery** tab is by default docked with other tabs. If not displayed, go to **View>Studio Tabs** and select the **Gallery** tab.

The Gallery has two parts: (1) an upper **Categories** drop-down menu and (2) a lower **Designs** window showing a list of thumbnails representing the designs in the selected category. You can adopt a design by dragging the thumbnail onto the page.

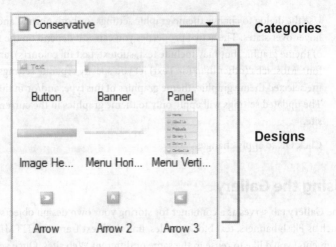

The Gallery tab also lets you store your own designs under My Designs (or in a user-defined category) if you would like to reuse them—the design is made available in any WebPlus project. You can add and delete any items stored in My Designs or one of its categories, with the option of naming elements to facilitate rapid retrieval by searching.

> Designs cannot be added to any pre-defined category.

To use a design from the Gallery:

- Click its thumbnail in the design category and drag it out onto the page. The Gallery retains a copy of the design until you expressly delete it.

To view your Gallery:

1. Click the Studio's **Gallery** tab.
2. Select a folder or category from the drop-down menu. The items from the folder's first listed category are displayed by default.

To add, delete, or rename My Design categories:

- With the Gallery tab selected, click the ▷ **Tab Menu** button and choose **Add category...**, **Delete category**, or **Rename category...** from the flyout menu.

If adding a category, you need to name the category in a dialog. For removal or deletion, simply pick the category in advance of picking the option.

⚠ All designs in a deleted category will also be lost.

To move or copy an object into the Gallery:

1.   Select My Designs or a gallery category into which you want to add the object. Use the Categories drop-down menu for this.

2.   To move, drag the object from the page and drop it in the window. To copy, press the **Ctrl** key before starting to drag.

3.   If **Prompt to Rename** is enabled (click the ▷ **Tab Menu** button and check the option), you'll be prompted to type a name for the design. (You can name or rename the design later, if you wish.) By default, unnamed designs are labelled as "Unnamed."

4.   A thumbnail of the design appears in the Designs group, and its name or label appears below the design.

To delete a design from the Gallery:

•   Click on the drop-down button in the bottom-right corner of a thumbnail (shown by hover over) and choose **Delete Design...** from the menu.

Setting site properties

Site properties allow settings to be made which will be applied across the entire Web site. Page settings, HTML output control, search engine optimization, author/copyright , and Web usage statistical information can all be set via the multi-tab Site Properties dialog. Generally speaking, decide on your Site property settings when you are planning your Web site—once set, the settings do not normally need to be modified (although you can at any time).

Some site properties such as page and search-engine optimization settings are also mirrored on individual pages (via Page Properties; see p. 64). This lets you override or complement the "global" Site Properties, respectively, and apply "local" settings to specific pages.

To view or change site property settings:

•   Choose **Site Properties...** from the File menu. The Site Properties dialog appears.

The dialog is arranged into separate tabs, with each tab reflecting an aspect of site properties.

Tab	Property
Options	**Default file extension** The default extension for published pages is .HTML. Some Web servers require you to use a different extension. **Default page alignment** WebPlus lets you set a default width and height for Web pages. **Force absolute text size** By default, text on your published Web pages will vary in size depending on the visitor's browser setting. You can override this, forcing text to appear at the same point sizes used in your layouts. **Default Page Size** Default Width and Height settings determine the dimensions of new master pages. **HTML Output** Control how your web pages are output by choosing from different encoding methods and controlling how HTML IDs are generated.
Search	**Search engine descriptors** Include optional descriptive information and keywords for your site.
Search Engine	**Sitemaps and robots** Informs search engines or robots if they can crawl, analyze and index Web pages in your Web site. A Sitemap file will include Web pages to be indexed whereas a Robots meta tag (or a robots.txt file) controls which pages are to be excluded from indexing.

Identification	**Author/copyright**
	Add details on ownership, legal notices (copyright statement) and publication dates as Meta Tags to your site's page headers.
Graphics	**Global image export options**
	WebPlus applies default settings when exporting graphics.
Favourites	**Favourites**
	Set an icon file (a graphic) for the Web site which will show when a web visitor bookmarks your Web site.
Summary/ Statistics	**Properties and statistics**
	View and change information for the current project file.
Site Analytics	**Web page statistics**
	Enable, then create and assign a Web Analytics profile which collects and displays Web statistics.
Site Base URL	**Absolute URLs**
	Defines the full URL address. This is a requirement for search engine optimization with sitemaps or RSS feeds.

Setting the default file extension

1. Choose **Site Properties...** from the File menu.

2. On the dialog's Options tab, select a different **Default file extension** if necessary.

Setting page size and alignment

Default site property settings for **Width** and **Height** determine the dimensions of master pages, and each master page in turn determines the size of pages that use it. A default site property setting for **alignment** (either Left or Centered) determines how page content lines up in a browser.

One of the first things you may want to do, when creating a new site from scratch, is to check the default dimensions and adjust them if necessary. You can also override the site setting for a given master page as needed. Individual pages that don't use a master page (for example, HTML pages you've imported) can have their own dimensions.

You can adjust the dimension settings at any time—but as a rule, make changes before you've gone too far with laying out page elements!

In general, use a **Width** setting that will fit on a standard monitor (750 pixels is usually safe) and won't force users to scroll horizontally.

As for **Height**, allow enough vertical distance to let you lay out the objects on your longest page. It's OK to allow more space than you expect to fill. As each individual page is published to the Web, WebPlus will truncate the page either at the specified Height setting or just below the bottom element on each page/master page, whichever is less. In other words, there's no danger of blank space below your bottom element—but don't let elements run outside the indicated page dimensions.

WebPlus lets you select one or more master page objects, and make them **Attach to Bottom of Page** (set in Arrange menu). This means that objects which should belong to the base of the page such as copyright information, bottom navbars, or navigation buttons will **always** show on the bottom of the web page irrespective of page height.

To set the site-wide page dimension settings:

- Choose **Site Properties...** from the File menu. On the dialog's **Options** tab, select different **Width** and/or **Height** values to apply to master pages.

You can also change the default page alignment setting as a site property, or override it for a given page.

To set the site-wide page alignment setting:

- Choose **Site Properties...** from the File menu. On the dialog's **Options** tab, select either "Left" or "Centered" in the **Default page alignment** drop-down menu.

For page dimension and alignment, you can override the site setting for a particular master page or normal page, as described in Setting page properties on p. 64.

Author and copyright information

- Use the **Identification** tab if you're planning on publishing some of your own material and would like declare legal ownership. Enter the **Author name** and site **Copyright message** into each box. The details are not published directly on the page but are added into each published page's header.

```
<meta name="author" content="Teeb Software, Inc.">
<meta name="copyright" content="The content of this Web
site are copyrighted to Teeb Software, Inc. See Terms
of Use Web page.">
```

- Check **Include the publication date in the header** to include the publication date along with the author and copyright details.

```
<meta name="date" content="2007-11-27T15:31:12+00:00">
```

Viewing and changing project information

WebPlus maintains basic properties and statistics for each project file.

To view or change project properties:

1. Choose **Site Properties...** from the File menu.

2. Click the Summary tab to view or change fields for Author, Keywords, Comments, Title, or Subject.

3. Click the Statistics tab to view key dates, etc.

For tracking version history, especially if layout work is being shared, you may wish to display current properties so they show up on the screen or on a printout. Properties you can insert include Site title, Filename, Author, Last Edit Time, Revision Count, and Page Count.

To insert project information in your text:

1. Select the Pointer Tool and click in the text for an insertion point.

2. Choose **Information** from the Insert menu, then select **Site Info...** from the submenu. Select a property to insert and click **OK**.

If the project information changes, the information field in the text is automatically updated.

Add to Favourites

The favourites feature is used to include a graphical portrayal of your Web site, a company logo, or other distinguishable symbol, to precede any bookmark stored in a web visitor's browser favourites.

An .ICO file must have been previously created to represent your site.

To create a favourites icon for your site:

1. Choose **Site Properties...** from the File menu.

2. Click the Favourites tab and check the **Show a favourites icon..** option.

3. **Browse** for an .ICO file, and in the Open dialog, select the file and click **Open**.

4. Check **Embed file** if you want to incorporate the icon file into your WebPlus project file.

5. (Optional) Set **Export Options** to define an exported file name and physical location. (See Setting image export options on p. 189.).

Controlling HTML Output

For HTML output, it is possible to set a language-specific site-wide encoding type, remove spacing from resource file names, let your browser choose to line break after hyphens, and control the generation of HTML IDs for various objects.

To set the encoding type:

1. Choose **Site Properties...** from the File menu.

2. Click the Options tab and select an encoding type from the **Code page** drop-down menu. Choosing a language-specific option is important for correct form handling on exported pages created in a specific language.

It may be necessary to export files (e.g., pictures, movies, JavaScript files) without spaces in their file names (your ISP may not support the upload of files with spaces present). By default, spaces are honoured but you can remove spaces for resource files if necessary.

To remove spaces from resource files or make file names lower case:

1. Choose **Site Properties...** from the File menu.

2. On the dialog's Options tab, check the **Remove spaces from resource file names** and/or **Make resource file names lower case** option.

To allow a browser to insert a line break after any hyphen, WebPlus can optionally export a <WBR> Word Break tag after each hyphen instance. If this isn't a requirement, you can export text containing just the hyphen (without the trailing <WBR> tag)—this removes a source of HTML validation failures (since WBR tags are a Microsoft extension) but text with hyphenated words may overlap its frame boundaries.

To switch off exporting word break tags:

1. Choose **Site Properties...** from the File menu.

2. From the Options tab, uncheck **Write <WBR> tags for hyphens**.

For advanced object manipulation (e.g., by scripting) you can control whether automatic HTML ID generation for object, text column, table row or cell takes place or not.

To manage HTML ID generation

1. Choose **Site Properties...** from the File menu.

2. Click the Options tab. ID generation is turned on for each object, text column, table row or cell. If required, uncheck any of the ID generation options to prevents IDs from being generated for that option.

Analyzing web statistics

Site Analytics, involving the gathering and presentation of Web page statistics, can be enabled for your Web site over a set time period, i.e. over one or more months (or even years!). This lets you assess whether the Web site meets its original objectives and perhaps the success of a Web site launch (re-launch). Either way, statistics let you make choices about how to improve your Web site.

Site Analytics can be presented in various categories. In particular:

- **Visits**: show the popularity of the Web site as a Site Visits bar chart showing number of visits by date.

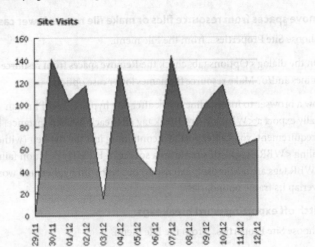

In addition, you can view your top five visitors, landing or exit pages (first/last page that a web visitor arrives at/leaves). Top five visitors show the visitor's IP address or, where possible, the visitor's computer host name.

- **Browsing environments**: shows a breakdown of Web visitor's browser programs used, screen resolutions, operating systems, and whether Flash is enabled on browsers, all expressed in percentages.

- **Referrers**: lists the top and most consistent referrers, i.e. the addresses of Web pages that have been used to arrive at your own Web pages.

- **Search Terms**: shows the top search engines and most used keywords and search terms.

Web statistics are enabled via Site Properties by linking to a profile specifically created for the Web site. Generated statistics can then be accessed in an **Analytics** Smart Object either via WebPlus's Smart Object Tool (Web Objects toolbar) or via the serifwebresources.com Web site (at any time).

Use the Site Visits bar chart to indicate web server outage—days with no site visits may indicate server unavailability.

To enable Web page statistics:

1. Choose **Site Properties...** from the File menu.

2. From the Site Analytics tab, check **Enable web analytics**.

3. Click the **Set Analytics Profile** button, then select either:

   - A new profile: enter a profile name in the Create New Profile input
     box, click the **Add New Profile** button, then select from the list.
     OR

   - An existing profile: Pick directly from the profile list.

4. Click **OK**, then **OK** again.

To view Web statistics:

1. Click the ![icon] **Smart Object Tool** button on the Web Objects toolbar and
   login.

2. Select the object from the My Smart objects Library pane.

3. In the adjacent window, select the ⎣ Manage... ⎦ button under the
   object preview.

4. Select a statistics category from the drop-down menu, then a time period
   over which the statistics have been collected.

Defining an absolute URL

Normally, there's no real need to declare your Web site's root URL from
within WebPlus. However, some exceptions include:

- If your ISP hosts Web sites inside an iFrame, you can set absolute URLs
  in your hyperlinks to site pages, files, anchor, and navigation elements.

- When using search engine sitemaps the root URL is specified (and then
  indexed) to allow search engine users to navigate to your Web site from
  their search results.

- Similarly, if an RSS feed/podcast you manage is being referenced from a
  third-party Web site or Internet browser, the Absolute URL will allow
  contact to be made with your feed. (See RSS feeds and podcasts on
  p. 270).

To set an absolute URL:

1. Choose **Site Properties...** from the File menu.

2. From the Site Base URL tab, enter the base URL that users would expect to navigate to, e.g. www.sailaway.com, www.discount.co.uk, etc.

3. (Optional) Check **Turn all local URLs into absolute URLs** to use absolute URLs instead of relative URLs.

> Hyperlinks can be made absolute hyperlinks by checking the **Absolute URL** option for a Site page, file, anchor, or navigation element. If the Site Base URL is not already set, you'll be prompted to declare the URL when publishing.

> Don't enter a URL with a subfolder or page name appended to the base Web address.

Setting page properties

Your WebPlus site has its own general framework, consisting of the **site** itself; one or more **master pages**; and a number of individual **pages**. Each aspect of the framework has various **property** settings that contribute to the look and behaviour or your site when it's published. Whether you start with a WebPlus template or from scratch, you can choose whether to stick with the default property settings or alter them to suit your needs.

Page properties of individual pages can be viewed either via the Site tab, by right-clicking on the active page in your workspace, or via the Site Manager. The Site Manager offers a more powerful method of not just viewing but modifying the properties of multiple pages at the same time—simply check you chosen pages and alter one or more page properties. All checked pages will adopt the new settings.

To view master page property settings:

*   Click the 📄 **Master Page Manager** button above the Master Pages window on the Site tab. The Master Page Manager appears.

To view normal Web page property settings:

- Right-click the page in the workspace and choose **Page Properties....**
  OR
  On the Studio's **Site** tab, single-click to select the page in the Site
  Structure tree, right-click the page entry and choose **Page Properties....**
  OR
  Choose the item from the Edit menu.

The Page Properties dialog appears.

Tab name	Property
Page	**Page and file name**
	Each page has a "visible" page title or file name shown in Site tab's Site Structure tree. Use the Page Properties dialog (Page tab) to change the page name, specify a different HTML title, and/or change the file name.
	Include in navigation
	By default, all pages are included in navigation (they can be linked to by navigation elements like navbars).
	Page alignment
	Alignment determines how the page content appears in a browser. Use the Site's default page alignment setting (Use Site setting), or choose Left or Centered as an override.
	Master page
	Use to assign a specific master page to a specific page, or set a page to use no master page.
	Width and Height
	Each master page determines the size of pages that use it. In the Master Page Manager (Properties button), you can override the site setting for a given master page. For individual pages that don't use a master page you can set custom page dimensions. For pages using a master page, only the Height can be set.

Active document frame

Pages can be opened in an active document frame if the frame has been created previously.

Background   **Background sound**

Choose a sound to load and play automatically when a specific page is first displayed.

Background   **Background colour/picture/On-page colour**

Sets a custom colour/picture for off-page background and a colour for on-page background. Use for pages that don't use a master page. When using master pages, adjunct scheme settings are applied by default.

Search   **Search engine descriptors**

Include optional descriptive information and keywords on individual pages, which override the site's search engine settings.

Search Engine   **Sitemaps and robots**

Informs search engines or robots if they can crawl, analyze and index the current page. A Sitemap file will include the current page in indexing whereas a Robots meta tag (or a robots.txt file) will exclude the page. These settings override the site's search engine settings.

Page Security   **Page Security**

Apply access control to your Web page(s) by assigning to a user list or user group (via Serif Web Resources Access Control Smart object).

Redirect   **Redirect**

After a configurable time interval a web page is redirected to a new hyperlink destination (another page, image, email, etc.).

Page Transitions   **Page Transitions**

Page entry and exit transitions can be applied as you navigate from one web page to another.

Page properties via Site Manager

The Site Manager lets you view and apply properties to individual or multiple Web Pages. You can set Include pages in navigation, assign master pages, set page alignment and size, rename pages, set a background/on-page colour, add sounds, optimize pages for search engines, and apply redirections, transitions, or access control. Master pages can also have their page size, background and page transitions managed via Site Manager.

To view Page/Master page properties via Site Manager:

1.   For Normal Web Pages or Master Pages, respectively:

     *   Select **Site Manager>Page Properties...** from the Tools menu. The **Site Manager** is launched with Page Properties shown by default. OR

     *   Select **Site Manager>Master Page Properties...** from the Tools menu. The **Site Manager** shows Master Page Properties by default instead.

         Alternatively, click the [icon] **Site Manager** button on the Hintline at the bottom of your workspace, then choose Page or Master Page Properties as a menu option.

2.   Pick a submenu item (e.g., Background) reflecting the type of page property.

3.   From the main Properties pane, you can edit individual page properties or those of multiple pages.

     *   For individual pages, click on the relevant column on a page entry. Depending on the setting (an input box, drop-down list, check box, or pop-up dialog) edit the page accordingly.

     *   For multiple pages, check the check box at the start of each page entry (For all pages, just click the **Page** column header). At the bottom of the property's column, click to set the property via input box, drop-down list, etc.

4.   Click the **Close** button.

Using Site Manager

WebPlus's **Site Manager** hosts a whole range of useful site-wide information available from a single menu-driven dialog. The tool lets you view Page/Master Page Properties, and pick from a selection of Management tools for viewing and editing hyperlinks (see below), resources, text, fonts, and more.

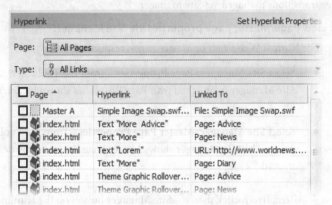

Powerful features of Site Manager include:

- The ability to control the scope and to manage an individual, a selection or all pages in your site equally.

- Any column can be sorted up or down which offers a quick way of reordering information.

- Find and Replace. Where available, this is a powerful way of applying text changes across all Web pages simultaneously.

While most management tools are beneficial at any point in Web site development, the management of resources and text, as well as use of the Site Checker, are essential for checking your Web site just prior to Web publishing.

To launch Site Manager:

- Click the 🖼️ **Site Manager** button on the Hintline at the bottom of
  your workspace.
  OR

  Click the 🖼️ Site Manager button on the Pages context toolbar.
  OR

  Select **Site Manager** from the Tools menu, and choose a manager type
  from the submenu (e.g. Resource Manager). This opens Site Manager
  with the chosen Manager displayed automatically.

A quick summary gives an indication of what each management feature can
do for you.

Type of Management	Let's you...
Page/Master Page Properties	Include pages in navigation, assign master pages, set page alignment and size, rename pages, set a background, add sounds, optimize pages for search engines, and apply redirections, transitions, or access control.
Hyperlink	View and edit hyperlinks, jump to hyperlinks on the page, find and replace destination links.
Resources	View images, media, links, HTML code resources, scripts, or applets in your site. Jump to each resource on the page, swap between linked/embedded image status, replace or resample images.
Text	View and edit text (in WritePlus), name stories, reformat text, apply styles, convert creative frames and tables to HTML-compatible text.
Font	View fonts and their availability, jump to fonts on the page, and substitute fonts.
E-Commerce	View E-Commerce objects on pages across your site.

Anchor	View and edit anchors, jump to anchors, find and replace anchor links.
File	Display the Web site structure with page file names rather than page names.
Site checker	Display common layout problems discovered in your Web site.

Access control

Access control lets you apply security across your Web site or, more typically, to specific pages which may host confidential information. How you apply access control to pages is dependent on the complexity and nature of your Web site—simple Web sites can usually adopt a basic level of access control, whereas larger multi-purpose Web sites might use more advanced access control. Each method can be further described as follows:

- **Basic access control**: log in to a password-protected page from a user login dialog. The login details are stored in a **user list** associated with the page. These lists are simply lists of username/password combinations.

- **Advanced access control**: Either:

    - login to a password-protected page from a user login dialog. The login details are stored in a **user group** associated with the page which contains a static list of users; the list is controlled by the Web manager of the Web site. The use of groups lets you assign a selection of users the same access control rights to pages.
      OR

    - login to the Web site from an on-the-page sign in box—this allows access to any user group set to "add new users on sign up" and therefore any pages associated with those user groups. No manual user management is normally required.

The subject of access control can be a little daunting so the following illustration helps to show the relationships between users, Web pages, user lists, and user groups.

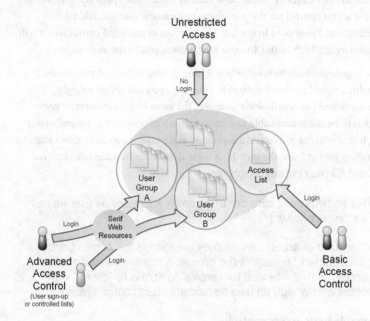

Advanced access control is carried out via Serif Web Resources by using a Smart object, called **Access Control**, which can be created to manage user groups and users, and to optionally insert a user login onto your page for user sign in (after self-registration sign up).

As a brief reminder, Serif Web Resources is a secure online service hosted by Serif that securely stores adopted Smart objects (see p. 306) and any generated data. You can manage your Access Control Smart object, as any other Smart object, via **www.serifwebresources.com** at any time.

Basic access control

The simplest form of access control within WebPlus is page-level access controlled via configurable user lists. Typically of use in personal Web sites or small enterprise Web sites, you can allow free access to most of your site, with only a limited set of pages accessible to selected Web visitors. For example, a

Photo Gallery page of your family can be made "private" but still be shared with your relatives (under password control).

User lists can be created at the same time as setting your page security. Simply enable access control for the page then create a new user list, adding a username and password to the list. The username/password combination will be used by the Web visitor to login and allow access to the Web page.

Two approaches can be taken when setting up username and passwords. If you don't need to control visitors to your page you can set up a single username and password—everyone uses the same login. However, if your page is to be made accessible to a known group of people, e.g. a membership list, it makes sense to allocate a username and password to each individual. As members join or leave the member's login details can be added or removed without affecting existing members.

> For known users, consider using email addresses as user names for better traceability.

> This form of access control does not involve the Access Control Smart object and associated groups, a more advanced method of access control intended for controlling access to "zones" with optional user sign up (see Advanced access control below).

To enable basic access control:

1. With the Web page currently in view, click the **Page Security**
    button on the Pages context toolbar.
    OR
    Right-click the page in the Site tab, and choose **Page Properties...**, then
    select the Page Security tab.

2. Check **Protect page with password** to enable access control. You'll notice
    that the **Change/Manage** button becomes active. Click this button.

3. From the dialog, create your new user list by entering a Name (e.g.,
    "PhotoGallery_Login") and a Description "Login access to family
    photos", then click the **Add New List** button.

4.   From the next dialog, enter a Username and Password for your new Web visitor, then click the **Add User** button. Repeat for other logins if necessary. The User List is incremented as each new username/password entry is added. You'll also be able to rename your user list by editing the list name in the box and clicking the Rename button.

5.   Click **OK**, then **OK** again to exit the dialogs.

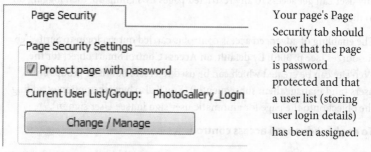

Your page's Page Security tab should show that the page is password protected and that a user list (storing user login details) has been assigned.

To edit a user list:

*   From the User Lists and Groups dialog, click the **Manage** button with a user list selected from the upper window. The next dialog lets you:

    *   **add** users. Enter a Username and Password for your new user, then click the **Add User** button. Repeat for other logins. The list is incremented as each new username/password entry is added.

    *   **delete** an entry. From the dialog, select an entry, then click **Delete** button.

Uncheck **Protect page with password** if you want to set up user lists without protecting the current page.

Advanced access control

Advanced access control is intended for more complex Web security scenarios where one set of Web pages belong to one **user group**, with another set of pages belonging to another. Each user group is then associated with a group of users—all with the same permission to access that group's set of pages. By establishing a range of user groups which reflect the distinct areas in your site, you have versatile control over visitor access. For example, a medium-sized business Web site can be set up to have separate password protection on pages for personnel information, VPN access, internal telephone lists, software downloads, etc.

Even more powerful is the ability to use a common login/logout input box throughout your site, typically by adding to your master page. This means that any user can get access to any restricted pages by signing up, then logging on to the site.

The enabling of advanced access control is carried out via login to Serif Web Resources (see p. 306). By default, an Access Control Smart object for the Web site can be created which can be used to create new user groups and users (and manage them subsequently). You'll also have the option of adding the object onto the page for automatic user sign in (see User sign in).

To enable advanced access control:

1. Click the Smart Object Tool button on the Web Objects toolbar.

2. Login to Serif Web Resources (See Using Smart objects; p. 306). This assumes you have a valid login; otherwise you have to register.

3. From the dialog, select the **New...** button at the bottom of the My Smart objects Library pane.

4. In the Create Smart object dialog, use the scroll bar to navigate the list of Smart objects, then select **Access Control**, then click **OK**.

5. (Optional) Name your Access Control smart object and modify colours for text, buttons, background, or border. Click **Create**. Your new Smart object is listed in your Smart objects Library.

6. Either:

   - If an on-the-page user login is not required, click **Exit** to logout of Serif Web Resources.

     OR

   - If an on-the-page user login is required, click the **Insert** button. See User sign in on p. 80.

To create a user group:

1. Click the   **Smart Object Tool** button on the Web Objects toolbar.

2. With your Access Control Smart object selected, in the Object Preview pane, click the object's **Manage...** button to reveal the Manage Access Control dialog.

3. (Optional) If user sign in is required, enable CAPTCHA then click the **Update** field. CAPTCHA is an anti-spamming technique where arbitrary server-generated text is displayed; the Web visitor enters the text for subsequent validation.

4. Enter a **Group Name** in the **Create New Group** section; this should reflect the type of users that will belong to the group, e.g. "Downloads".

   Create New Group

   Group Name: Downloads

   Add new users on signup: ☑   Automatic login/logout: ☐

   ---

5. Some group-related settings can be configured, i.e.

   - **Group Smart object** (not shown): Use only if you're setting up a forum's moderator group or restricting comments posted on a blog. Select the forum or blog name as appropriate.

   - **Add new users on signup**: Check for direct user sign up—the user login details are added to the user group. When unchecked, the user group has to be manually populated with the user's email (the Web Manager will need to know user email addresses in advance).

- **Automatic login/logout**: If you've got a forum on the same page as your user login, check the option to automatically login to the forums as well when a user signs in. You'll need to publish your Web site to check this is set correctly due to web browser security restrictions.

6. Click the **Create Group** button, verify dialog settings then click **Done**. The group will be added to the **Group** drop-down menu in User Group Management (see below).

To manage a user group:

- In the User Group Management section, select the group name from the **Group** drop-down menu, then click **Manage Group**.

From the dialog, you can rename, link to an existing forum/blog, enable user sign up to groups, and automatically login to pages hosting forums. Number and names of group users are also displayed. Make changes by clicking the **Update Group** button, or remove the group with the **Delete Group** button.

Adding users to groups

For each user group that is created, a group of **users** can be added to each user group by manual entry (by Web manager), import from a comma-delimited text file (again by Web Manager) or automatically by user sign up. All options are possible when managing the Access Control Smart object.

- **manual entry**: Users are included in groups by manual addition.

- **import user lists**: Another manual method for adding users, but an existing set of users is imported into your site from a comma-delimited file (.CSV format).

- **user sign up**: Web visitors create their own user accounts at login and then access the page once their email address has been verified. No manual addition of users is need.

It's your choice which of the above methods you use. Typically manual user control is great for controlled environments such as small businesses, organizations, or clubs where users are "known". Conversely, user sign in is intended for more public access where controlling users is impractical—instead user sign up (self-registration) is used, with the option to manage users within their groups via the Access Control Smart object.

> You can add more than one user to the same user group. The same user can belong to multiple user groups.

Any user can be deleted whether the user belongs to a group or not. A user can also be temporarily suspended for breaking site rules (e.g., for posting defamatory statements on a hosted public forums). The next time the user tries to log on the message "Your account has been suspended" is displayed.

If more drastic action is required, a user's IP address can be banned from accessing Serif Web Resource objects (e.g., forums, etc.). As a last resort, even the ISP or organization to which the owner of the email address belongs to can be banned from access. This latter option is not recommended normally but may be necessary to prevent institutional malpractice such as professional spamming.

To add a user manually:

1. Click the ⚙ **Smart Object Tool** button on the Web Objects toolbar.

2. With your Access Control Smart object selected, in the Object Preview pane, click the object's **Manage...** button to reveal the Manage Access Control dialog.

3. From the **Add New User** section at the bottom of the dialog, enter the user's email address in the **Email** box and click the **Add User** button.

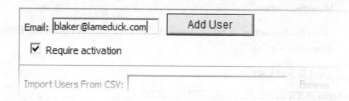

The user is added to the User Group Management's **Users** field.

4. With **Require activation** checked, an activation link will be emailed to the user along with an auto-generated password. When unchecked, only an auto-generated password will be emailed.

5. To assign to a group, select the group from the Group drop-down list, then add the selected user from the Users box to the Group box by clicking the **Add** button (if adding all users, click **Add All**). The user will now belong to the user group. To remove, use the **Remove** (or **Remove All**) buttons from the group.

To import a user list from a text file:

1. Follow the above procedure but from the **Add New User** section at the bottom of the dialog, click the **Browse...** button to locate an existing text file which contains comma-delimited username/password combinations. Select the file and click **Open**.

2. Click the **Import** button to populate the **Users** left-hand pane (in User Group Management) with the file's contents.

To import a user list from a mailing list:

1. Select a mailing list Smart object, right-click and select **Manage...**.

2. To synchronize, click the **Sync To Access Control** button.

3. From the dialog, pick a named Access Control Smart object from the drop-down list and click **Proceed...**. The stored email addresses are copied to this Smart object.

To delete a user:

1. With your Access Control Smart object selected, click the object's **Manage...** button.

2. From the bottom of the dialog, select a user for deletion from the **Email** drop-down menu.

3. Click **Delete User**.

To suspend a user:

• As for deletion of a user (above), but click the **Suspend User** button instead of the **Delete User** button. Use the **Unsuspend User** button to make the user login active again.

> Suspended users will be shown with an asterisk in the Manage Access Control dialog's user groups.

To ban a user(s):

- by IP address: As for deletion of a user (above), but select **IP address** from the drop-down list, then click the **Ban** button.

- by ISP/Organization: As for deletion of a user (above), but first click the **Lookup User** button (this locates the user's ISP/organization network address in the scrolling window above the button) then select **ISP/organization** from the drop-down list, then click the **Ban** button.

> To allow banning to take place, the user must have been logged onto Serif Web Resources previously.

If a user's IP address, ISP or Organization is currently banned, it will appear in an **Unban** drop-down list. This lets you review current bans. Of course, banning may be reversed if a particular IP address or network is no longer considered suspect.

To unban a user(s):

- Select a specific IP address (for an individual user) or network IP address (for ISP/organization) from the **Unban** drop-down list. A specific IP address will end with a number other than zero (e.g., 80.6.91.234), whereas a network address for an ISP/organization will always ends with zero (e.g., 80.6.91.0). The entry will also include the date the address was banned.

- Click the **Unban** button. The IP address will be removed from the list.

User sign in

Login

Email

[   ]

Password

[   ]

Sign up | Reset password

[Sign in]

A user login box can be added to the page to allow registered users to Sign in to **all** groups that are "sign up enabled", otherwise restricted pages will be protected.

A new visitor to the site can sign up to become a registered user (click the Sign up link).

> Add the login box to the Web site's master page. Any Web page will then offer the user the opportunity to sign up to the site.

To add a user login for sign up:

1. Follow the procedure for To enable access control (see p. 70) but instead of exiting the dialog, pick a page to place your login box, then click the **Insert** button.

2. Position the ⊕ 🔲 **Paste** cursor where you want the user login box, then click the mouse to insert the object at a default size.

3. Right-click the login box and choose **Manage Smart object....**

4. Enter a **Group Name** in the **Create New Group** section; this should reflect the type of users that will belong to the group, e.g. "Homeworker".

5. Check **Add new users on signup**—on user sign up, the user's account login details are added to the user group.

6. Click the **Create Group** button, verify dialog settings then click **Done**. The group will be added to the **Group** drop-down menu in User Group Management.

As users are signing up by themselves you don't need to manually add users in the Add New Users section (although you can still add manually; see To add a user manually p. 77). When users sign up they will appear automatically in every user group which is "user sign up enabled."

To sign up as a registered user:

1. From the User Login box, click the **Sign Up** link.

2. Agree to Serif Hosted Objects and Form Redirection Services **Terms and Conditions** by checking the check box.

3. From the dialog, enter the user login details, choosing a valid email address, screen name, and memorable password (at least six characters long). If you've enabled CAPTCHA verification, enter the displayed text in the box.

4. Click the **Signup** button. An activation email is sent to the user—click the link to activate the new user login.

> If you've not been emailed your activation link check your Junk, Trash, Bulk, or equivalent mail folder. Your email may have been incorrectly treated as a "spammed" message and therefore deleted.

Once logged into the site, you can revisit the login area on your page to **Change screen name**, **Change Password**, or simply log out. The screen name is the name other users see when the user makes public postings on forums or blogs.

Search engine optimization

Indexing involves the automatic collection of information about your Web pages by search engines such as Google, Yahoo!, Live Search, and many more. By "harvesting" this information at the search engine, search engine users can make use of this indexed information to obtain quick and accurate site search results which match the search criteria entered by the user.

By default, the contents of each published Web page (especially heading text) will be indexed. However, in an Internet world of billions of Web pages all being constantly indexed, Web developers can optimize this indexing process to allow a Web site's pages to appear higher in a user's search results.

Optimization of Web pages for search engines is possible in several ways:

- **Meta Tags**: Tags store **search engine descriptors** (i.e., keywords and a description) for the site and/or an individual page. These tags are used to allow better matching between entered search engine text (like you might enter into Google) and the keywords you've associated with your Web site or page. Additionally, a **robots meta tag** also lets you include/exclude the site or pages from being indexed; hyperlinks to other pages can also be prevented from being explored (crawled by "spiders").

- **Robots**: Pages (or folders) can be **excluded** from search-engine indexing by using a robots file. This works in an equivalent way to the robots meta tag but uses a text file (robots.txt) to instruct robots or spiders what **not** to index. The file simply lists excluded Web site page/folder references.

- **Sitemaps**: The opposite of the "robots" concept; pages can be **included** to aid and optimize intelligent crawling/indexing. Web site page references are stored in a dedicated sitemap file (sitemap.xml).

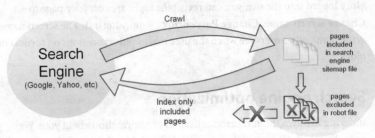

Whether you are using Meta tags, robots, or sitemaps independently or in combination, WebPlus makes configuration simple. As these settings can be established or modified for the whole site (Site Properties; Search Engine tab) any newly created page will adopt site's search engine settings. If you change the site settings, all Web pages will update to the new settings automatically. However, you can override the site's settings on a specific Web page (Page Properties; Search Engine tab) at any time. The page's override means that subsequent changes to site settings will always be ignored.

Using search engine descriptor Meta Tags

Although they're optional, if you want to increase the likelihood that your Web site will be "noticed" by major Web search services, you should enter Meta Tag **search engine descriptors**. Search services maintain catalogues of Web pages, often compiled through the use of "crawlers" or other programs that prowl the Web collecting data on sites and their content. By including descriptive information and keywords, you'll assist these engines in properly categorizing your site. You can enter descriptors for the site as a whole and/or for individual pages. For example, for a simple ornithological web site you could have the following descriptors, reflecting the content of your site or page, e.g.

	Site Properties	Page Properties
Description	American Birds Web	Egret and Heron species page
Keywords	Birds, America, Audubon	Cattle Egret, Blue Heron, Green-backed Heron

It's a good idea to plan which descriptors are used for the site and pages. If set, a site's descriptors will complement page-specific descriptors.

To enter search engine descriptors:

1. (For the site) Choose **Site Properties...** from the File menu.
   OR
   (For a page) Right-click the page in the workspace or Site tab and choose **Page Properties...** (or choose the item from the Edit menu).

2. Click the dialog's **Search** tab.

3. In the top window, type in a brief description of your site. Although the description can be any length, the first ten words or so are the most important.

4. In the next window, enter any number of keywords (separated by commas) that you think fairly categorize your site. Put yourself in the place of a potential visitor. What keywords might they enter if they were searching for exactly what your site or page has to offer?

5. Set a language code for your site from the drop-down menu to identify your site's language use. Most user's Internet search engines will permit language specific searches for web pages, so your site will show in search results according to its language code setting.

Excluding pages from indexing (robots meta tags)

A robots meta tag can be used by search engine robots to control how they access the Web site or page. The whole Web site (and pages) can be set to be indexed/not indexed, page hyperlinks followed/not followed, or any combination thereof. Site-wide settings are made by checking **Index pages on this site** and **Follow links from pages** or as overrides on specific page properties.

To enable robot Meta Tag generation:

1. (For the site) Choose **Site Properties...** from the File menu.
    OR
    (For a page) Right-click the page in the workspace or Site tab and choose **Page Properties...** (or choose the item from the Edit menu).

2. Select the Search Engine tab and check the **Create robots meta tags** option (for a page you'll need to override site-wide settings).

3. (For the site) Use the two suboptions to allow or prevent search engines indexing the entire site (check/uncheck **Index pages on this site** option) or to allow or prevent indexing of all pages linked from an indexed page (check/uncheck **Follow links from pages** option).
    OR
    (For the page) Check **Override site search engine settings** and **Create robots meta tag**, then check/uncheck the equivalent suboptions for the specific page.

Excluding pages from indexing (Robots file)

The objective of this method is the same as that for using a robots meta tag, but instead a robots.txt file is created and no robots meta tag is included in Web pages. The robots.txt file is stored in the Web site's root folder and can be viewed in any text editor to verify the excluded pages and folders.

To enable a robots.txt file:

1. (For the site) Choose **Site Properties...** from the File menu.
   OR
   (For a page) Right-click the page in the workspace or Site tab and choose **Page Properties...** (or choose the item from the Edit menu).

2. Check the **Create search engine robots file** option.

3. (For the site) To allow or prevent search engines indexing the entire site (check/uncheck **Index pages on this site** option).
   OR
   (For a page) To prevent search engines indexing the page, check **Override site search engine settings**, then uncheck the **Index this page** option.

Including pages in indexing

So far we've looked primarily at methods of excluding Web pages from indexing. Without these controls, Web pages will be indexed by discovering page hyperlinks and crawling through them, harvesting keywords, descriptions, and page text to be indexed. However, this process may not be efficient as there may be a limited number of inter-page hyperlinks present throughout your site. As a result, a search engine sitemap file (sitemap.xml) can be created to act as a local lookup for crawlers to begin investigating your site. The file simply lists pages in your Web site that you've decided can be indexed. The file also indicates to search engines when pages have been modified, informs when the search engine should check the page and how "important" pages are in relation to each other.

The Sitemap method is especially good for "advertising" your Web site pages—with a greater likelihood of your pages appearing high in a user's search results.

Just like the robots file, the setting of site and page properties creates the sitemap file (this is published with your Web site); the file is stored in the root Web folder (perhaps alongside a robots.txt file).

One requirement of using search engine sitemaps is the need to declare an absolute URL. This allows the proper URL address (e.g., www.helloworld.com) to be indexed, allowing search engine users to link through to your site from their search results.

To enable search engine sitemaps:

1. (For the site) Choose **Site Properties...** from the File menu.
    OR
    (For a page) Right-click the page and choose **Page Properties...**.

2. Check the **Create search engine sitemap file** option.

3. (Optional) When the above option is checked, the default sitemap.xml file can be renamed. Click the **Change...** button and edit accordingly.

4. (For the site) To populate the sitemap file with a list of all the site's Web pages (for improved page "discovery"), the **Index pages on this site** option is checked. Uncheck to create an empty sitemap.xml file.
    OR
    (For a page) To add the page to the sitemap file, check **Override site search engine settings**, then check the **Index this page** option. This assumes the site as a whole has not been listed in the sitemap.xml file.

5. Check/uncheck Sitemap settings including:

    •   Page's last modified date and time.

    •   Page change frequency (set drop-down menu to hourly, daily, weekly, monthly, yearly, or never): This suggests to the search engine how frequently the page is likely to change. The search engine will decide how often to index the page on the basis of this setting.

    •   Page priority rating: 0.0 (lowest) to 1.0 (highest). Sets a page priority relative to your other Web pages by which search engines are most likely to index. The default can be set on site properties with specific page overrides setting a priority higher or lower than the default.

Prioritizing text with Heading HTML tags

It is possible to assign paragraphs (or text styles) in your HTML frame or
HTML table with a preferred HTML tags (H1, H2, .., to H6) for export. The
tags can be assigned from **Paragraph...** on the Text menu (choose the
Paragraph>HTML option); simply pick a preferred HTML tag for your
paragraph from the drop-down menu. An advantage of this is that paragraphs
assigned such tags take priority over other "body" tags (e.g., those using the
<P> tag) when appearing in search engine results (the H1 tag is the highest
priority).

Searching Web sites

WebPlus uses a powerful search facility which matches user search terms with
text that appears in your Web site in artistic text, and HTML or creative text
frames or tables. This makes it easy to retrieve content from any hosted Web
pages.

The search feature works by using the Site Search Tool and Site Search Results
Tool, both hosted on the Web Objects toolbar's Search flyout. Each tool is
used to create objects that work together in combination.

Site Search object—the text box
in which users type the word or
phrase they want to search for.
This text box is usually added to
a master page and appears on all
pages of the site.

Site Search Results object—
creates a window in which the
search results are displayed.
Typically, this is placed and
sized onto its own page, and
does not appear in the site
navigation structure.

As an example, the search term "vitae" could retrieve search results showing Web pages which contain the search term. The user clicks the **Search** button to initiate any search.

> <u>Products</u>
> In eget sapien vitae Vivamus vel sapien.
> Maecenas Curabitur Nulla vestibulum elei
> nisl ...
>
> <u>Downloads</u>
> SoftwareDownloads Latest Reviews In e
> Morbi pellentesque Mauris purus Donec N
> Vivamus...
>
> <u>Services</u>
> Services List Overview Services List Aliq
> neque. Donec posuere tempus massa. C
> ornare non, v...

The search results show a hyperlinked page name heading plus associated Web page text for reference. Simply click the hyperlink to access the Web page.

With respect to security, all Web pages will be searchable by default. However, password-protected pages will always be excluded from search results. See Access Control on p. 70 for more information on password protection.

To add the Site Search object:

1. Click the 🔍 **Site Search Tool** on the Web Objects toolbar's Search flyout.

2. On the Web page or master page, move the ⊹▨ place cursor to a chosen position and click to place your Site Search object. Your search object appears on the page.

> 💡 Add the search object to the top of your master page to allow site-wide access to the search feature.

Site search is useless without some means of displaying the search results to the user. This is possible by using the Site Search Results object which, like the Site Search object, can be placed on a Web page under a place cursor. However, the object is typically resized to full page size before placement (it needs to display multiple Web page hits consecutively). It also makes sense to keep the search results on a separate, perhaps new, page which can also have its own look and feel (double-click the object to alter page appearance).

To add Site Search Results to a new page:

1. On the **Site** tab, in the [+] ▼ **Add** drop-down list, click **New Blank Page**.

2. Right-click the new page and then click **Page Properties....** In the **Page Properties** dialog, on the **Page** tab, name your search results page and clear the **Include in Navigation** check box.

3. Click the ⊞ **Site Search Results Tool** on the Web Objects toolbar's Search flyout.

4. Move the ⊹▦ place cursor to a chosen position, then click and drag to place your search results window.

Working
with Text

Understanding text frames

Typically, text in WebPlus goes into **text frames,** which work equally well as containers for single words, standalone paragraphs, or multipage articles or chapter text. You can also use **artistic text** for standalone text with special effects, or **table text** (see Creating text-based tables on p. 127) for row-and-column displays.

What's a text frame?

A text frame is effectively a mini-page, with:

- Margins and column guides to control text flow.

- Optional preceding and following frames.

- Text and optional inline images that flow through the frame (from the previous frame and on to the next).

The text in a frame is called a **story**.

- When you move a text frame, its story text moves with it.

- When you resize a text frame, its story text reflows to the new dimensions.

Frames can be linked so that a single story continues from one frame to another. But text frames can just as easily stand alone. Thus in any Web site, you can create text in a single frame, spread a story over several frames, and/or include many independent frame sequences, e.g.

When you select a frame you'll see its bounding box (see Frame 1 above), indicated by a grey border line plus corner and edge handles, and (if you clicked with the Pointer Tool) a blinking insertion point in the frame's text. In this mode, you can edit the text with the Pointer Tool. As in a word processor, double-clicking selects a word, and triple-clicking selects a paragraph.

HTML or Creative frames

Two types of frame can be added to the WebPlus page—the HTML text frame and the Creative text frame. These can be compared easily in the following table.

	HTML frames	Creative frames
Searchable by search engines (Google, etc.)	✓	✗
Script insertion for generating dynamic content	✓	✗
Margins and column guides	✗	✓
Breaks (column, page, and frame)	✗	✓
Resize/move frame	✓	✓
Crop frame	✗	✓

Rotate frame	✗	✓[1]
Frame linking	✗	✓
Columns	✗	✓
Export as text	✓	✓[2]
Copy and paste exported text	✓	✓
Solid fill and line colour	✓	✓
Gradient and bitmap fill	✗	✓
HTML-compliant Styles	✓	✗
Transparency	✗	✓[1]
Borders	✗	✓[1]
Warp	✗	✓[1]
2D/3D Filter Effects	✗	✓[1]
Instant 3D	✗	✓[1]

[1] If applied, will export frame as a graphic.

[2] Only if rotate, crop, transparency, a border or a filter effect is not applied.

The above table relates to the frame as an object, and not to text contained within. See for more information on frame text properties.

So how do you tell the difference between an HTML and Creative frame? Simply, HTML frames will always possess dark blue corner/edge handles when selected, while a Creative frame's handles will show as grey.

To select only the frame (no insertion point):

- Click the frame's bounding box. When only the frame is selected, you can move it more easily.

To move a text frame:

- Drag the frame's bounding box.
  OR

- Use the X or Y options in the Transform tab.

To resize a text frame:

- In any selection mode, drag a corner or edge handle.
  OR

- Use the W or H options in the Transform tab.

Creating frames

You add frames to a page as you would any other object. You can resize any frame, but cannot alter its basic shape.

To create a frame:

1. Click either the ▣ **HTML Frame Tool** or the ▣ **Creative Frame Tool** button from the Text Frames flyout on the Standard Objects toolbar.

2. Click on the page or pasteboard to create a new frame at a default size or drag to adjust the frame's dimensions.

> You can use the **Update Object Default** from the Format menu to set properties for future new frames you create. See Updating and saving defaults on p. 156.

To delete a frame:

- Select the frame and press the **Delete** key. (If there's a selection point in the text, pressing **Delete** will remove characters after the cursor.)
  OR

- With or without an insertion point, choose **Delete Object** from the Edit menu.

Putting text into a frame

You can put text into an HTML or Creative frame in one of several ways. For HTML frames, text will be converted to compliant HTML code.

WritePlus story editor:	To start **WritePlus**, right-click on a frame and choose **Edit Story** (shortcut **Ctrl+E**).
	OR
	Click the [A↨] **WritePlus** button on the Frame context toolbar.
	This opens the WebPlus integrated story editor useful for typing, formatting, and proofing large amounts of text. If the frame already contains text, it is automatically loaded into WritePlus for editing.
Importing text:	Right-click on a frame and choose **Text File...** (shortcut **Ctrl+T**) to import text.
Typing into the frame:	Select the Pointer Tool, then click for an insertion point to type text straight into a frame, or edit existing text. (See Editing text on the page on p. 108.)
Pasting via the Clipboard:	Select the Pointer Tool and click for an insertion point in the text, then press **Ctrl+V**.
Drag and drop:	Select text (e.g. in a word processor file), then drag it onto the WebPlus page.
	If you drop onto a selected a frame, the text is pasted inline after existing text. Otherwise, a new frame is created for the text.

Creative frame setup and layout

The **frame layout** of a Creative frame controls how text will flow in the frame. The frame can contain multiple **columns**. When a frame is selected (and **Frame Edges** is switched on in the View menu), its column margins appear as dashed grey guide lines when values for column blinds and margins are defined.

Note that unlike the page margin and row/column guides, which serve as layout guides for placing page elements, the frame column guides actually determine how text flows within each frame. Text won't flow outside the column guides.

You can drag the column guides or use a dialog to adjust the top and bottom **column blinds** and the left and right **column margins**.

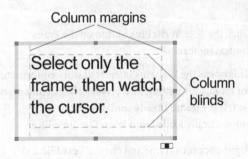

To edit frame properties directly:

- Select the frame, then drag column guide lines to adjust the boundaries of the column.

(1)   (2)   (3)

The illustration shows how the cursor will change when hovering over the bounding box (**1**), after dragging inwards the column margin can be adjusted (**2**), and after dragging downwards, the top margin blind can be moved (**3**).

To edit frame properties using a dialog:

1. Select the Creative frame and click the 📝 **Frame Setup** button on the Frame context toolbar.

2. From the dialog, you can change the **Number of columns**, **Gap** distance between columns, **Left Margin**, **Right Margin**, and enable/disable text wrapping around an object.

3. To change the column widths and blinds (top and bottom frame margins), click a cell in the table and enter a new value.
    Hint: If the frame has more than one column, you only need to enter top/bottom values for the first one. Then click **Top** and/or **Bottom** to repeat the entries instantly in the cells below.

How a story flows through Creative frames

> Stories cannot flow between HTML frames, as they do not support linking (text can only overflow a single frame).

You can have just one Creative frame on its own, or you can have many frames. Frames can be connected in linked **sequences** so that the **story** associated with a given frame sequence flows through the first frame on to the next and keeps flowing into frames in the link sequence.

A key difference from a word processor is that WebPlus does not normally add or remove frames according to the amount of text. The text simply flows until the text runs out (and some frames are left empty), or the frames run out (and some text is left over).

If the text runs out before the last frame, you'll have some empty frames. These frames will be filled with text if you add more text to the story, or if you increase the size of the story text.

WebPlus keeps track of multiple linked frame sequences, and lets you flow several stories in the same site. The Site Manager's Text menu item (accessed via the Tools menu) provides an overview of all stories and lets you choose which one you want to edit.

AutoFlow

When importing text, it's a good idea to take advantage of the **AutoFlow** feature, which will automatically create text frames and pages until all the text has been imported. This way, enough frames are created to display the whole story. Then you can gauge just how much adjustment will be needed to fit the story to the available "real estate" in your site. You can make the major changes first, then proceed to the fine-tuning.

To AutoFlow story text on the page:

- Click the ⬚⊞ **AutoFlow** button just to the left of the frame's **Link** button (showing ⬚⬚.)

WebPlus creates additional pages and frames as needed to accommodate the story text.

Fitting text to frames

If there's too much story text to fit in a frame sequence, WebPlus stores it in an invisible **overflow area** and the **Link** button on the last frame of the sequence displays ⬚⬚; an **AutoFlow** button appears next to the Link button. You might edit the story down or make more room for it by adding an extra frame or two to the sequence. Clicking the AutoFlow button adds additional frames and pages as needed.

The Frame context toolbar includes several tools that can simplify the task of fitting text to frames:

AutoFit

Click to scale the story's text size so it fits exactly into the available frames. You can use this early on, to gauge how the story fits, or near the end, to apply the finishing touch. AutoFit first applies small point size changes, then small leading changes, then adjustments to the paragraph space below value, until the text fits. Other settings are not affected. (Also see Note below.)

Tip: You can also press **Ctrl+Alt+X** to apply AutoFit.

Enlarge Story Text

Click to increase the story's text size one increment. Click for a bigger increase.

Shrink Story Text

Click to reduce the story's text size one increment. Click for a greater reduction.

Linking Creative frames

When selected, a text frame includes a **Link** button at the bottom right which allows you to import text files or control how the frame's story flows to following frames. The icon inside each frame's Link button denotes the state of the frame and its story text:

No Overflow
The frame is not linked to a following frame (it's either a standalone frame or the last frame in a sequence) and the end of the story text is visible.

Overflow
The frame is not linked (either standalone or last frame) and there is additional story text in the overflow area.

Continued
The frame is linked to a following frame. The end of the story text may be visible, or it may flow into the following frame.
Note: The button icon will be red if the final frame of the sequence is overflowing, or green if there's no overflow.

There are two basic ways to set up a linked sequence of frames:

- You can link a sequence of empty frames, then import the text.
  OR

- You can import the text into a single frame, then create and link additional frames into which the text automatically flows.

> When frames are created by the AutoFlow option when importing text, they are automatically linked in sequence.

To create a link or reorder the links between existing frames, you can use the **Link** button or the controls on the Frame context toolbar. Remember to watch the cursor, which changes to indicate these operations.

To link the selected frame to another frame as the next frame:

- Click the frame's **Link** button (showing ▭▭.)

  OR

  Select the frame, then click the [▣] **Link Frame** button on the Frame context toolbar.

- Click with the Textflow cursor on the frame to be linked to. Only empty frames are valid frames to link to.

To unlink the selected frame from the sequence:

- Click the [▣] **Unlink Frame** button on the Frame context toolbar.

  OR

  Click on the frame's **Link** button, then click with the Textflow cursor on the same frame.

Story text remains with the "old" frames. For example, if you detach the second frame of a three-frame sequence, the story text remains in the first and third frames, which are now linked into a two-frame story. The detached frame is always empty.

> If you click on a frame's **Link** button, and then change your mind about linking or unlinking, press the **Esc** key or click on a blank area of the page or pasteboard to cancel.

To navigate from frame to frame:

- Click the [▣] **Previous Frame** or [▣] **Next Frame** button on the Frame context toolbar.

Graphic properties of frames

Like graphics, all frames have **line** and **fill** properties initially an outline of zero weight and a clear fill. Although HTML frames cannot possess transparency, Creative frames can (initially set to None). As with graphics, you can edit these properties, for example adding a grey or light-coloured fill as shading behind a frame's text. You can also import images **inline** with frame text.

Note that the text inside a frame can take a solid colour, but doesn't have line and fill properties as such for fancy line/fill effects with text, you can employ **artistic text** (see p. 104).

Controlling overflowing text (HTML frames)

As HTML frames have to comply with HTML standards, they are not capable of linking stories (as for Creative frames). As a result, a decision has to be made about what happens in the event of overflowing text. Overflowing HTML frames are clearly indicated—when selected, the **Link** button at the bottom right of the frame indicates ☐ **Overflow**.

If you see this, you can choose to leave the text **Hidden**, let it **Overflow**, or let all the text be viewable with the help of a scroll bar.

To control overflowing text:

1. Select your overflowing HTML text frame.

2. Right-click on your frame, and go to **Format>Overflowing text** and choose:

    - **Hidden** - The frame as it is displayed on your page will be shown in a browser. Text will continue to be hidden.

    - **Overflow** - The frame will overflow (be extended) to allow all text within the frame to be shown.

    - **Scroll bar** - A navigation scroll bar is displayed permanently but will be greyed out if text does not overflow.

    - **Auto** - A navigation scroll bar is displayed only when text overflows the frame.

It's always a good idea to preview your HTML frames (via Preview in Window or via your browser)—especially if **Overflow** is selected.

Using artistic text

Artistic text is standalone text you type directly onto a page. Especially useful for headlines, pull quotes, and other special-purpose text, it's easily formatted with the standard text tools.

ABCDEF

Here are some similarities between frame text and artistic text. Both text types let you:

- vary character and paragraph properties, apply named text styles, edit text in WritePlus, and import text.

- apply different line styles, fills (including gradient and bitmap fills), and transparency.

- embed inline images.

- apply filter effects and rotate/flip.

- use proofing options such as AutoSpell/Spell Checker, Proof Reader, and Thesaurus.

- manage their content and track font usage via the Site Manager.

And some differences:

- You can initially "draw" artistic text at a desired point size, and drag it to adjust the size later. Frame text reflows in its frame upon frame resize.

- Artistic text can be applied to a path but frame text cannot.

- Artistic text won't automatically line wrap like frame text.

- Artistic text doesn't flow or link the way frame text does; the Frame context toolbar's text-fitting functions aren't applicable to artistic text.

To create artistic text:

1. Choose the **Artistic Text Tool** from the Tools toolbar's Text flyout.

2. Click anywhere on the page for an insertion point using a default point size, or drag to specify a particular size as shown here.

3. Set initial text properties (font, style, etc.) as needed before typing, using the Text context toolbar, Text menu, or right-click (choose **Text Format>**).

4. Type directly on the page to create the artistic text.

Once you've created an artistic text object, you can select, move, resize, delete, and copy it just as you would with a text frame. Solid colours, gradient/bitmap fills and transparency can all be applied.

To resize or reproportion an artistic text object:

- Drag the object's handles to resize it while maintaining the object's proportions. To resize freely, hold down the **Shift** key while dragging.

To edit artistic text:

- Select a range of text by dragging. Double-click to select a word, or triple-click to select a paragraph.

Now you can type new text, apply character and paragraph formatting, edit the text in WritePlus, apply proofing options, and so on.

> With artistic text, the **vertical alignment** setting anchors a particular part of the object—for example, a "top" setting anchors the top line and forces new text to come in below, while a "bottom" setting anchors the bottom (most recent) line and pushes previous lines up as you type new lines.

Putting text on a path

"Ordinary" straight-line artistic text is far from ordinary—but you can extend its creative possibilities even further by flowing it along a curved path. The resulting object has all the properties of artistic text, plus its path is a Bézier curve that you can edit with the Pointer Tool as easily as any other line! In addition, text on a path is editable in some unique ways, as described below.

To apply a preset curved path to text:

1. Create an artistic text object.

2. With the text selected, click the **fx ▾** **Path flyout** on the Text context toolbar and choose a preset path.

The text now flows along the specified path.

To add artistic text along an existing line or shape:

1. Create a freehand, straight, or curved line (see Drawing and editing lines on p. 159) or a shape (see Drawing and editing shapes on p. 165).

2. Choose the **A** **Artistic Text Tool** from the Tools toolbar's Text flyout.

3. Bring the cursor very close to the line. When the cursor changes to include a curve, click the mouse where you want the text to begin, and the line changes as shown at below.

> If you don't want text on a path, you can override the cursor response by holding down the **Alt** key.

4. Begin typing at the insertion point. Text flows along the line, which has been converted to a path.

> The original line object no longer exists. To recover it, use **Undo** at this point.

To fit existing text to an existing line or shape:

1. Create an artistic text object.

2. Create a freehand, straight, curved line or a shape.

3. Select both objects and choose **Fit Text to Curve** from the Tools menu. The text now flows along the specified path.

To create text and path at the same time:

1. Choose one of the Path Text tools from the Text flyout:

 The **Freehand Path Text Tool** lets you sketch a curved line in a freeform way.

 The **Straight Path Text Tool** is for drawing a straight line.

 The **Curved Path Text Tool** lets you join a series of line segments (which may be curved or straight) using "connect the dots" mouse clicks.

> These three tools work almost exactly like their equivalents on the Line flyout. To use the first two, simply drag to define a line on the page. The Curved Path Text Tool is a bit more complex (and lets you use the Curve Creation context toolbar to define individual segments).

2. Create a line on the page. Your line appears as a path with an insertion point at its starting end (for a curved path you can either type directly onto any part of the path or press **Esc** or double-click to get the insertion point at the start of the path).

3. Begin typing at the insertion point. Text flows along the path.

Editing text on the page

You can use the Pointer Tool to edit frame text, table text, or artistic text directly. On the page, you can select and enter text, set paragraph indents and tab stops, change text properties, apply text styles, and use Find and Replace (see p. 111). For editing longer stories, and for more advanced options, choose WritePlus.

Selecting and entering text

The selection of frame text, artistic text, and table text follows the conventions of the most up-to-date word-processing tools. The selection area is shaded in semi-transparent blue for clear editing.

> Nulla vestibulum eleifend
> nulla. Suspendisse potenti.
> Aliquam turpis nisi, venenatis
> non, accumsan nec, imperdiet
> laoreet, lacus.

Double- or triple-click selects a word or paragraph, respectively. You can also make use of the **Ctrl**-click or drag for selection of non-adjacent words, the **Shift** key for ranges of text.

To edit text on the page:

1. Select the Pointer Tool, then click in the text object. A standard insertion point appears at the click position (see below).
    OR
    Select a single word, paragraph or portion of text (see above).

2. Type to insert new text or overwrite selected text, respectively.

Nulla vestibulum eleifend
nulla. Suspendisse potenti.
Aliquam turpis nisi, venenatis
non, accumsan nec, imperdiet
laoreet, lacus.

To start a new paragraph:

- Press **Enter**.

To start a new line within the same paragraph (using a "line break" or "soft return"):

- Press **Shift+Enter**.

The following two options apply only to frame text. You can use these shortcuts or choose the items from the **Insert>Break** submenu.

To flow text to the next column (Column Break) or frame (Frame Break):

- Press **Ctrl+Enter** or press **Alt+Enter**, respectively.

To switch between insert mode and overwrite mode:

- Press the **Insert** key.

To repeat a text action:

- Choose **Repeat** from the Edit menu, or press **Ctrl+Y**.

For example, if you've applied new formatting to one paragraph, you can click in another paragraph and use the **Repeat** command to apply the same formatting there.

Copying, pasting and moving text

You can easily copy frame text and paste into the same or a different text frame. Text stored on the clipboard can additionally be pasted into a new frame.

Drag and drop support for frame text allows text to be moved into a different location within the same frame or a different text frame in your site.

To copy and paste text:

1. Select the text to be copied.

2. Select **Copy** from the Edit menu. This places the text onto the clipboard.

3. Place an insertion point in a different location in your story or artistic text.

4. Select **Paste** from the Edit menu.

> If you don't place an insertion point, the text can be pasted into a new text frame directly.

To move text by drag and drop (text frames only):

1. Select the text to be moved.

2. Hover over the selected text and hold your mouse button down. A cursor is shown.

3. Move the cursor to the location (in the same or different frame) you wish to place the text—an insertion point should be displayed.

4. Release the mouse button to place your text.

Setting paragraph indents

When a text object is selected, markers on the horizontal ruler indicate the left indent, first line indent, and right indent of the current paragraph. You can adjust the markers to set paragraph indents, or use a dialog.

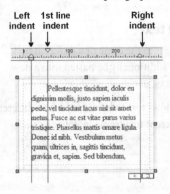

- The **Left** indent is set in relation to the object's left margin.

- The **1st line** indent is in relation to the left indent.

- The **Right** indent is in relation to the object's right margin.

For details on setting frame margins, see Frame setup and layout on p. 97.

To set the indents of the current paragraph:

- Drag the appropriate ruler marker(s).
  OR

  For quick left indents, select the 📑 **Increase Level** or 📑 **Decrease Level** button to increase or decrease indent, respectively. Indent is by the currently set default tab stop distance.
  OR

  To adjust indent settings via a dialog, choose **Text>Paragraph...** from the Text menu (or **Text Format>Paragraph...** from the right-click menu). In the Indentation box, you can enter values for Left, Right, 1st Line, or Hanging indents.

Working with Unicode text

WebPlus fully supports **Unicode**, making it possible to incorporate foreign characters or special symbols.

- To paste Unicode text from the Clipboard to the page, use **Edit>Paste Special...**, then select "Unformatted Unicode Text".

- Insert Unicode characters directly into your text by typing your Unicode Hex value and pressing **Alt+X**. The Alt+X keyboard operation toggles between the displayed character (e.g., @) and its Hex value (e.g., U+0040) equivalent.

- To export text in Unicode format, use WritePlus.

Using Find and Replace

You can search site text for an extraordinary variety of items: not just words or parts of words, but a host of character and paragraph attributes such as fonts, styles, alignment, bullets and numbering, missing fonts, drop caps... ...

even inline graphics and more! Using the Find and Replace dialog—which remains open without interrupting your work until you click its **Close** button—you can replace globally, or on a case-by-case basis.

To use Find and Replace:

1. Choose **Find & Replace...** from the Edit menu or press **Ctrl+F**.

2. In the dialog, type the text to be found in the **Find** box and its replacement text (if any) in the **Replace** box. Click the down arrows to view recent items. Click either box's button to use flyout menus to select formats or special characters, or define a regular expression (for a wildcard-type search).

3. Select the Range to be searched: **Current Story** (just the currently selected text object or story), or **All Stories** (all text), or **Current Selection** (only used with the Replace All function to operate on currently selected text).

4. Select **Match whole word only** to match character sequences that have **white space** (space, tab character, page break etc.) or punctuation at each end, or which are at the start/end of a paragraph. Select **Match case** for case-sensitive search. Select **Regular expressions** to treat the contents of the Find box as an expression, rather than as a literal string to be found.

5. Click **Find Next** to locate the next instance of the Find text.
    OR
    Click **Select All** to highlight all instances of matching text simultaneously.

6. Click **Replace** if you want to substitute the replacement text.
    Alternatively, click **Find Next** again to skip to the next matching text. Continue using the Replace option as required until you reach the end of your document.
    OR
    Click **Replace All** to replace all instances of the Find text with the replacement text at the same time.

7. Click **Close** to dismiss the Find and Replace dialog.

The Find and Replace dialog also lets you perform a wildcard-type search by using a **regular expression**—a formula for generating a set of strings—to specify complex search criteria. This is covered in more detail in the WebPlus Help.

Formatting Characters and Paragraphs

Formatting
Characters and
Paragraphs

Setting text properties

WebPlus gives you a high degree of control over the fine points of typographic layout, whether you're working with frame text, table text, or artistic text.

To apply basic text formatting:

1. Select the text.

2. Use buttons on the Text context toolbar to change typeface, point size, font, attributes, paragraph alignment, or level.
   OR
   Right-click the text and choose **Text Menu>Text Format**, then select from the submenu: **Character...**, **Paragraph...**, **Bullets & Numbering...**, or **Vertical Alignment**. (You can also select these items from the Text menu.) The Text Style dialog (see below) is displayed with the selected menu option shown by default.
   OR
   Use the Character tab to adjust point size, spacing (tracking), leading, and language.

By default, text on your published Web pages is set to vary in size depending on the visitor's browser setting. If you wish, you can override this as a global option in WebPlus, so that text will appear in the browser at exactly the same point sizes used in your layouts. To check or change the setting, choose **Site Properties...** from the File menu. On the Options tab, check **Force absolute text size** to override the variable-text default.

> If a font is unavailable and has been substituted, its font name on the Context toolbar is prefixed by the "?" character.

To clear local formatting (restore plain/default text properties):

- Select a range of text with local formatting.

- Click on the **Clear Formatting** option on the Text context toolbar's text styles drop-down list (or Text Styles tab).

Using fonts

One of the most dramatic ways to change your document's appearance is to change the fonts used in your artistic text, frame text, or table text. Applying different fonts to a character or entire paragraph can communicate very different messages to your intended readership.

Lorem Ipsum

LOREM IPSUM

Lorem Ipsum *Lorem Ipsum*
Lorem Ipsum

Font assignment is very simple in WebPlus, and can be done from the **Fonts** tab, Text context toolbar, or in the **Character** dialog (via right-click, or from the Text menu). However, the Fonts tab lets you:

- Pick fonts easily without dialog navigation.

- Save your favourite fonts (by right-click).

- View most recently used, Websafe, and your favourite fonts at the same time.

- Assign a font to be Websafe, rasterize on export, or resolve in Site Checker. (by right-click)

- Search for installed fonts via search box.

- Hover-over preview of fonts on your document's text (optional).

- Change a font for another throughout your Web site (by right-click Select All).

- Access Serif Font Manager (if purchased).

The Fonts tab is automatically hidden by default, but can be viewed by clicking the arrow button at the left of your workspace.

Websafe fonts are a specially selected and configurable subset of fonts which offer the best font matches between your Web site (during design) and your web visitors' computers (during browsing). On publishing, Websafe fonts are only referenced (and not rasterized) as they are assumed to be available on a Web visitor's computer.

Generally speaking, it is advisable to keep to the standard list of Websafe fonts shown in the Fonts tab unless you can be sure of font usage amongst your target audience. These fonts are grouped together under the tab's Websafe category (an equivalent category exists on the text context toolbar's Font drop-down menu).

Using text styles

It's a good idea to establish the main text and graphic formatting to be used in your site early in the creative process. WebPlus facilitates this by letting you adopt named **text styles** (pre- or user-defined), which can be applied to frame text, table text, or artistic text. A text style is a set of character and/or paragraph attributes saved as a group. When you apply a style to text, you apply the whole group of attributes in just one step. For example, you could use named paragraph styles for particular layout elements, such as "Heading," "Quote," or "Body," and character styles to convey meaning, such as "Emphasis," "Code," or "Reference." Using styles not only speeds the task of laying out a site but ensures consistency and ease of updating.

Styles can be applied to characters or paragraphs using either the Text context toolbar or the Text Styles tab. Both paragraph and character styles can be managed from the **Text Style Palette**.

The Text Styles tab also lets you create new styles from scratch, create named styles from existing text properties, and swap a style for another across your Web site in one operation. Any style can be previewed against any selected paragraph directly on the page. See online Help for more details on these features.

Paragraph styles and character styles

A **paragraph style** is a complete specification for the appearance of a paragraph, including all its font and paragraph format attributes. Every paragraph in WebPlus has a paragraph style associated with it.

- WebPlus includes one built-in paragraph style called **"Normal"** with a specification consisting of generic attributes including left-aligned, 12pt Verdana. Initially, the "Normal" style is the default for any new paragraph text you type. You can modify the "Normal" style by redefining any of its attributes, and create or adopt any number of new or pre-defined styles having different names and attributes.

- Applying a paragraph style to text updates all the text in the paragraph except sections that have been locally formatted. For example, a single word marked as bold would remain bold when the paragraph style was updated or changed.

A **character style** includes only font attributes (name, point size, bold, italic, etc.), and you apply it at the character level—that is, to a range of selected characters—rather than to the whole paragraph.

- Typically, a character style applies emphasis (such as italics, bolding or colour) to whatever underlying font the text already uses; the assumption is that you want to keep that underlying font the same. The base character style is shown in the Text Styles tab (or palette) as **"Default Paragraph Font,"** which has no specified attributes but basically means "whatever font the paragraph style already uses." Suppose a paragraph uses a style called "Body," and the "Body" style uses regular 10pt Arial. Then the "Default Paragraph Font" style for that particular paragraph means regular 10pt Arial.

- Applying the Default Paragraph Font option from the Text Styles tab (or the Text context toolbar's Styles box) will strip any selected local character formatting you've added and will restores original text attributes (paragraph styles are not affected).

- As with paragraph styles, you can define any number of new character styles using different names and attributes (or adopt a pre-defined character style).

Working with named styles

Normal ▾ The named style of the currently selected text is displayed in either the Text Styles tab or the drop-down Styles box on the Text context toolbar. A character style (if one is applied locally) may be shown; otherwise it indicates the paragraph style. You can use either the tab, the drop-down Styles box, or a dialog to apply a particular style to the existing text. The Text Style Palette lets you modify an existing style, import styles, or define a new style.

By default, a limited set of styles are shown in the Text Styles tab, although you can display all styles by checking the tab's **Show All** option (or via **Tools>Options; UI Settings**). The Default Paragraph Font, some common styles, and your document's currently used styles (plus any associated styles) will always be shown. You can preview any style and then apply it to a word, paragraph, or story.

To apply a named style:

1. Using the Pointer Tool, click in a paragraph (if applying a paragraph style) or select a range of text (if applying a character style). If you apply a paragraph style, it will be applied to the whole paragraph regardless of the amount of text selected. If you've selected text in more than one paragraph, the change takes place in all selected paragraphs.

2. Display the Text Styles tab and select a style from the style list.
   OR
   On the Text context toolbar, click the arrow to expand the Styles drop-down list and select a style name..

The applied style appears in the tab's style list.

Creating a bulleted or numbered list

For any text frame it's possible to apply bullets and numbering to lists and paragraphs alike. Bullets are especially useful when listing items of interest in no specific order of preference and numbered lists for presenting step-by-step procedures (by number or letter). WebPlus lets you apply the list style to normal text (as local formatting) or to text styles equally.

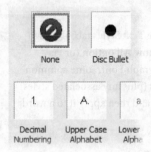

Within HTML text frames, basic bullet icons, numbers (numeric and Roman) and letters can be applied.

However, if you're using Creative text frames you can adopt basic as well as complex **bulleted** or **numbered** lists either by selecting presets (see below) or creating your own custom list style (these let you select your own symbols, numbers and letter formats). You then have the option of replacing an existing preset with your own preset based on your custom list style.

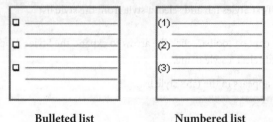

Bulleted list   **Numbered list**

To create a bulleted or numbered list:

1. Select one or more paragraphs.
    OR
    Click in a paragraph's text.

2. Select **Text>Bullets & Numbering...** from the Text menu.

3. From the Text Style dialog, either:

- For text in HTML text frames, click in a preset icon from the dialog (see above).
  OR

- For text in Creative text frames, pick **Bullet** or **Number** from the **Style** drop-down menu, then select one of the preset formats shown by default.
  OR

- For a custom list, select a preset then click the **Details** button to alter custom options.

4. Click **OK** to apply list formatting.

Each time you insert a following return, a new line will begin with the specified symbol or number. In addition, typing two returns in a row (pressing **Enter** twice) cancels bullets or numbers and resumes regular paragraph formatting.

To restart list numbering (Creative frame text only):

1. Click to place an insertion point in the list to set the restart position, then select **Text>Bullets & Numbering...** from the Text menu.

2. From the Presets or Details page, check **Restart Numbering** to reset the number or letter sequence back to 1 or A, respectively.

3. Click **OK**.

To turn off bullets or numbering formatting:

1. Select the paragraph with list formatting.

2. Select **Text>Bullets & Numbering...** from the Text menu.
   OR
   Right-click the paragraph and from the **Text Format** option, choose **Bullets & Numbering...**.

3. In the **Text Styles** dialog, click the **None** preset option.

WebPlus also lets you assign bullets and numbers to styles. (See WebPlus help.)

Inserting a symbol

You can insert symbol characters using either the Insert menu or (for common symbols) keyboard shortcuts.

As a rule for Web page use, don't employ symbols outside the standard character set, or in non-standard fonts.

To insert a symbol character using the Insert menu:

1. Select the Pointer Tool and click in the text for an insertion point.

2. Choose **Symbol...** from the Insert menu, and select a symbol name from the submenu.

3. If you need a symbol not shown on the submenu, select **Other...** to display an **Insert Symbol** dialog. The dialog remains open so you can continue editing in the workspace as you select symbols.

   - Select a **Font** to display its full character set, and then scroll the font table to view characters. You can choose from the **Subset** list to jump to a particular range within the character set.

   - Click any individual character (or select it while browsing using the arrow keys on your keyboard) to view the character's name and Unicode Index at the bottom of the dialog. You can also enter any Unicode hex value and click **Go** to jump to that particular character in the current font.

   - To insert a character into your text, double-click it (or select it and click **Insert**).

The memory row below the font table keeps track of characters you've recently inserted. Double-click any character in the row to insert it again.

Trouble inserting a character? Check your insertion point to ensure it is still placed in your chosen text position.

Inserting date/time

You can insert a date/time field into your text, stamped with current date/time information, by using **Information>Date** or **Time...** from the Insert menu. Various date and time formats are available. By default, the date/time field updates itself automatically when the site is saved or loaded. You can turn auto-updating off if necessary.

Inserting user details

You can take advantage of the User Details dialog to store frequently-used or updated user information so you don't need to keep re-entering it—think of how often a mobile phone number or email address may change over time! The dialog lets you review all your User Details at a glance, and will update fields directly.

To review or change User Details:

1. Choose **Set User Details...** from the Tools menu.

2. Enter new information into the spaces on the **Business**, **Home**, or **Custom** tab (a **Calendars** tab will appear if there is a calendar in your site).

The **Custom** tab of the User Details dialog includes blank, renameable fields where you can enter any information you may frequently need to "plug into" your sites.

To insert a User Detail field:

1. Select the Pointer Tool and click in the text for an insertion point.

2. Choose **Information** from the Insert menu, then select **User Details...** from the submenu.

3. Select a User Detail entry, and optionally any text **Prefix** or suffix (**Postfix**) to include with your user details, e.g. *Name:*.

4. Click **OK**.

To update fields:

- Enter new information in the User Details dialog (via **Tools>Set User Details**).

- Click the **Update** button to automatically update any altered field currently placed in your site or template. This field will remain linked to User Details until it is deleted.

Working with Tables

Creating text-based tables

Tables are ideal for presenting text and data in a variety of easily customizable row-and-column formats, with built-in spreadsheet capabilities.

Quantity	Description	Code
12	Geraniums	34W-6YY
3	Plant Posts (small))	44X-123

Each cell in a table behaves like a mini-frame. Like frame text you can vary character and paragraph properties, apply named text styles, embed inline images, apply text colour fills, and use proofing options such as AutoSpell/Spell Checker, Proof Reader, and Thesaurus. Some unique features include number formatting and formula insertion.

HTML or Creative tables

Two types of table can be applied to the WebPlus page—the HTML table and the Creative table. These can be compared easily below—some features can be applied to both, or just to one or the other.

	HTML tables	Creative tables
Searchable by search engines (Google, etc.)	✓	✗
Script insertion for generating dynamic content	✓	✗
Resize/move table	✓	✓
Crop table	✗	✗
Rotate table	✗	✓[1]
Rotate table text (in cell)	✗	✓[1]

Sort table contents	✓	✓
Solid fill and border colour	✓	✓
Gradient and bitmap fill	✗	✓
HTML-compliant Styles	✓	✗
Transparency	✗	✓[1]
Borders	✗	✓[1]
Warp	✗	✓[1]
2D/3D Filter effects	✗	✓[1]
Instant 3D	✗	✓[1]
QuickClear/QuickFill/AutoFormat	✓	✓
Edit cell text in WritePlus	✓	✓
View cell text in Site Manager	✓	✓
Import of Excel and text files	✓	✓

[1] If applied, will export table as a graphic.

So how do you tell the difference between an HTML and Creative table? Simply, HTML tables will always possess dark blue corner/edge handles when selected, while a Creative table's handles will show as grey.

To create a table:

1. Choose either the ⟨⟩ **HTML Table Tool** or ▦ **Creative Table Tool** from the Table flyout on the Standard Objects toolbar, and click on the page or pasteboard, or drag to set the table's dimensions. The Create Table dialog appears with a selection of preset table formats shown in the **Format:** window.

2. Step through the list to preview the layouts and select one. To begin with a plain table, select [**Default**].

3. Click **OK**.

The new table appears on the page, and the Table toolbar appears to assist with entering and formatting spreadsheet data.

WebPlus treats table text in three ways: as **numbers**, **formulas**, or **ordinary text**.

* **Numbers:** WebPlus can format numbers in special ways. See Formatting numbers in online Help.

* **Formulas:** WebPlus will treat any text entry beginning with an equal symbol (=) as a formula. Formulas can be formatted the same as numbers. See Inserting formulas in online Help.

* **Ordinary text:** Any other text entry, i.e. one that doesn't begin with "=".

Manipulating tables

Once you've created a table, you can select, move, resize, delete, and copy it as an object, just as you would with a text frame. Cell properties can also be modified.

To manipulate the table object:

* To select the table object, click its bounding box. Now you can resize it like a text frame by dragging a corner or side handle, or move it by dragging an edge.

- To delete the table object, select it and press the **Delete** key (you can also choose **Delete Object** from the Edit menu).
OR
Select any part of its text and choose **Delete** from the Table menu (**Table>Delete** from the right-click menu), then **Table** from the submenu.

- To duplicate the selected table object and its text, first make sure no text is selected (an insertion point is OK), then use the **Copy** and **Paste** commands. As a shortcut, select the object and drag with the **Ctrl** key pressed down.

To select and edit text in cells, rows, and columns:

- To select text in a single cell, double- or triple-click text (for word or paragraph selection) or drag over the text. See Editing text on a page on p. 108.

- To move to the next or previous cells, use the **Tab** or **Shift+Tab** keys, respectively, or the keyboard arrow keys.

- To enter text, simply type into a cell at the insertion point. You can also type or edit text via the Table toolbar's edit field.

  Click the ✔ **Accept** button to update the selected cell. Click ✕ **Cancel** to reset the edit field to the previous cell text. Cells expand vertically as you type to accommodate extra lines of text. To enter a Tab character, press **Ctrl+Tab.**

- To select a row or column, click its control button along the left or top of the table. To select more than one row or column, drag across their control buttons. You can also select cell(s) first, then choose **Select** from the Table menu (**Table>Select** from the right-click menu), then either **Row** or **Column** from the submenu.

- To select all text (all rows and columns), choose **Select** from the Table menu (**Table>Select** from the right-click menu), then **All** from the submenu.

- To copy, paste and delete selected table text within the same table (or between different tables), use the **Copy**, **Paste** and **Delete** commands as you would for frame text. You can also right-click on a cell containing text and choose **Text Menu>Copy**—select a new cell then pick **Paste** from the Edit menu.

  QuickFill lets you fill a span of cells with the contents of an initially selected cell's contents. This one-to-many "replicating" operation is possible by dragging the bottom right-hand QuickFill handle of the initially selected cell outwards to encompass a contiguous block of cells either on the same row or column. Conversely, **QuickClear** clears adjacent cells.

  The copy and paste of Microsoft Excel spreadsheet cell contents into any WebPlus table is also possible.

- To move cell contents within the same table, select the cell(s), and hover over the cell border(s) until the move cursor is shown—click and drag the cell to its new cell location.

- To format selected text, apply character and paragraph properties or text styles as with any text. Note that cell text with mixed formatting (for example, some bold and some plain) will revert to plain if you edit it via the Table context toolbar.

- To rotate selected text in Creative tables, right-click and choose **Table>Cell Properties**. On the **Orientation** tab, use the rotation dial to set a rotation angle or enter a specific value into the input box.

- Table text can be sorted by row, column, multi-row, multi-column regions or entire table using the **Sort** button from the context toolbar. For more details, see online Help.

- Characters as part of creative table text can take line, gradient, and bitmap fill properties, although HTML table text cannot.

- Table text shares default properties with frame text. For details, see Updating and saving defaults on p. 156.

- 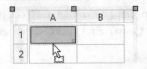 To format numbers and insert formulas, switch on the **Spreadsheet functions** button on the Table toolbar. See online Help for more information.

To change the table's structure and appearance:

- To select a cell, click on the edge of the chosen cell. To select more than one cell, click in one cell and drag across the others, one row or column at a time.

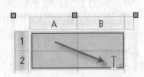

- To **adjust row or column size**, drag the ↔ control button shown when hovering over the separating lines in the table row or column headings. Note that you can adjust a row's height independent of the amount of text it contains. For absolute row/column sizing, choose **Set column width(s)** or **Set row height(s)** from the Table menu (or use the right-click menu). For individual columns, click the column or row header's ▼ button, choosing **Set width** or **Set height**. You can resize your columns without affecting the overall table width by adjusting the column heading with **Ctrl**-drag.

- To **distribute** rows or columns, select the entire table or just a selection of rows or columns, then choose **Evenly Distribute** from the **Evenly distribute>Rows** or **Evenly distribute>Columns** from the Table menu (or use the right-click menu). To honour table width, a cell's text may wrap when distributing columns.

  To evenly distribute rows in an individual column, click the column's ▼ button and choose **Evenly Distribute Rows**. Conversely, use the equivalent button (and **Evenly Distribute Columns** command) at a row header to distribute columns on the chosen row.

- Choose **Autofit Column(s) to Contents** from the Table menu (or right-click menu) to reduce or increase the size of selected columns to fit to the text of the greatest width. An equivalent option exists for rows. For an individual column or row, click the column or row header's 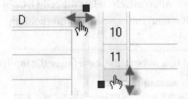 button, choosing **Autofit Row to Contents** or **Autofit Column to Contents**, respectively.

- To **delete** multiple rows or columns, select them (or cell text), then choose **Delete** from the Table menu (**Table>Delete** from the right-click menu), then either **Row(s)** or **Column(s)** from the submenu. For an individual column or row, click the header's ⧩ button and choose **Delete**.

- To **insert/remove** columns in an existing table, click and drag left/right on the header after the end of the last table column; columns are added or removed as you drag. For insertion of rows, drag up/down on the header at the end of the last row.

Alternatively, select one or more cells, then choose **Insert** from the Table menu (**Table>Insert** from the right-click menu), then either **Rows...** or **Columns...** from the submenu. In the dialog, specify how many to add, and whether to add them before or after the selected cells.

- To **merge** cells into larger cells that span more than one row or column (for example, a column head), select a range of cells and choose **Merge Cells** from the Table menu (**Table>Merge Cells** from the right-click menu). The merged cell displays only the text originally visible in the top-left selected cell. The original cells and their text are preserved, however—to restore them, select the merged cell and choose **Separate Cells** from the Table menu (**Table>Separate Cells** from the right-click menu).

  To merge all cells in an individual column or row, click the column or row header's ▼ button, choosing **Merge Cells**. Do the equivalent with the **Separate Cells** command to split cells.

- To **copy** cells (including text, formatting, borders, and colours) to a new cell in the same table, select the cell(s), press the **Ctrl** key and hover over the cell border(s) until the copy cursor is shown—click and drag the copied cell to its new cell location. Alternatively, select the cell(s), Copy and then Paste (both via the Edit menu) into a new cell while holding down the **Shift** key.

- To apply a coloured background to a whole table, hover over the top-left hand corner of the table until you see a ✥ cursor—click once, and then use the Colour tab or Swatches tab to apply a colour fill. (See Applying solid colours on p. 213).

- To apply a coloured background to specific cells, select the cell(s) and again use the Colour tab or Swatches tab to colour the cells.

Using AutoFormat

To use style presets to customize the table's appearance:

- Choose **AutoFormat...** from the Table menu (**Table>AutoFormat...** from the right-click menu). The dialog presents a list of sample tables, which differ in their use of **Lines** (inner and outer cell borders), **Fill** (cell and table), **Font** (bold, italic, etc.), **Alignment** (left, centre, etc.) and **HTML editing** support.

- You can pick any sample and use the checkboxes to specify which of the sample's attribute(s) to apply to your actual table. This lets you "mix and match," for example by applying (in two passes) the Colour from one sample and the Font from another.

- To restore plain formatting, choose [**Default**].

Setting Cell Properties

To customize the appearance of one or more cells "by hand":

1. Select the cell(s), row(s) or column(s).

2. Click  **Cell Properties** button on the Table toolbar.
   OR

   For a whole column or row only, click the column or row header's button, choosing **Cell Properties...**.

3. Use the dialog's **Border**, **Fill**, **Transparency**, **Margins** and **Orientation** tabs to apply cell formatting, then click **OK**.

Inserting a calendar

The **Calendar Wizard** helps you design month-at-a-glance calendars for use on your Web page.

The wizard lets you set up the month/year and calendar style/format, and controls the inclusion of personal events and/or public holidays.

The calendar is created as a scalable text-based table so you can edit text using the standard text tools. The properties of a selected calendar are similar to those of a table, and can be modified identically (see Manipulating tables on p. 129).

For calendar-specific properties, a context toolbar lets you change an existing calendar's month/year, modify calendar-specific properties, and manage calendar events (both personal and public holidays).

You can update calendar details throughout your Web site via Set User Details—in the same way that you'd set up the date (along with the time) on some alarm clocks. This is especially useful if you want to update the year on a year-to-view Web page, composed of 12 monthly calendars—you only need to change the year in one place.

To insert a calendar:

1. Click the Table flyout on the Standard Objects toolbar and choose [31] **Insert Calendar**.

2. Click again on your page, or drag out to indicate the desired size of the calendar.

3. From the displayed **Calendar Wizard**, define options for your calendar including setting the year and month, calendar style (square, or in single or double column format), week start day, room to write, display options, switching on personal events/holidays, and calendar format.

    To have your country's public holidays shown, check **Add public holidays** in the wizard and select a **Region** from the associated drop-down menu. To add personal events, check **Add personal events** additionally.

4. Click **Finish** to complete the wizard.

To edit a selected calendar's properties:

1. Click the **Edit Calendar** button on the Calendar context toolbar.
    OR
    Right-click on a selected calendar, and choose **Table>Edit Calendar...**.

2. Choose an appropriate tab (Date, Style, Events, etc.) and make your modification, then press **OK**.

Right-click on a calendar and choosing **Table** lets you select, insert, distribute, and delete rows and columns, but take care not to corrupt your table formatting!

To update calendar details globally:

1. Select **Set User Details...** from the Tools menu.

2. From the dialog's Calendars tab, select the **Year** that all your calendars will adopt from the drop-down menu.
   OR

3. In the Events section, check **Show public holidays** and/or **Show personal events** if all calendars are to adopt the holidays and events already configured in the **Calendar Event Manager** (to modify personal events, click the **Events** button).

Adding public holidays

When you create a calendar you can set up the appropriate public holidays for the country you reside in. The holidays will show up in your calendar automatically. You can also swap to a different country's public holiday settings for any existing calendar if needed.

> Remember to ensure that **Add public holidays** is checked in Calendar Properties.

To swap public holidays:

1. Select a calendar.

2. Click the **Edit Calendar** button on the context toolbar.

3. On the **Events** tab, select a different region from the **Region** drop-down menu.

Adding personal events

You can complement your public holiday listings (e.g., Easter holidays) by adding personal events such as birthdays, anniversaries, and bill payments (unfortunately!) so that the events show up on your calendar—simply use the **Calendar Events** button on a selected calendar's context toolbar. Events show automatically on your calendar under the chosen date.

3	Tue	Update Cash ISA
4	Wed	
5	Thu	Cassie's Birthday
6	Fri	Good Friday
7	Sat	
8	Sun	Easter Sunday
9	Mon	Easter Monday

To add an event:

1. Select a calendar.

2. Click **Calendar Events** on the context toolbar.

3. (Optional) Check **Show events by date** to add, edit, or delete events using a traditional calendar layout. Leave unchecked for a row-by-row Date/Event listing. If using the latter method, enable the **Show personal events** button.

4. Click the 📆 **New event** button.

5. From the dialog, type, use the up/down arrows, or click the ⋯ **Browse** button to select a date.

6. Enter your event text into the text input box—click to add an insertion point, then begin typing. The entered text will display in your calendar under the chosen date.

7. If the event is a birthday or other annual event, check **Event recurs annually**.

8. Click **OK**.

9. When you have finished adding events, click the **Save** button.

   Use the 📆 **Edit Event** or ✕ **Delete Event** buttons to modify or delete an existing event.

Remember to ensure that **Add personal events** is checked in Calendar Properties.

Editing Objects on the Page

Selecting an object

Before you can change any object, you need to select it using one of these tools from the Tools toolbar:

Pointer Tool

Click to use the **Pointer Tool** to select, move, copy, and resize objects.

Rotate Tool

Click to use the **Rotate Tool** to rotate an object around its centre. Select the object, then drag one of its handles. You can also use the Rotate Tool to move and copy objects. See Rotating an object.

Square Crop and Irregular Crop tools

Choose either **Crop** tool from the Effects flyout to crop (or trim) objects. Select the object, then drag one of its handles inward. You can also use a Crop tool to move and copy objects. See Cropping and combining objects.

To select an object:

- Click on the object using one of the tools shown above. A grey bounding box appears, with small "handles" defining the object's corners and edges.

- If objects overlap, click with the **Alt** key down until the desired object is selected.

When selecting a text object with the Pointer Tool:

- Clicking on a text object with the Pointer Tool selects the object and also positions the blinking text selection cursor within the object's text. In this mode, you can edit the text.

- Double-click to select a word, and triple-click to select a paragraph.

- Press the **Delete** key to delete characters after the cursor. To delete the frame itself, choose **Delete Object** from the Edit menu.

To select only the frame (for example, to adjust its margin and column guides), click the frame's bounding box.

Simply clicking on any member of a group selects the group object. In general, any operation you carry out on a selected group affects each member of the group. However, you can also select and edit an individual object within a group.

To select an individual object within a group:

- **Ctrl**-click the object.

Ruler regions

When you click to select an object, blue ruler regions indicate the left, right, top, and bottom edges of the object.

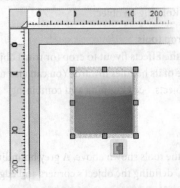

For details on using the rulers, see Rulers on p. 45.

Selecting multiple objects

Selecting more than one object at a time (creating a **multiple selection**) lets you:

- Position or resize all the objects at the same time.

- Create a **group object** from the multiple selection, which can then be treated as a single object, with the option of restoring the individual objects later. See Creating Groups on p. 154.

To create a multiple selection:

- Click in a blank area of the page and drag a "marquee" box around the objects you want to select. Repeated **Shift**-drags add to the selection region.
  OR
  Hold down the **Shift** key and click each object in turn.

To add or remove objects from a multiple selection:

- Hold down the **Shift** key and click the object to be added or removed.

To deselect all objects in a multiple selection:

- Click in a blank area of the page.

To select all objects on the page (or master page):

- Choose **Select All** from the Edit menu (or press **Ctrl+A**).

To select all objects of one type on the page (or master page):

- Hold down the **Ctrl** key and double-click one object of that type.
  OR
  Click on an object to select it and choose **Select Similar** from the Edit menu.

Copying, pasting, and replicating objects

Besides using the Windows Clipboard to copy and paste objects, you can duplicate objects easily using drag-and-drop, and replicate multiple copies of any object in precise formations. You can also transfer the formatting of one object to another, with the option of selecting specific attributes to be included when formatting is pasted.

To copy an object (or multiple selection) to the Windows Clipboard:

- Right-click the object and choose **Copy** from the submenu.
  OR

  Select the object, click the [image: Copy icon] **Copy** button on the Standard toolbar, press **Ctrl+C**, or choose **Copy** from the Edit menu.

If you're using another Windows application, you can usually copy and paste objects via the Clipboard.

To paste an object from the Clipboard:

- Right-click on the page and choose **Paste** from the submenu.
  OR

  Press **Ctrl+V**, or choose **Paste** from the Edit menu, or click the
  Paste button on the Standard toolbar.

The standard Paste command inserts the object at the insertion point or (for a separate object) at the centre of the page. To insert a separate object at the same page location as the copied item, use the **Paste in Place** command (**Ctrl+Alt+V**).

To choose between alternative Clipboard formats:

- Choose **Paste Special...** from the Edit menu.

To duplicate an object:

1. Select the object, then press the **Ctrl** key.

2. Drag the outline to a new location on the page. You can release the **Ctrl** key once you've started the drag.

3. To constrain the position of the copy (to same horizontal or vertical), press and hold down the **Shift** key while dragging. A duplicate of the object appears at the new location.

Replicating objects

Duplicating an object means making just one copy at a time. The **Replicate** command lets you create multiple copies in a single step, with precise control over how the copies are arranged, either as a linear series or a grid. You can include one or more transformations to produce an interesting array of rotated and/or resized objects. It's great for repeating backgrounds, or for perfectly-aligned montages of an image or object.

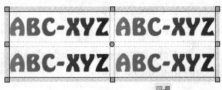

To replicate an object:

1. Select the object to be replicated and choose **Replicate...** from the Edit menu. The Replicate dialog appears, with a preview region at the right.

2. To arrange copies in a straight line, select **Create line**. For an X-by-Y grid arrangement, select **Create grid**.

3. Specify **Line length** (the number of objects including the original) in the arrangement, or the Grid size. Note that you can use the Line length setting to include an odd number of objects in a grid.

4. Set spacing between the objects as either an **Offset** (measured between the top left corners of successive objects) or a **Gap** (between the bottom right and top left corners). You can specify **Horizontal** and/or **Vertical** spacing, and/or an angular **Rotation**. To set a specific horizontal or vertical interval, check **Absolute**; uncheck the box to specify the interval as a percentage of the original object's dimensions.

5. Click **OK**.

The result is a multiple selection. Click its **Group** button if you want to keep the separate objects linked for additional manipulations.

Pasting an object's formatting

Once you have copied an object to the Clipboard, you can use the **Paste Format** to apply its formatting attributes to another **selected** object. **Paste Format Plus** displays a "master control" dialog that lets you select or deselect specific attributes to be included when formatting is pasted. See the WebPlus Help for more information on the Paste Format Plus feature.

To paste one object's formatting to another:

1. Copy the source object.

2. Select the target object and choose **Paste Format** from the Edit menu (or press **Ctrl+Shift+V**).

The target object takes on any formatting attributes and settings of the source object that are currently defined in Paste Format Plus (see below).

Moving objects

To move an object (including a multiple selection):

- Click within the object (not on a handle) and drag it to the new location while holding down the left mouse button.

  OR

  Drag the object's grey bounding box.

The view automatically re-centres itself as you drag objects to the edge of the screen.

To constrain the movement of an object to horizontal or vertical:

- Select the object and use the keyboard arrows (up, down, left, right).

  OR

  Press and hold down the **Shift** key after you begin dragging the object.

  Release the **Shift** key after you release the left mouse button.

  💡 Use the Transform tab for fine-tuning the position of an object.

Resizing objects

WebPlus provides several methods of resizing lines, shapes, artistic text, frame objects, and table objects. Click-and-drag is the simplest—watch the Hintline for context-sensitive tips and shortcuts! For extremely precise resizing, use the Transform tab.

💡 To set two or more objects to the same horizontal or vertical size as the last selected object, select the objects and then use **Arrange>Size Objects...**.

To resize an object (in general):

1. Select the object.

2. Click one of the object's handles and drag it to a new position while holding down the left mouse button.

Dragging from an edge handle resizes in one dimension, by moving that edge. Dragging from a corner handle resizes in two dimensions, by moving two edges. You can also constrain the resizing—note that pictures normally behave differently from lines, shapes, and text objects.

Text in frames and tables doesn't change size when the container object is resized.

To resize freely:

- Drag from a corner (or line end) handle.

To constrain a shape, frame object, or table object when resizing:

- Hold the **Shift** key down and drag from a corner (or line end) handle.

Resizing pictures

These objects are normally constrained when resized, since you'll typically want to preserve their proportions.

To resize while maintaining aspect ratio (proportions):

- Drag from a corner handle.

To resize freely:

- Hold the **Shift** key down and drag from a corner handle.

Resizing groups

You can resize a group object. The size of images, graphic objects, and text objects in the group will change. The size of text inside frames or tables won't change, only the size of the text container.

> Use the Transform tab for fine-tuning the position of an object.

Rotating an object

You can rotate objects, including text objects and groups. (You cannot rotate a multiple selection.)

To rotate an object:

1. Select the 🔄 **Rotate Tool** on the Tools toolbar.

2. Click to select the object, hover over one of its handles until you see the rotate pointer (below).

3.   Hold the mouse button down and drag the pointer in the direction in
     which you want to rotate the object, then release (use **Shift** key for 15°
     rotation intervals).

To unrotate (restore the original orientation):

●   Double-click the object.

●   To restore the rotated position, double-click again.

To rotate an object 90 degrees left or right:

●   Select the object and choose the **Rotate Left** or **Rotate Right**
     command from the Arrange menu. You can also right-click the object
     and use the **Flip/Rotate** submenu.

To prevent a picture object from accidentally being rotated:

●   Right-click on the object and check **Arrange>Lock Objects**.

Cropping and combining objects

Cropping means masking (hiding) parts of an object or group, for example to
improve composition or to create a special effect. The underlying object is
intact. You can use either the **Square Crop Tool** or **Irregular Crop Tool** from
the Tools toolbar to crop while preserving an object's original square (or
rectangular) outline or crop by distorting the object's original crop outline,
respectively.

Another cropping option is the **Crop to Shape** command, which lets you crop
one object to the outline of another.

The **Combine Curves** command, like Crop to Shape, starts with more than
one object, but creates a special composite object with one or more "holes" on
the inside where the component objects' fills overlapped one another—useful
for creating mask or stencil effects.

To crop using the object's original outline:

1. Click to select the object or group.

2. Select the ⊡ **Square Crop Tool** from the Tools toolbar's Effects flyout.

3. Drag one of its edge or corner handles inward (the aspect ratio of the original object is maintained). Press the **Shift** key for free (unconstrained) cropping.

To crop by modifying the object's outline:

1. Select the object or group.

2. Select the ⊡ **Irregular Crop Tool** from the Tools toolbar's Effects flyout. You'll now see the nodes and connecting segments that define the object's crop outline.

3. Modify the outline as follows:

   - To move a node (control point) where you see the $\overset{\shortmid}{}$ cursor, drag the node.

   - To move a line segment (between two nodes) where you see the ▶⌄ cursor, drag the segment.

   - ◇ ◇ To convert an outline from straight lines to curves and vice versa, click the **Fit Curves** and **Straighten All Lines** button on the Crop context toolbar.

   - To adjust the curvature of a segment, drag the control handle(s) of the adjacent nodes.

   - For more complex outlines:

   - To add a node, double-click on any line segment; double-click on a node to remove it.

   - To move the object relative to its crop outline, drag its interior when you see the hand cursor.

For information on different corners segment types and other options hosted on the context toolbar, and a more detailed look at editing lines, see Drawing and editing lines on p. 159.

To pan the visible portion of a cropped object within the crop area:

- Select the object and drag its centre area.

To uncrop (restore full visibility):

- Click the **Remove Crop** button on the Crop context toolbar.

Cropping one shape to another

The **Crop to Shape** command works with exactly two objects selected. Either or both of these may be a group object. The lower object (the one behind the other) gets clipped to the outline of the upper object, leaving a shape equivalent to the overlapping region. Note that you can't crop a mesh-warped object, but can use one to crop another object. Use **Combine Curves** to use one shape to punch a "hole" in another.

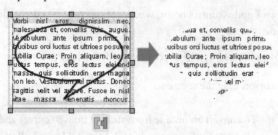

To crop one shape to another:

1. Place the "clipping" object in front of the object to be cropped, using the Arrange menu and/or Arrange toolbar as needed. In the illustration above, a QuickShape is in front of a text frame.

2. With both objects selected (or grouped), choose **Crop to Shape** from the Tools menu.

Combining lines and shapes

Combining curves is a way of creating a composite object from two or more lines or drawn shapes. As with cropping to a shape, the object in front clips the object(s) behind, in this case leaving one or more "holes" where the component objects overlapped. As with grouping, you can apply formatting (such as line or fill) to the combined object and continue to edit individual nodes and segments with the Pointer Tool. Unlike those other methods, a combined object permanently takes the line and fill properties of the front object. Combining is reversible, but the component objects keep the line and fill properties of the combined object.

Combining is a quick way to create a mask or stencil cutout:

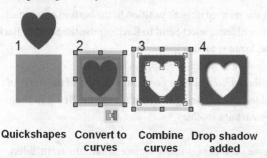

1	2	3	4
Quickshapes	Convert to curves	Combine curves	Drop shadow added

To combine two or more selected lines or drawn shapes:

1. Draw two QuickShapes.

2. Place the "clipping" object in front of the object to be cut out, using the Arrange menu and/or Arrange toolbar as needed.

3. Select (or group) both objects and choose **Tools>Convert to Curves**.

4. Choose **Combine Curves** from the Arrange menu.

To restore the original shapes from a combined object:

- Select the combined object and choose **Split Curves** from the Arrange menu.

Ordering objects

As objects are created, they are **ordered** in a stack, such that the most recently created object will overlap earlier ones. You can change the stacking order, which affects how objects appear on the page

To change the object's position in the stacking order:

- Right-click on the object and choose **Arrange**.
  OR
  Click the **Arrange** menu (with object selected).

Then:

- 🔲 To shift the selected object's position to the bottom of the stack, behind all other objects, select **Send to Back** (or use the **Send to Back** button on the Arrange toolbar).

- 🔲 To shift the selected object's position to the top of the stack, in front of all other objects, select **Bring to Front** (or use the **Bring to Front** button on the Arrange toolbar).

- 🔲 To shift the object's position one place toward the front, select **Forward One** (or use the **Forward One** button on the Arrange toolbar).

- 🔲 To shift the object's position one place toward the back, select **Back One** (or use the **Back One** button on the Arrange toolbar).

Aligning and distributing objects

Alignment involves taking a group of selected objects and aligning them all in one operation—the operation is applied to all of the objects selected. You can perform the following:

- Align the edges of any two or more objects with one another. For example, top alignment will align objects to the top edge of the top-most object in the selection. Bottom alignment would align to the bottom edge of the bottom-most object.

- Space objects out at certain intervals. Lets you **distribute objects**, so that your objects (as a multiple selection) are spread evenly between the endmost objects on your page. Alternatively, check the **Spaced** option and corresponding measurement value to set a specific distance between each object.

- Align objects with the page margin or edge. Rather than work within the current selection area you can align to page margins (if set) or just the page edge.

Alignment controls are available in either the Align tab or from **Arrange>Align Objects...**.

It's also possible to align a single object either to the top, bottom, left, or right page edge or centre the object vertically or horizontally.

To align the edges of two or more objects:

1. Using the Pointer Tool, **Shift**-click on all the objects you want to align, or draw a marquee box around them (or use **Edit>Select All**), to create a multiple selection.

2. Select the Align tab.

3. Select an option for vertical and/or horizontal alignment. Choose **Top**, **Bottom**, **Left**, **Right**, **Centre Horizontally** or **Centre Vertically**.

To distribute two or more objects:

- Choose **Space Evenly Across** or **Space Evenly Down** to spread selected objects uniformly across the either the whole page (horizontally or vertically, respectively) or by a set measurement (choose **Spaced** and set a value in any measurement unit).

To align one or more objects with the page edge:

- Follow the steps above, but check **Include Margins**. (If only one object is selected, the option is checked by default.)

To align one or more objects with set page margins:

- Set page margin guides in Layout Guides (Context toolbar) then follow the steps above, then check **Include Margins**. Objects will then align to margins rather than the page edge.

Creating groups

You can easily turn a **multiple selection** (see Selecting multiple objects on p. 142) into a group object. When objects are grouped, you can position, resize, or rotate the objects all at the same time.

To create a group from a multiple selection:

• Click the [icon] **Group** button below the selection.**Group Objects...**

To ungroup (turn a group back into a multiple selection):

• Click the [icon] **Ungroup** button below the selection to turn back to a multiple selection.

Simply clicking on any member of a group selects the group object. In general, any operation you carry out on a selected group affects each member of the group. However, the objects that comprise a group are intact, and you can also select and edit an individual object within a group.

To select an individual object within a group:

• **Ctrl**-click the object.

Locking an object's size or position

To prevent accidentally moving, resizing, flipping, or rotating an object, you can lock it in position.

To lock an object:

• Right-click on the object and choose **Arrange>Lock Objects**, or select the command from the Arrange menu.

To unlock an object:

• Right-click on it and choose **Arrange>Unlock Objects**, or choose the command from the Arrange menu.

Snapping

The **Snapping** feature simplifies placement and alignment by "magnetizing" grid dots and guide lines. When snapping is on, the edges and centres of objects you create, move, or resize will jump to align with the nearest visible grid dot or guides. Objects normally snap to the page edge, too.

Guide lines include ruler guides as well as layout guide lines based on page margins, rows, and columns (see Using layout aids on p. 44).

You may notice that with snapping enabled, when you move a guide, any "snapped to" objects will move with the guide. This object "stickiness" is enabled by default (with the Sticky Guides feature) but can be disabled permanently or temporarily as necessary (in **Tools>Options>Layout**). It is especially useful for selectively repositioning objects in bulk by guide movement, without any unnecessary grouping operations.

To turn snapping on and off:

- Click the 🔲 **Snapping** button on the Hintline. When the button is down, snapping is on.

Selective snapping

You control which points and lines are snapped to by showing or hiding the individual guide elements (i.e., Rulers, Guide lines, Frames, Dot Grid, etc.), and by changing options settings for those visible elements.

To show or hide guide elements:

- Enable (or disable) the element name's button on the View menu.

To set which visible elements are snapped to:

1. Choose **Options...** from the Tools menu, and select the Snapping option.

2. Check the **"Snap to:"** box, then check/uncheck the elements you want to snap to. The choices include **Grid dots**, **Page/Bleed edge**, **Page margins**, **Ruler guides**, **Row/column guides** and **Nearest Pixel**.

Updating and saving defaults

Object defaults are the stored property settings WebPlus applies to **newly created** objects, e.g. text, graphics, and frames. When you create text in your site, it will have default properties for font, size, colour, alignment, etc. New graphics or frames will have their own default properties. You can easily change the defaults for any type of object.

Default settings are always **local**—that is, any changed defaults apply to the current site and are automatically saved with it, so they're in effect next time you open that site. However, at any time you can use the **Save Defaults** command to record the current defaults as **global** settings that will be in effect for any new site you subsequently create.

To set local defaults for a particular type of object:

1. Create a single sample object and fine-tune its properties as desired—or use an existing object that already has the right properties.

2. Select the object that's the basis for the new defaults and choose **Update Object Default** or **Update Text Default** from the Format or Text menus, respectively.

Or, for line and fill colours, including line styles:

1. With no object selected, choose the required line and/or fill colours from the Colour or Swatches tab (see Applying solid colours on p. 213). Use the Line tab to set a default line weight, style, and corner shape.

2. Draw your object on the page, which will automatically adopt the newly defined default colours and styles.

To view and change default text properties:

1. Choose **Text Style Palette...** from the Text menu.

2. Click **Default Text**, then click **Modify...** to view current settings.

3. Use the Text Style dialog to alter character, paragraph, and bullet/list properties.

To save all current defaults as global settings:

- Choose **Save Defaults** from the Tools menu, then click **OK** to confirm that you want new sites to use the current site's defaults.

Lines, Shapes, and Effects

Lines, Shapes, and Effects

Drawing and editing lines

WebPlus provides Pencil, Straight Line, Pen, and QuickShape tools for creating simple graphics.

Using the **line tools** (found on a Standard Objects toolbar's Line flyout), you can draw single lines, connect line segments together, or join line ends to **close** the line, creating a **shape** (see Drawing and editing shapes on p. 165 for details). Use the Pointer Tool and the Curve context toolbar to resize or reshape lines once you've drawn them.

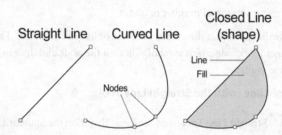

Straight Line   Curved Line   Closed Line (shape)

Line

Fill

Nodes

 The **Pencil Tool** lets you sketch curved lines and shapes in a freeform way.

 The **Straight Line Tool** is for drawing straight lines; rules at the top and/or bottom of the page; or horizontal lines to separate sections or highlight headlines.

 The **Pen Tool** lets you join a series of line segments (which may be curved or straight) using "connect the dots" mouse clicks.

Drawing lines

To draw a freeform line (with the Pencil Tool):

1. Click the Line flyout on the Standard Objects toolbar and choose the **Pencil Tool.**

2. Click where you want the line to start, and hold the mouse button down as you draw. The line appears immediately and follows your mouse movements.

3. To end the line, release the mouse button. The line will automatically smooth out using a minimal number of nodes.

4. To extend the line, position the cursor over one of its red end nodes. The cursor changes to include a plus symbol. Click on the node and drag to add a new line segment.

To draw a straight line (with the Straight Line Tool):

1. Click the **Straight Line Tool** from the Lines flyout on the Standard Objects toolbar.

2. Click where you want the line to start, and drag to the end point. The line appears immediately.

> To constrain the angle of the straight line to 15° increments, hold down the **Shift** key as you drag. (This is an easy way to make exactly vertical or horizontal lines.)

3. To extend the line, position the cursor over one of its red end nodes. The cursor changes to include a plus symbol. Click on the node and drag to add a new line segment.

To draw one or more line segments (with the Pen Tool):

1. Click the Line flyout on the Standard Objects toolbar and choose the **Pen Tool** from the flyout. The Curve Creation toolbar appears, with three buttons that let you select which kind of segment you'll draw next.

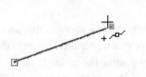

A **Straight** segment is simply a straight line connecting two nodes. (**Shortcut:** Press **1**)

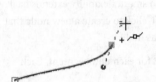

A **Bézier** segment is curved, displaying control handles for precise adjustment. (**Shortcut:** Press **2**)

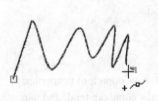

Smart segments appear without visible control handles, using automatic curve-fitting to connect each node. They are especially useful when tracing around curved objects and pictures. (**Shortcut:** Press **3**)

2. Select a segment type, then click where you want the line to start.

- For a **Straight** segment, click again (or drag) for a new node where you want the segment to end. **Shift**-click to align the segment at 15° intervals (useful for quick right-angle junctions).

- For a **Bézier** segment, click again for a new node and drag out a **control handle** from it. (Control handles act like "magnets," pulling the curve into shape. The distance between handles determines the depth of the resulting curved line.) Click again where you want the segment to end, and a curved segment appears. Pressing the **Shift** key while you're drawing causes the new node's control handles to "snap" into orientation at 15° intervals with respect to the node.

- For a **Smart** segment, click again for a new node. The segment appears as a smooth, best-fitting curve (without visible control handles) between the new node and the preceding node. Before releasing the mouse button, you can drag to "flex" the line as if bending a piece of wire. If the preceding corner node on the line is also smart, flexibility extends back to the preceding segment. You can **Shift**-click to create a new node that lines up at 15° intervals with the previous node.

3. To extend an existing line, repeat Step 2 for each new segment. Each segment can be of a different type.

4. To end the line, press **Esc**, double-click, or choose a different tool.

See WebPlus help for information on editing lines.

Setting line properties

All lines, including those that enclose shapes, have numerous properties, including colour, weight (width or thickness), scaling, cap (end) and join (corner). You can vary these properties for any freehand, straight, or curved line, as well as for the outline of a shape (see Drawing and editing shapes). Text frames, tables, and artistic text objects have line properties, too.

To change line properties of a selected object:

- Use the Swatches tab to change the line's colour and/or shade. (If changing the outline colour of a shape or other object, click the **Line** button so that the line, not the fill, will change.) Click a gallery sample in the tab's Publication or standard palettes to apply that colour to the selected object. Alternatively, use the Colour tab to apply a colour to the selected object from a colour mixer.

- Use the Line tab or Line context toolbar (shown when a line is selected) to change the line's weight (thickness), type, or other properties. Select a line width with the slider, and use the drop-down boxes to pick the type of line. The context toolbar can also adjust line-end scaling as a percentage.

On the Line tab or context toolbar, the middle **Line Styles** drop-down menu provides the following styles: **None**, **Single**, **Calligraphic**, and several **Dashed** and **Double** line styles as illustrated below.

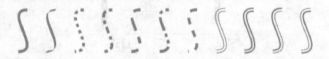

Several techniques offer additional ways to customize lines:

For dotted/dashed lines, select from one of five line styles (see above).
OR
(Tab only) Drag the **Dash Pattern** slider to set the overall pattern length (the number of boxes to the left of the slider) and the dash length (the number of those boxes that are black). The illustrations below show lines with dash lengths of (**1**) 4 and 2, and (**2**) 5 and 4:

For Double lines, select from one of four **Double** line styles (see above).

(Tab only) For Calligraphic lines of variable width (drawn as if with a square-tipped pen held at a certain angle), select the calligraphic line style (opposite) from the drop-down menu then use the **Calligraphic Angle** box to set the angle of the pen tip, as depicted in the examples below.

The Line tab also lets you vary a line's **Cap**(end) and the **Join** (corner) where two lines intersect. Both properties tend to be more conspicuous on thicker lines; joins are more apparent with more acute angles. The button icons clearly communicate each setting:

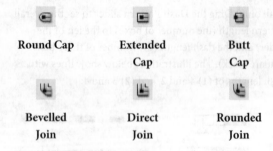

Round Cap	Extended Cap	Butt Cap
Bevelled Join	Direct Join	Rounded Join

To access all Line properties:

- Click the ✎ **Line/Border** button on the Tools toolbar's Fill flyout.

- In the **Line and Border** dialog, the **Line** tab lets you adjust all line properties as described above plus line end scaling.
  Note: The Border tab (see Adding borders on p. 176) provides a variety of other options for decorative outlines.

- To apply a border to specific edges of the object, use the dialog's Border Edges tab.

Drawing and editing shapes

WebPlus provides Pencil, Pen, Straight Line, and QuickShape tools for creating simple graphics. **QuickShapes** are pre-designed objects that you can instantly add to your page, then adjust and vary using control handles. Another way of creating shapes is to draw a line (or series of line segments) and then connect its start and end nodes, creating a **closed shape**. Once you've drawn a shape, you can adjust its properties—for example, apply gradient or bitmap fills (including your own bitmap pictures!) or apply transparency effects. You can even use sliding handles to create variations on the original QuickShape.

It's also possible to use the always-at-hand QuickShape context toolbar situated above the workspace to swap QuickShapes, and adjust a QuickShape's line weight, colour, style, and more. New shapes always take the default line and fill (initially a black line with no fill).

QuickShapes

The QuickShape flyout contains a wide variety of commonly used shapes, including boxes, ovals, arrows, polygons and stars. You might use the **QuickShape** button for:

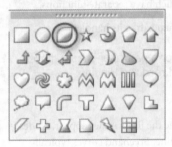

- Decorative circles or polygons.

- Functional arrows, stars, callouts.

- Web buttons... any QuickShape will do, but try the unique **QuickButton** (circled at left) for creating stylish button outlines. Add hyperlinks or hotspots to make your shapes "clickable."

- A border framing your page, e.g. a box around the whole page.

- Shaded panels, also known as screens, behind pictures/text to draw attention to them.

To create a QuickShape:

1. Click the **QuickShape** button on the Tools toolbar and select a shape from the flyout. The button takes on the icon of the shape you selected.

2. Click on the page to create a new shape at a default size. Drag to adjust its dimensions.

3. When the shape is the right size, release the mouse button. Now you can alter the shape by dragging on its displayed handles.

To draw a constrained shape (such as a circle):

- Hold down the **Shift** key as you drag.

All QuickShapes can be positioned, resized, rotated, and filled. What's more, you can adjust their designs using the Pointer Tool. Each shape changes in a logical way to allow its exact appearance to be altered. The ability to alter the appearance of QuickShape objects makes them more flexible and convenient than clipart pictures with similar designs.

To adjust the appearance of a QuickShape:

1. Click on the QuickShape to reveal one or more sliding handles around the shape. These are distinct from the "inner" selection handles. Different QuickShapes have different handles which have separate functions.

2. To change the appearance of a QuickShape, drag its handles.

> To find out what each handle does for a particular shape, move the Pointer Tool over the handle and read the Hintline.

Closed shapes

As soon as you draw or select a line, you'll see the line's nodes appear. Nodes show the end points of each segment in the line. Freehand curves typically have many nodes; straight or curved line segments have only two (**1**). You can make a shape by drawing a line between node end points (**2**), or by simply closing the curve (**3**).

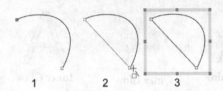

To turn a selected line into a shape:

You can go the other way, too—break open a shape in order to add one or more line segments.

To break open a line or shape:

1.   With the Pointer Tool, select the node where you want to break the shape.

2.   Click the ![icon] **Break Curve** button on the Curve context toolbar. A line will separate into two lines. A shape will become a line, with the selected node split into two nodes, one at each end of the new line.

3.   You can now use the Pointer Tool to reshape the line as needed.

See WebPlus help for information on editing shapes.

Using 2D filter effects

WebPlus provides a variety of **filter effects** that you can use to transform any object. "3D" filter effects let you create the impression of a textured surface and are covered elsewhere (see p. 171). Here we'll look at 2D filter effects exclusively. The following examples show each 2D filter effect when applied to the letter "A."

A	A	A	A
Drop Shadow	**Inner Shadow**	**Outer Glow**	**Inner Glow**
A	A	A	A
Inner Bevel	**Outer Bevel**	**Emboss**	**Pillow Emboss**
A	A	A	A
Gaussian Blur	**Zoom Blur**	**Radial Blur**	**Motion Blur**
A	A	A	A
Colour Fill	**Feather**	**Outline**	**Reflection**

WebPlus additionally provides the Shadow Tool for applying a shadow to an object directly on your Web page.

To apply 2D filter effects:

1. Select an object and click the **Filter Effects** button on the Tools toolbar's Effects flyout.

2. To apply a particular effect, check its box in the list at left. For certain effects, also select an effect type from the drop-down list. You can apply multiple effects to a given object.

3. To adjust the properties of a specific effect, select its name and vary the dialog controls. Adjust the sliders or enter specific values to vary the combined effect. (You can also select a slider and use the keyboard arrows.) Options differ from one effect to another.

4. Click **OK** to apply the effect to the selected object, or **Cancel** to abandon changes.

Creating reflections

A simple way to add creative flair to your page is to apply a vertical reflection on a selected object. The effect is especially eye-catching when applied to pictures, but can be equally impressive on artistic text, such as page titles or text banners. A combination of settings can control reflection height, opacity, offset and blurring.

Creating outlines

WebPlus lets you create a coloured outline around objects, especially text and shapes (as a **filter effect**). For any outline, you can set the outline width, colour fill, transparency, and blend mode. The outline can also take a gradient fill, a unique **contour** fill (fill runs from the inner to outer edge of the outline width), or pattern fill and can also sit inside, outside, or be centred on the object edge.

As with all effects you can switch the outline effect on and off. You'll be able to apply a combination of 2D or 3D filter effects along with your outline, by checking other options in the Filter Effects dialog.

Blur

Various blur effects can be applied to WebPlus objects. The Types of blur include:

- **Gaussian**: the effect smooths by averaging pixels using a weighted curve.

- **Zoom**: applies converging streaks to the image to simulate a zoom lens.

- **Radial**: applies concentric streaks to the object to simulate a rotating camera or subject.

- **Motion**: applies straight streaks to the object to simulate the effect of camera or subject movement.

Using the Shadow Tool

Shadows are great for adding flair and dimension to your work, particularly to pictures and text objects, but also to shapes, text frames and tables. To help you create them quickly and easily, WebPlus provides the **Shadow Tool** on the Tools toolbar's Effects flyout. The tool affords freeform control of the shadow effect allowing creation of adjustable **basic** or **skewed edge-based shadows** for any WebPlus object.

Basic (left) and skewed shadows
(right) applied to a square
QuickShape.

Adjustment of shadow colour, opacity, blur, and scaling/distance is possible using controllable nodes directly on the page (or via a supporting Shadow context toolbar). Nodes can be dragged inwards or outwards from the shadow origin to modify the shadow's blur and opacity. For a different colour, select the Colour node then pick a new colour from the Colour or Swatches tab. Depending on if a basic or skewed shadow is required, the origin can exist in the centre (shown) or at the edge of an object, respectively.

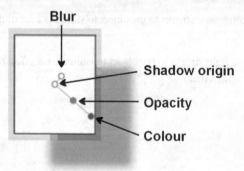

Blur

Shadow origin

Opacity

Colour

Once you've created a shadow, you can also fine-tune it as needed using the Filter Effects dialog.

Using 3D filter effects

3D filter effects go beyond 2D filter effects (such as shadow, glow, bevel, and emboss effects) to create the impression of a textured surface on the object itself. You can use the **Filter Effects** dialog to apply one or more effects to the same object. Keep in mind that none of these 3D effects will "do" anything to an unfilled object—you'll need to have a fill there to see the difference they make!

Overview

To apply a 3D filter effect to a selected object:

1. Click the *fx* **Filter Effects** button on the Tools toolbar's Effects flyout.

2. Check the **3D Effects** box at the left. The **3D Lighting** box is checked by default.

✓ 3D Effects
　　3D Bump Map
　　　　Function
　　　　　　Advanced
　　2D Bump Map
　　3D Pattern Map
　　　　Function
　　　　　　Advanced
　　2D Pattern Map
　　Transparency
✓ 3D Lighting

• **3D Effects** is a master switch, and its settings of **Blur** and **Depth** make a great difference; you can click the "+" button to unlink them for independent adjustment.

• **3D Lighting** provides a "light source" without which any depth information in the effect wouldn't be visible. The lighting settings let you illuminate your 3D landscape and vary its reflective properties.

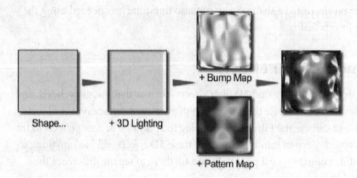

You'll notice that Bump Maps and Pattern Maps come in two varieties: "2D" and "3D." They are all three-dimensional effects—the 2D/3D distinction refers to how each one achieves its result. With the "2D map" variants, you begin by selecting a bitmap from a gallery. With the "3D" Bump Maps and Pattern Maps, you first pick a mathematical function. The function-based maps include data about the interior of the "space," while the bitmap-based maps describe only surface characteristics.

Multiple effects. You can combine multiple 3D filter effects, as in the illustration above. The effects are applied cumulatively, in a standard "pipeline" sequence: 3D Bump > 2D Bump > 3D Pattern > 2D Pattern > 3D Lighting.

3D Bump Map

The **3D Bump Map** effect creates the impression of a textured surface by applying a mathematical function you select to add depth information, for a peak-and-valley effect. You can use 3D Bump Map in conjunction with one or more additional 3D filter effects—but not with a 2D Bump Map.

2D Bump Map

The **2D Bump Map** effect creates the impression of a textured surface by applying a greyscale bitmap you select to add depth information, for a peak-and-valley effect. You can use 2D Bump Map in conjunction with one or more additional 3D filter effects—but not with a 3D Bump Map.

3D Pattern Map

The **3D Pattern Map** effect creates the impression of a textured surface by applying a mathematical function you select to introduce colour variations. You can use 3D Pattern Map in conjunction with one or more other 3D filter effects. (See the overview above for background and technical details on these effects.)

2D Pattern Map

The **2D Pattern Map** effect creates the impression of a textured surface by applying a greyscale bitmap you select to introduce colour variations. You can use 2D Pattern Map in conjunction with one or more other 3D filter effects.

Transparency

The uniform transparency of an object (with 3D filter effects applied) can be controlled via the Transparency tab (see first example below). However, for more sophisticated transparency control, especially for simulating reflective lighting effects on glass objects, transparency settings can instead be set within the 3D filter effects dialog (check the **Transparency** option). Transparency can be adjusted independently for both non-reflective surfaces (typically an object's edge shadows shown when side-lit) and top-lit surfaces (see second example below).

50% Transparency   Filter Effect Transparency

3D Lighting

The **3D Lighting** effect works in conjunction with other 3D effects to let you vary the surface illumination and reflective properties.

Adding dimensionality (Instant 3D)

Using the **Instant 3D** feature, you can easily transform flat shapes (shown) and text into three-dimensional objects.

WebPlus provides control over 3D effect settings such as:

- **bevelling**: use several rounded and chiselled presets or create your own with a custom bevel profile editor.

- **lighting**: up to eight editable and separately coloured lights can be positioned to produce dramatic lighting effects.

- **lathe effects**: create contoured objects (e.g., a bottle cork) with the custom lathe profile editor and extrusion control.

- **texture**: control how texture is extruded on objects with non-solid fills.

- **viewing**: rotate your object in three dimensions.

- **material**: controls the extent to which lighting has an effect on the object's surfaces (great for 3D artistic text!).

An always-at-hand 3D context toolbar hosted above your workspace lets you configure the above settings—each setting contributes to the 3D effect applied to the selected object. For on-the-page object control you can transform in 3D with use of a red orbit circle, which acts as an axis from which you can rotate around the X-, Y-, and Z-axes in relation to your page. Look for the cursor changing as you hover over the red circles' nodes or wire frame.

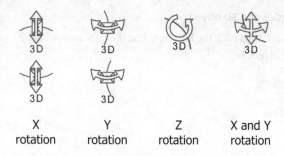

X	Y	Z	X and Y
rotation	rotation	rotation	rotation

Transform about your 3D objects' axes instead of your pages' axes by holding the **Ctrl** key down as you transform.

You can also adjust the angle and elevation of each "active" light on the page by dragging the light pointer to a position which simulates a light source.

After any transformation, the underlying base object remains editable.

To add dimensionality:

1. Select an object and click the Instant **3D** button from the Tools toolbar's Effects flyout (or choose **Instant 3D...** from the Format menu). The object immediately adopts 3D characteristics with a red orbit circle displayed in the object's foreground.

2. Click a 3D effect category from the first drop-down menu on the 3D context toolbar; the bar's options change dynamically according to the category currently selected. See the WebPlus Help for more details.

If you're not happy with how your 3D object is looking, you can revert to the object's initial transformation by either clicking the **Reset Defaults** button on the context toolbar.

To switch off 3D effects:

-   Click the **Remove 3D** button on the context toolbar. You can always click the Tool toolbar's **Instant 3D** button at any time later to reinstate the effect.

To edit base properties of a 3D object:

- Select the 3D object, then click the **Edit** button at the bottom right-hand corner of the 3D object, i.e.

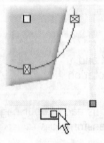

The object is shown without its 3D effect, allowing its selection handles to be manipulated for resizing and rotating.

Adding borders

A **border** in WebPlus is a repeating, decorative element that can be set to enclose an object, giving the appearance of a picture frame. Borders work especially well with imported pictures.

To add a border to an object:

1. Click the **Line/Border** button on the Tools toolbar's Fill flyout.

2. If you want to apply the border to specific edges of the object, use the **Border Edges** tab. The preview at the left indicates with bolding which edges of the selected object's border will be updated with the current **Border** tab settings when you click **OK**.

- To select all edges or no edges, click the corresponding icon on the top row.

- To toggle a single edge, click the corresponding icon in the bottom row.

3. To define the border, select the **Border** tab. In the **Side** drop-down list, select a border preset. You can use the up/down arrows to move through the list, and preview each border in the window at the right. To remove a border, select "None."

4. To keep the corner pattern the same as the side, leave **Keep side and corners the same** checked. To mix and match, uncheck the box and select a preset from the "Corner" list.

5. Choose an **Alignment** setting to fit the border to the **Outside** or **Inside** of the object, or straddling the **Middle** of its bounding box.

6. Set other properties as needed:
   • To vary the border width, select or type a value in the **Weight** list.
   • If **Behind contents** is checked, the inner half of the border extends behind the object. If unchecked, the whole border appears in front (the wider the border, the more it encroaches on the filled region).
   • If **Scale with object** is checked, both border and object change together if you resize the object. If unchecked, the border weight remains constant during resizing.

7. Click **OK** when you're done.

Using object styles

Object styles benefit your design efforts in much the same way as text styles and colour schemes. Once you've come up with a set of attributes that you like—properties like line colour, fill, border, and so on—you can save this cluster of attributes as a named style. WebPlus remembers which objects are using that style, and the style appears in the **Styles tab**.

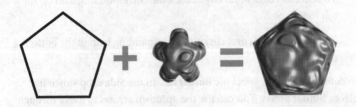

Here's how object styles work to your advantage:

- Any time you want to alter some aspect of the style (for example, change the line colour), you simply change the style definition. Instantly, all objects in your site sharing that style update accordingly.

- Object styles you've saved globally appear not only in the original site but in any new site, so you can reuse exactly the same attractive combination of attributes for any subsequent design effort.

As a bonus, the Styles tab ships with multiple galleries of pre-designed styles that you can apply to any object, or customize to suit your own taste!

Each object style can include settings for a host of object attributes, such as line colour, line style, fill, transparency, filter effects, font, and border. The freedom to include or exclude certain attributes, and the nearly unlimited range of choices for each attribute, makes this a powerful tool in the designer's arsenal.

To apply an object style to one or more objects:

1. Display the **Styles** tab.

2. Expand the drop-down menu to display a tree-structure menu showing 3D, Filter effect and Materials categories. Navigate the menu to select a category while previewing available styles as thumbnails in the lower panel.

3. Click a style thumbnail in the panel to apply it to the selected object(s).

Choose **Format>Object Style>Create** to create a new object style based on an existing object's attributes.

Images, Animation, and Multimedia

Importing images

WebPlus lets you insert images from a wide variety of file formats. Here's a quick overview:

- **Bitmapped** images, also known as **bitmaps** or **raster** images, are built from a matrix of dots ("pixels"), rather like the squares on a sheet of graph paper. They may originate as digital camera photos or scanned images, or be created (or enhanced) with a "paint" program or photo editor.

- **Draw** graphics, also known as **vector** images, are resolution-independent and contain drawing commands such as "draw a line from A to B."

- **Metafiles** are the native graphics format for Windows and combine raster and vector information.

You can also acquire images directly from PhotoCDs or via TWAIN devices (scanners or digital cameras).

Inserting images

There are several ways to bring an image into WebPlus. You can drag a file from an external Windows folder directly onto your page, drag a thumbnail from WebPlus's Media Bar (see p. 185), paste from the pasteboard, or import an image as a file via a dialog.

- **Detached** images float freely on a page, while **inline** images are incorporated with the text flow in a text object.

- **Embedded** images become part of the WebPlus project, while **linking** places a reference copy of the image on the page and preserves a connection to the original file. Each approach has its pros and cons (see Embedding vs. Linking on p. 184).

WebPlus lets you place your image onto the page at its original size. The image will be uncropped by default but you have the option to crop the image, and adjust the image's picture frame properties with respect to image positioning and scaling within the picture frame.

To add an image from the Media Bar:

• Drag an image thumbnail onto the page from the currently displayed album(s) shown in WebPlus's Media Bar (expand the Media Bar from the bottom of your workspace). You can also drag onto an existing image to replace it.

To import an image from a file:

1. (Optional) If you want to place the image inline, click for an insertion point in a text object. For a detached image, make sure text objects are deselected.

2. **In the main window**:

   • Click the ⬚ **Import Picture...** button on the Standard Objects toolbar's Picture flyout.
   OR

   In WritePlus:

   • Choose **Picture File...** from the Insert menu.

3. Use the dialog to select the image file to open.

4. Select either **Embed Picture** or **Link Picture**. See

5. Click **Open**.

6. If there's a text insertion point in the main window, you'll be prompted whether to insert the image at the current cursor position. Click **Yes** if that's what you want.

   ⬚ If there was no insertion point (or you answer "No" to the insertion prompt), you'll see the mouse pointer change to the **Picture Paste** cursor. What you do next determines the initial size and placement of the detached image.

7.   To insert the image at its original pixel size, simply click the mouse.
     OR
     To set the size of the inserted image, drag out a region and release the
     mouse button. Use the **Shift** key for unconstrained placement (normal
     operation is to maintain the image's aspect ratio).

> For multi-image pasting, select multiple images in the Open dialog,
> then paste each image one by one onto the page (by consecutive
> clicks).

Replacing images

The replace picture option lets you swap an image at any time, especially
useful when you want to retain an image's position and dimensions on the
page but want to update the image itself. It can be used on any image
(uncropped or cropped).

To replace an image:

*   Click the 🖼 **Replace Picture** button directly under the selected image,
    locate and select an image. Click **Open**.

To replace an image via Media Bar:

*   Drag an image thumbnail onto an existing image from the currently
    displayed album(s) shown in WebPlus's Media Bar (expand the Media
    Bar from the bottom of your workspace first).

Adjusting cropped images

WebPlus provides additional options for working with cropped images—
either pictures you've cropped with the Crop tools (Tools toolbar) or
replaceable pictures already present in design templates. For example, you can
pan or zoom to adjust the portion of the image that displays inside its "frame,"
or you can change the way the image is scaled and aligned by adjusting its
frame properties.

When you select a cropped image with the **Pointer
Tool**, a control bar displays below the image,
offering panning, rotation, zoom in, zoom out, and
replace picture options.

- To reposition a cropped image inside its "frame," click [icon], and then click and drag on the image.

- To rotate an image in 90° anti-clockwise increments, click the [icon] button.

- To zoom in or out of an image, click one of the [icons] zoom in/out tools.

- To replace an image, click [icon], then browse to locate the new image and click **Open**.

To alter frame properties:

1. Right-click on a cropped image and choose **Frame Properties....**
   OR
   Select the image and choose **Frame Properties** on the Picture context toolbar.

2. In the dialog, you can scale to maximum/minimum, **Stretch to Fit**, or use the original image's size (**No Scale**).

3. To change the vertical alignment of the image within the frame, select **Top**, **Middle**, or **Bottom**.

4. For horizontal alignment, select **Left**, **Centre**, or **Right**.

> Selecting an uncropped picture offers only a Replace Picture button.

Embedding vs. linking

Embedding means the image in WebPlus is now distinct from the original file. Embedding results in a larger WebPlus file, and if you need to alter an embedded image you'll need to re-import it after editing. Still, it's the best choice if file size isn't an issue and graphics are final.

Linking inserts a copy of the image file into the WebPlus Web site, linked to the actual file so that any changes you later make to it in the native application will be automatically reflected in WebPlus. Linking is one way of avoiding "bloat" by limiting the size of the project file. On the other hand, you'll need to manage the externally linked files carefully, for example making sure to include them all if you move the WebPlus file to a different drive.

By default, WebPlus prompts you to embed images that are <256 KB, by pre-selecting the "Embed Picture" option in the Insert Picture dialog (but you can always select "Link Picture" instead). If you like, you can change the threshold file size or even switch off the automatic selection.

You can check resources via Site Manager later on, to change an item's status from linked to embedded, or vice versa.

For dragging images from the Media Bar, images <256 KB are embedded, while images >256 KB are linked. However, you can change embed or link status with the **Shift** key as you drag.

To preselect embedding or linking based on file size:

1. Choose **Options...** from the Tools menu. Select the **General** menu option.

2. To preselect the "Embed Picture" option for images under a certain size, select the threshold size in the "Embed if smaller than" list. ("Link Picture" will be pre-selected for images larger than the threshold.)

3. To choose whether to embed or link each image, uncheck **Suggest embed/link picture**. You can still select either option in the import dialog; it will now remember and preselect the last setting you used.

Using the Media Bar

The Media Bar acts as a "basket" containing photos for inclusion in your Web site. Its chief use is to aid the design process by improving efficiency (avoiding having to import photos one by one) and convenience (making photos always-at-hand). For photo-rich Web sites in particular, perhaps based on a WebPlus design templates, the Media Bar is a valuable tool for dragging photos directly onto unwanted pictures to replace them.

The Media Bar can be used as a temporary storage area before placing photos in your Web site, or it can be used to create more permanent **photo albums** from which you can retrieve stored photos at any time. By default, photos are added to a **temporary album** but remember to click the **New Album** button if you want to save your album for later use. Each time you start WebPlus you simply load that saved album (or any other saved album) or just work with a temporary album—the choice is yours!

You can import an unlimited number of photos by file or by whole folders, and whether photos are embedded or linked to your project in advance of photo placement on the page.

For large photo collections, searching throughout albums for photos by file name and EXIF, IPTC or XMP metadata is possible; even edit XMP metadata from within WebPlus.

> The currently loaded album shown on your Media Bar will remain visible irrespective of which document you have open.

Thumbnails can be dragged from the Media Bar directly onto an existing picture on your page, replacing it in the process. Alternatively, a picture can be added as new, being placed at its original size.

To view the Media Bar:

- Unless already displayed, click the ▬▬▲▬▬ handle at the bottom of your workspace.

To add photos to a temporary album:

1. With the Media Bar visible and a temporary album loaded, click on the Media Bar's workspace to reveal an **Import Picture** dialog.

2. From the dialog, navigate to a photo or folder, select photo(s), and optionally choose whether your photos are to be placed at native or 96 dpi, or embedded or linked (embedding may increase your file size significantly).

3. Click **Open**. Your photos appear as thumbnails in the Menu Bar workspace.

> Unless you save it, the temporary album and its photo contents will not be saved when you close WebPlus.

> You can drag one or more files from any Windows folder directly into the Media Bar window. If you right-click an image in the Media Bar and choose Locate in Explorer you'll open the photo's folder via Windows Explorer—great for drag and drop or just general file management!

To save a temporary album to a named album:

1. Click the down arrow on the ⊞ Add To ▼ button. From the menu, select **New Album**.

2. In the **New Album** dialog, in the **Album Name** box, type a name to identify your album in the future.

3. (Optional) For any photo you can alter the resolution (native or 96 dpi), or embed/link status in advance of placement on your page—click a photo's setting (DPI, Placement) and use the setting's drop-down menu to change. You can also change these settings during drag/drop onto the page.

4. Click **OK**.

To include a temporary album's photos in an existing saved album, click the **Add To** button and choose a named album from the menu.

To create a named album:

1. Click the bar's 🖼️ New Album button.

2. In the dialog, in the **Album Name** box, type a name to identify your album in the future.

3. Click the 🖼️ **Add Image...** or 🖼️ **Add Folder...** button.

4. In the dialog, navigate to a photo or folder and optionally choose whether your photos are to be placed at native or 96 dpi, or embedded or linked (embedding increases your file size significantly). Click **Open**.

5. The **New Album** dialog lists the files for inclusion. Optionally, alter DPI and Embed options by clicking on each photo's setting, then selecting from the drop-down menu.

6. Click **OK**.

To load a saved album:

• Select a saved album name from the bar's top-right drop-down menu. The album's photos will display in the workspace.

🖼️ Manage   A saved album can be selected as above and then modified via the **Manage** button (only shown for existing saved albums). You can add photos/folders, delete photos, change DPI, and alter embed/link status.

To rename or delete an album:

• Right-click an existing album name in the top-right drop-down menu and choose **Rename Album** or **Delete Album**.

To sort results from an album:

• In the **Sort By** search box, choose Filename, Rating, or Date Taken to reorder the photos accordingly to option.

Adding photos to the page

To add a photo to your page:

1. Display the Media Bar's temporary album or load a saved album from the top-right drop-down menu.

2. Drag an album's photo thumbnail onto the page and release your mouse button.

Setting image export options

When you export your project as a Web site, WebPlus applies certain global settings to determine how each image—whether drawn, pasted in, or imported—ends up as a separate bitmap displayed on the Web page.

Here's a quick summary of the conversion settings as they're initially defined for Web publishing:

- Each referenced image is exported as a separate file.

- Any image you inserted as a GIF, JPEG, or PNG is exported as the original file, using its original file name.

- Inserted metafiles and all other graphics are regenerated as PNG images.

You can alter these settings, but before doing so you should review the "logic" WebPlus applies to publishing Web graphics. First, WebPlus has one **default format** to which **all** graphics will be converted on export—but you can make exceptions to this rule by specifying that certain image types should remain as their original file. Initially, PNG is the default format, but with **overrides** set for GIFs. That's why, using the initial settings above, GIFs stay as they are while all other graphics get converted to PNGs.

You can check and change these settings in the **Site Properties** dialog (File Menu). The settings there are global and apply to all graphics in the site—but again you can make exceptions, in this case for individual graphics. To do so, for a selected graphic you could:

- Use the **Image Export Options...** (Format menu) or the **Image Export Manager** (Tools menu) to set the export format of particular images on a case-by-case basis.

  OR

  Convert certain images to a specific format beforehand using the **Tools>Convert to Picture**.

This combination of global and local settings gives you almost total control (if you care to exercise it) over how your graphics make it onto your Web pages! Let's look first at how the global settings work.

To set global export options for Web graphics:

1. Choose **Site Properties...** from the File menu and select the Graphics tab. Then set options as follows:

2. Check **Optimize overlapping graphics** to have WebPlus analyze the site and (where a smaller file would result) output overlapping graphics as a single graphic. Whether this option makes sense will depend on your particular layout. Rather than use this global approach, you might consider using **Tools>Convert to Picture** in specific cases.

3. In the **Placed Graphics** section, to override conversion for images of certain formats (inserted JPEGs, GIFs, and/or PNGs), check which format(s) to preserve. Checking a format means that any image you've placed on a page using that format will stay in its original file format—exempt from conversion to the default format. The reused file will be given a checksummed name to avoid redrawing small images as larger files (making the site more efficient).

4. In the **Generated Graphics** section, select a preferred export format. This is the default format to which all graphics will be converted on export unless you set overrides. For JPGs, you can set a compression value. For PNGs, **Use PNG transparency** and **Use compatibility hack..** options let you allow PNG transparency and properly render PNG alpha transparency (in Internet Explorer 5.5 and 6.0), respectively.

5. For exporting original graphic file names, check **Use original names of graphics files**. Graphics will be stored in the root of your published Web site.

Setting export options, title, and alt text for each graphic

The **Image Export Manager** is a Wizard that lets you set the export file format for individual graphics in the site, or for objects such as rotated text that will be converted to images on export. These local, image-by-image settings **override** the global settings (as set in **File>Site Properties**) which WebPlus uses to determine the export format. You can run the Wizard to check a single selected image, the current page, or the entire site. For each image, you can save it using different methods. Either:

- Choose a specific format (GIF, JPEG, or PNG) to export to (or just defer to site default settings). For JPEG, you can choose a level of compression. OR

- Save the file to a chosen path and file name on export. Perhaps you want to add more meaningful descriptive names to images on export (especially useful when maintaining your Web site) instead of having the images export with automatically generated image names.

Let your own eye be the judge. Your best bet is to retain the **Use site default settings** option for all images to start with. Using the original global settings, this means that GIFs, JPEGs, and PNGs will be exported as their original files, while any others, including QuickShapes and closed shapes, will be published as PNGs. Then preview your site and determine if you want to vary the global settings or try a different output format for specific images.

Even if you don't change any format settings, you can set a picture **title** which will normally appear as a tooltip when the image is moused over in a browser. You can also enter **alternativee text** (manually or automatically) for accessibility reasons.

To set export format, title, and/or alternative text:

1. If you're checking just a single image, you can select it first and choose **Image Export Options...** from the Format or right-click menu. OR
    To review Web export options for images throughout your site, choose **Image Export Manager...** from the Tools menu.

2. (Only if you're using the Image Export Manager) Select whether you are checking a selected object, current page or entire site in the Wizard, then click **Finish**. The Wizard cycles through graphics in the specified range, and displays each one in turn along with the Image Export Options dialog.

3. In the dialog's **Save Picture As** section, you can choose to enable either:

   • **Save to a format and name chosen by WebPlus**. The format of the graphic is as defined in Site properties (Generated Graphics; Default Format); the name is generated automatically, e.g. wp479d0ea6.

   • **Save in this format with a name chosen by WebPlus**.
     Click a GIF, JPEG, or PNG radio button to specify the export format for the current graphic. Enable **Use site default settings** if the site's default format is to be maintained but named automatically by WebPlus. If selecting JPEG, choose a compression quality from the **Compression** drop-down menu.

   • **Save to my chosen path and name**.
     Click the **Choose File...** button. The displayed dialog lets you export with the original image file name (enable **Use default name**) or choose a new image name (enable **Choose name** button and enter a new file name). For either method, you can navigate to the folder where you want to save the exported image. The file format used will be that set in the site default settings. You can still override the site default setting by altering the file extension in the Choose name field, e.g. change .GIF to .PNG.

4. Check the **Exclude this picture from optimization..** option if you don't want the image to be combined into one exported image if overlapping with another image in your project.

5. (Optional) Choose from one of several resampling methods—WebPlus can resample when needed, the file will always be resampled (e.g., when a JPG is resized) or will never be resampled (original image will be used). Enable the appropriate radio button as needed. Changing the format will always resample.

6. To enter a title for a graphic, view the Alt and Title tab, and enter the appropriate text. This is shown when hovering over an exported image.

7. In the same tab, assign an ALT text string to your image for Web accessibility. The string is read out by screen reader on hover over. You can assign text by entry into the input box or you can check **Use default ALT text** instead. For the latter, the image is exported as follows:

   - If the images is decorative (contains no text) it will have no ALT text.
     OR

   - If the image is a clickable graphic such as a labelled button (e.g. Back, Forward, etc.), text on the image is automatically taken, exported as ALT text (i.e., Back, Forward) and presented to a screen reader. If a title graphic is specified, the title text is used as the ALT text.

8. Click **OK**.

Applying image adjustments

The **Picture context toolbar** appears automatically when you select an image on the page. You can use the toolbar to improve the appearance of any image appearing in your drawing by adjusting **brightness** and **contrast** directly, setting levels and contrast automatically, fixing red eye or by applying **Image adjustments**. The context toolbar also hosts other photo manipulation tools.

Image adjustments are made possible with a comprehensive mix of colour correction/adjustment tools for use on your newly imported images. Levels, Colour Balance, Channel mixer, Dust and Scratch Remover and Hue/Saturation/Lightness corrective adjustments, amongst others, are available. Effect-inducing adjustments also range from the artistic Diffuse Glow to various blur effects. In fact, over 20 adjustments can be directly applied to your image not only individually but cumulatively.

Adjustments are managed in the **Image Adjustments** dialog. The gallery offers a one-stop shop for applying your adjustments—all supported by a dynamic preview window!

Adjustments can be applied to imported pictures as well as objects converted to pictures within WebPlus.

If you're looking to carry our some more advanced photo editing and have Serif's PhotoPlus software (10.0 or above) installed, you can use the **Edit in PhotoPlus**.A button on the Picture context toolbar to load the image directly into PhotoPlus. You can carry out your edit and save the file in PhotoPlus—if embedded or linked, the newly altered image is refreshed and updated in WebPlus automatically.

Adding an image adjustment

Adding an adjustment is as easy as choosing an option from a drop-down menu in the Image Adjustments dialog. To assist in the selection of an appropriate adjustment the list is separated into corrective adjustments (in the first half of the list), and effect-inducing adjustments (in the second half). As soon as an adjustment is selected it is added to a stack where additional adjustments can be added and built up cumulatively. Any adjustment can be switched on/off, deleted or reordered in this list. The order in which they appear in the stack may produce very different results—if you're not happy with your current order—WebPlus lets you drag and drop your adjustment into any position in the stack.

Adjustments are applied such that the most recently added adjustment always appears at the bottom of the list and is applied to the picture last (after the other adjustments above it). In the above example, the Diffuse Glow effect is applied to the picture first, followed by Levels.

To add an image adjustment:

1. Select the picture that you want to apply an adjustment to.

2. Click the ✐ Image Adjustments button on the Picture context toolbar.

3. In the Image Adjustments dialog, click 🞤 **Add Adjustment**.

4. From the drop-down list, select an adjustment. The adjustment is added to the scrollable window.

5. Select the adjustment. There are three methods to configure properties depending on the adjustment selected:

   Adjust settings by moving available sliders (if present)
   OR
   Enter different values into the input boxes.
   OR

   🖹 For more complex adjustments, make changes in a pop-up dialog (click **Advanced Properties** to access).

   NOTE: Some adjustments have no properties and are applied directly as they are selected.

6. Click the **OK** button.

Add more than one adjustment to the picture by repeating the above procedure.

To delete an image adjustment:

• With an adjustment selected, click the ✕ Delete Adjustment button.

Switching on/off adjustments

⊖ In the same way in which a layer's contents can be made visible/invisible, the **Mute** button can be used to temporarily make an adjustment invisible or visible.

Modifying adjustments

The properties of any selected adjustment can be changed in one of two ways:

- Properties will be displayed alongside the adjustment appearing in the stack (in Image Adjustments dialog)—you can alter and experiment with these.

- 📑 The properties of an applied adjustment can be changed by clicking the **Advanced Properties** button alongside the effect (in Image Adjustments dialog)—this is because some effects are more complex to modify by their nature and need to be presented in a separate dialog.

Reordering adjustments

Adjustments can be moved around the stack to change the order in which they are applied to the picture. Drag an adjustment name to another position in the list while holding down the mouse button. A dark line indicates the new position in which the entry will be place if the mouse button is released.

Importing TWAIN images

If your scanner or digital camera provides **TWAIN** support, you can scan pictures directly into WebPlus using the TWAIN standard, or save the scanned image as a TIFF or PCX and then import into WebPlus.

To set up your TWAIN device for importing:

- See the documentation supplied with your scanner for operating instructions

To import a scanned image:

- Choose **Picture** from the Insert menu, then select **TWAIN** then **Acquire...** from the submenus to open a file selection dialog.

If you have more than one TWAIN-compatible device installed, you may need to select which source you wish to scan with.

To select a different TWAIN source for scanning:

1. Choose **Picture** from the Insert menu, then select **TWAIN** then **Select Source** from the submenus.

2. Identify the device you want to use as your TWAIN source.

Adding animation

WebPlus lets you add several varieties of eye-catching animation effects to any web page: **animated marquees**, **GIF animations**, and **Flash** (.SWF) files. For any of the animation effects, you can preview the animation and/or customize the effect. Once placed into your Web site, the animations appear static, but they will spring to life once the site has been exported and a visitor views your page in a Web browser.

> Bear in mind that animations do add to the "overhead" or load time your page requires, and may not display as quickly on the Web as when previewed.

Animated marquees

Animated marquees are an impressive way to add horizontally scrolling motion to a headline or catch phrase. You can choose the background colour, enter from one to three lines of text, define text properties (choose from any installed font), scroll direction, speed and alignment for each line. If you like, you can define any link destination type for the marquee (see Adding hyperlinks and anchors on p. 225). For the most compelling effect, select two lines with strongly contrasting text colours and opposing scroll directions.

Animated marquees appear as static graphics on the WebPlus page. You can cut, copy, move, and resize them just like other graphics. They will animate when previewed or viewed in a Web browser.

To create an animated marquee:

*   Click the [ANIM] **Insert Animated Marquee** button on the Web Objects toolbar's Media flyout.

To edit an animated marquee you've already defined:

- Double-click the marquee. The Insert Animated Marquee dialog redisplays, with the current settings in place.

GIF animations

WebPlus lets you select and preview any animated GIF. They are particularly useful to illustrate particular themes or just add some fun to your page! All GIF animations appear as static images on the WebPlus page and, just like any image, you can cut, copy, move, and resize them just like other graphics. They will animate when previewed or viewed in a Web browser.

To preview and insert an animated GIF:

1. Click the ▥ **Insert Animated GIF** button on the Web Objects toolbar's Media flyout.

2. Use the dialog to select the image file to open. Check **Preview** to examine images in the window at right.

3. If you check the **Place at native dpi** option and the image has a different internal setting, WebPlus will scale the image accordingly; otherwise it applies a default screen resolution setting of **96 dpi**.

4. To keep the image separate from the WebPlus file (using a link to the source file) check **Link picture**. To include the image in the WebPlus project, check **Embed picture**.

5. Click **Open**.

6. You'll see the ▥ Picture Paste cursor. Click to insert the animation at a default size or drag to a custom size.

Flash files

A Flash (*.SWF) file is a viewable movie using the Flash™ Player format. (Flash is a vector-based program designed to create and display small files on the Web.) Flash files can be added to your page (much like an image) and will play within your page view without the need for previewing in your browser (or WebPlus preview window). You can cut, copy, move, and resize them just like other graphics.

To see some Flash files in action, the Gallery tab hosts a stunning collection of Flash banners (each with pre-assigned Flash parameters already set) which can be easily adopted. These banners are designed to allow you to customize their appearance (i.e., text, images, and scheme colours) without any prior Flash design experience.

To insert a Flash file:

1. Click the 🄵 **Insert Flash file** button on the Web Objects toolbar's Media flyout.

2. Use the dialog to select the Flash file to open (click **Browse...** then select your .SWF file). Click **Export Options** to optionally define a different file name and/or file location. To keep the animation separate from the WebPlus file (using a link to the source file) uncheck **Embed Flash file in site**.

3. (Optional) In the Parameters window, click the **Add...** (or **Edit...**) button to add parameters as name/value pairs.

4. (Optional) In the Additional Files window, build up a library of files (e.g., images) which are used to make up your Flash movie. Think of it as a local library in which supporting files are easily at hand and easily referenced. Click the **Add...** button to navigate to then select files for addition (use Ctrl-click or Shift-click for contiguous or non-contiguous file selection, respectively).

5. (Optional) The Display box controls how the Flash movie is presented on your WebPlus page. Experiment with the options for different looping, transparency, alignment, scaling, and quality options.

6. Click **OK**.

7. You'll see the ⬚ Picture Paste cursor. Click to insert the file at a default size or drag to set a custom size region.

To edit a Flash banner:

1. Double-click your Flash movie.

2. (Optional) Change **Export Options...** and whether you want to embed the file in your WebPlus project.

3. In the Parameters box select any parameter **Name** in the list and click the **Edit** button (you don't need to use the **Add...** button when editing Flash banners). Depending on the Flash banner chosen, you can edit several types of parameter value, i.e.

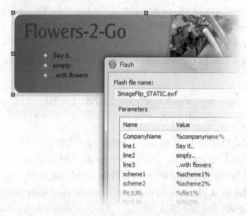

- Text values can be changed from their placeholder text, e.g. a placeholder text value for "line 1" can be overwritten with your own text (e.g., "Say it.."). You can equally use a token as a replacement value (e.g. a token of *%companyname%* will automatically show the company name set in User Details in your banner—in this case "Flowers-2-Go").

- Scheme values can be altered by again editing token values, e.g. to use your project's scheme colour 2 instead or scheme colour 1 you can edit %scheme1% to be %scheme2%.

- Parameter values for pictures work slight differently to text and schemes. Flash banners are arranged in the Gallery tab in folders representing the number of pictures used in the banner design, i.e. "1 Image", "2 Image" and "3 Image". Each picture that makes up your banner is referenced in the parameters list, e.g. for "3 Image" banners, Pic1URL, Pic2URL, and Pic3URL represents the first, second and third pictures listed in the **Additional Files** list. You can either reorder pictures in the Additional Files list (**not** the Parameters list) using the **Up** or **Down** buttons to make pictures appear in a different sequence or use the right-most **Add...** button to add new files to the Additional Files list to replace currently referenced pictures. There's no need to edit the Parameter values at all—the key is to set the pictures and their order in the Additional Files list only.

> Remember to remove any unwanted pictures from the Additional Files list.

4. (Optional) Uncheck **Embed files in site** if you don't want additional files to be included in your project.

5. (Optional) The Display box controls how the Flash movie is presented on your WebPlus page. Experiment with the options for different looping, transparency, alignment, scaling, and quality options.

6. Click **OK**.

The selected Flash banner is shown with any previously made edits applied.

> If you experience any playback problems when Flash files are placed on your page, it is possible to uncheck **Load Flash previews** in **Tools>Options** (Layout menu option). Exported web pages containing Flash files are unaffected.

Adding sound and video

WebPlus lets you augment your Web pages with sound and video files in a variety of standard formats, including both **non-streaming** and **streaming** media. In addition, WebPlus lets you include third-party videos already hosted on www.youtube.com.

Sound

- There are actually two sound playback options—**background sound**, where a sound loads and plays automatically when a specific page is first displayed in the visitor's Web browser, and **linked sound**, triggered by a mouse click (for example on an icon or hyperlinked object). The supported audio formats are .AIFF, .AU, MIDI (.mid, .midi), .MP3, RealAudio (.ra, .ram), and .WAV.

Video

- **Linked video** works like linked sound. Supported video formats are .AVI, QuickTime (.mov, .qt), MPEG (.mpg, .mpeg, .mpe, .mpv), and RealVideo (.ram, .rv). (Non-streaming files must download in entirety to a user's computer before they begin playing; streaming files require a special player that buffers incoming data and can start playing before the whole clip has arrived.)

- **YouTube videos** which are already published on the Internet can be included on your Web page. Videos themselves are not be embedded in your project; instead, just the unique YouTube video ID is embedded in your page as you place the YouTube video on your page—a link is created from your Web page back to www.youtube.com. This lets you add media content to your pages while avoiding uploading large videos as part of your project.

With both background and linked sound (or video), you have the option of **embedding** the source file in your project file, as opposed to keeping it separate (remember that YouTube videos cannot be embedded in your project). Although embedding any file adds to the size of the project, it is the default option because you'll no longer have to worry about juggling separate files or the chance of accidentally deleting one of them. When you publish your site, WebPlus takes care of exporting and copying both embedded and non-embedded files.

To add background sound to a page:

1. Right-click the page in the workspace and choose **Page Properties...**

2. From the Background tab, check **Use sound file**, then from the Open dialog, browse to the sound file you want to add. Once the file is selected, click **OK**.

3. If you do <u>not</u> wish to embed the file, uncheck the **Embed sound file in site** option.

4. To have the sound play back as a continuous loop, check **Loop sound**. Otherwise, it will play just once.

5. (Optional) Set **Export Options...** to define an exported file name and physical location. (See Setting image export options on p. 189.).

The sound file will download and play back when the Web page displays in a browser.

The basic question is how you want the visitor to be able to trigger the playback of a given media file. WebPlus offers the same basic options for both kinds of media:

- **From a hyperlinked object (or hotspot):** You start with an existing object in the site, and hyperlink it to the media file, or use a hotspot over an image.

- **From a video thumbnail preview:** You click on an embedded video thumbnail which commences video playback (YouTube videos only).

- **From an icon:** WebPlus provides an icon pre-linked to the media file. You then position the icon on your page.

- **From a picture:** You select an external picture file, which WebPlus then imports and links to the media file.

- **Inline:** A media "player" will be visible on your published Web page (rather than appearing after the user clicks a link, icon, or picture). In WebPlus, you'll see a marker on the page where the player will appear.

With the first two options, the media file remains external and can't be embedded in your project. Options 3 to 5 give you the choice of embedding the media file.

To add linked sound or video to a page:

- To link from an object or hotspot, choose **Hyperlink...** from the Insert menu and select **A file on your hard disk** as the link target, then locate the media file.

To embed a YouTube video:

1. Open the www.youtube.com web site in your browser, and choose the YouTube video that you want to link to.

2. Copy the URL address for the video (or embed code). This contains an alphanumeric ID, e.g. ySnp4YXU6JQ, which uniquely identifies the video clip.

3. Click the　　**Embed YouTube Video** button on the Web Objects toolbar's Media flyout.
   OR
   Choose **Media** from the Insert menu and select **YouTube Video...** from the submenu.

4. From the dialog, paste the video URL into the input box, then click **OK**.

5. Position the　　**Paste** cursor where you want the top-left corner of your video to be placed.

6. To insert the video at a default size, simply click the mouse.
   OR
   To set the size of the inserted video, drag out the cursor and release the mouse button. The video resizing will be unconstrained but you can maintain the video's aspect ratio by pressing the **Shift** key as you drag.

Some Web sites may require their YouTube video(s) to be swapped for another on an occasional or more regular basis. For example, the site may host a regularly changing top 10 or videos with topical content. Either way, WebPlus can replace videos without affecting their placement.

To swap your YouTube video for another, double-click an existing YouTube video. From the dialog, paste a previously copied video URL into the input box.

To link from an icon, picture, or inline player:

1. Click the ⊙ **Insert Sound Clip** or 🎞 **Insert Video Clip** button on the Web Objects toolbar's Media flyout.

2. Browse to locate the media file name.

3. Select a link display option (icon, inline, or picture).

4. If you do **not** wish to embed the file, uncheck the "Embed picture file in site" option.

5. Click **OK** to close the dialog, then click (or click and drag) with the cursor to place the icon, picture, or marker on your page.

Using the Flash™ Photo Gallery

The simultaneous expansion of digital camera usage and Broadband services has created a fantastic opportunity for publishing photo collections on Web pages. There are a multitude of reasons for doing so but some common ones include:

- hosting family photos for access by geographically distant relatives

- Special occasions (parties, Christmas, meetings, holidays)

- cataloguing collections (e.g., of animals, stamps, etc.)

In WebPlus you can add a Flash™ photo gallery to any Web page. By using the power of Flash you can also adopt some eye-catching gallery styles, each offering different ways of cycling through photos. Photo galleries let you navigate via a top or bottom control bar or, depending on gallery style, by using:

- thumbnail rollovers (scrollable; with/without reflections)

- vertical thumbnails (scrollable; with/without slide-ins)

- photo grid (scrollable; with slide-ins)

- photo stack (below)

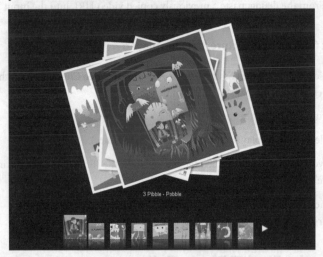

3 Pibble - Pobble

Photos can be imported by file or folder, or from a TWAIN device (digital camera/scanner). Once arranged in a gallery structure the photo's thumbnails can be manipulated in a variety of ways. It's possible to:

- Reorder by drag and drop, or using arrangement buttons.

- Rotate (in 90° anti-clockwise increments)*.

- Temporarily expand thumbnail size for review.

- Add captions.

- Apply image adjustments.

- *Automatic rotation of digital camera images (landscape to portrait) is possible (if supported by camera)

Creating the Gallery

The Photo Gallery is inserted on the page, just like an individual image, after collecting your images together from file, folder, camera, or scanner.

> All the images are output as JPGs regardless of the original image type and the settings in **File>Site Properties>Graphics**.

To insert a Photo Gallery:

1. Click the ![icon] **Insert Flash Photo Gallery** button on the Standard Objects toolbar's Picture flyout.

2. From the dialog, choose whether to:

   - **Add individual files**
     Click the **Add Files** button to navigate to then select the image file(s) to open. Use **Ctrl**-click or **Shift**-click to select multiple non-adjacent or adjacent files. Use the **Preview** window to examine the images as you add to your current selection.
     OR

   - **Add all photos in a folder**
     Click the **Add Folders** button to navigate to a folder then select it to add its contents.
     OR

   - **Add from a digital camera or scanner**
     Click the **Add TWAIN** button. If needed, select your TWAIN source in advance of the Acquire process via **Select Source...** from the drop-down menu. Click **Acquire...** to get your photos.

   - To delete one or all thumbnails, use the **Delete** or **Delete All** button, respectively.

   Your images display as thumbnails in the **Flash Photo Gallery** dialog.

> Any selected thumbnail can be resized by dragging from its lower right-hand corner. Drag when you see the cursor change.

Large images are automatically scaled down (to 800 x 600 pixels; 96dpi) to reduce file sizes (and improve upload times).

3. (Optional) Select one or more gallery thumbnail for manipulation, i.e.

    - Reorder the thumbnails by drag and drop.
      OR

      Use the △ **Up**, ▽ **Down**, ◸△ **Top** and ▽= **Bottom** buttons in the Arrangement box.

    - Rotate the selected image in 90° clockwise intervals with multiple clicks of the **Rotate** button.

    - Add a caption under the selected image with the **Caption** button (captions only show during preview or on live site).

    - Click the **Adjustments** button to apply image adjustments. The flyout menu offers some commonly used basic image adjustments but you can select **Custom...** to access WebPlus's Image Adjustment dialog.

4. To include selected photos within your WebPlus project file, check **Embed Images**. By default, photos are kept separate from the WebPlus file (using a link to the source file).

5. Click the **Next>** button.

6. Select a Gallery style from the **Gallery Style** pane running across the top of the displayed dialog. Each type offers a different style for photo navigation—try each one out until you find one you like in the accompanying Preview window. You'll notice a control bar on each style which allows for user navigation of photos after publishing.

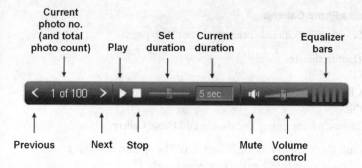

The last three options only show if background music is used.

7. (Optional) For the selected style, use the **Settings** pane to modify various gallery-wide options (accompanying background music, font colour, AutoPlay, etc.). Some options are specific to a gallery style such as enabling/disabling thumbnail rollovers, number of thumbnails shown, photos per stack, etc. Blur amount controls how much blurring occurs between photos. AutoPlay will automatically start photo display at a set but configurable time interval (in seconds). Otherwise, the control bar shown on the photo gallery after publishing can initiate photo playback.

8. Click the **Finish** button.

9. To insert the gallery at a default size, position the displayed cursor where you want the gallery to appear on the page, then simply click the mouse.

   OR

   To set the size of the inserted gallery, drag out a region and release the mouse button.

Editing the Photo Gallery

Once added to the web page, the Photo Gallery can be edited. Images can be added, removed, rotated, captioned, or adjusted via Image Adjustments. You can also swap your existing gallery style for another, change background music, caption text colour, and set your gallery to autoplay (photos will automatically cycle).

To edit a Photo Gallery:

1. Select a gallery already present on your Web page.

2. Double-click the gallery.

   OR

   Click the **Edit Gallery** button from the context toolbar.

   OR

   Right-click the gallery and choose **Edit Photo Gallery....**

The Flash Photo Gallery dialog is displayed. The options available are the same as those available when the gallery was created.

Once a gallery is placed on the page it's also possible to drag a corner of the gallery object to resize. Use the **Ctrl** key while dragging to maintain the aspect ratio.

Linking remote images

It is possible to connect to any image currently available on the Internet. However, to prevent copyright infringement it's advisable to use images from a reliable image hosting service. Many exist on the Internet but services such as ImageShack are particularly popular. Of course you may be able to "hotlink" to other images (from a friend or colleague's Web site) where legal implications are not an issue but it's only polite to **ask for permission first!**

To insert a remote image:

1. Go to **Insert>Picture>Remote link....**

2. In the dialog, enter the absolute URL for the image.

3. Click **OK**.

4. You'll see the mouse pointer change to the ⊕ 🖼 Picture Paste cursor. What you do next determines the initial size and placement of the image.

5. To insert the image at a default size, simply click the mouse.

   OR

   To set the size of the inserted image, drag out a region and release the mouse button.

Colour, Fills, and Transparency

Applying solid colours

WebPlus offers a number of ways to apply solid colours to objects of different kinds:

- You can apply solid colours to an object's **line** or **fill**. As you might expect, QuickShapes and closed shapes (see Drawing and editing shapes on p. 165) have both line and fill properties, whereas straight and freehand lines have only a line property.

- Characters in text objects can have a colour, and text frames and table cells can have a background fill independent of the characters they contain.

You can use the Colour tab, Swatches tab or a dialog box to apply solid colours to an object.

To apply a solid colour via the Colour tab:

1. Select the object(s) or highlight a range of text.

2. Click the **Colour** tab and select one of several colour modes (RGB, CMYK, or HSL) from the drop-down list.

3. Click the ▭ **Fill** or ▬ **Line**, or **A** **Text** button at the top of the tab to determine where colour will be applied. The colour of the underline reflects the colour of your selected object. For frame text, the Fill will be the background text colour (but not the frame's background colour).

4. Select a colour from the colour spectrum or sliders depending on colour mode selected.

> You can't apply a Fill as a background colour to artistic text.

> In RGB colour mode, you can use decimal colour coding by selection from the Colour tab's ▷ Tab Menu button.

To apply a solid colour via the Swatches tab:

1. Select the object(s) or highlight a range of text.

2. Click the **Swatches** tab.

3. Click the ⬓ **Fill** or ▬ **Line**, or **A** **Text** button at the top of the tab to determine where colour will be applied.

4. Select a colour swatch from the **Publication Palette** (commonly used colours and those previously applied in your site) or **Palette** (standard RGB or themed palette presets such as WebSafe colours).

Alternatively, use **Format>Fill...** to apply colour via a dialog.

To change a solid colour's shade/tint (lightness):

1. Select the object and set the correct Fill, Line or Text button in the Colour tab.

2. From the Colour mode drop-down menu, select **Tinting**.

3. Drag the Shade/Tint slider to the left or right to darken or lighten your starting colour, respectively (the original colour is set at 0%). You can also enter a percentage value in the box (entering 0 in the input box reverts to the original colour).

| 0% ▶ | Object tinting can also be applied via the Swatches tab—adjust the percentage tinting via slider or direct input.

WebPlus automatically adds used colours to the Publication Palette in the Swatches tab. This palette is loaded by default but instead you can view and adopt colours from a standard RGB, WebSafe, or selection of themed palettes by clicking the tab's **Palette** button. Colours can be added, edited or deleted from the Publication Palette but not from other palettes.

Using colour schemes

Each WebPlus site uses a global colour scheme which you can manage using the **Scheme Manager**. Each scheme has a name and consists of five complementary **basic colours** which you can apply to any design element. (These work like a paint-by-numbers system, as explained below.) In addition, each scheme includes **adjunct colours** which apply specifically to hyperlinks (default, followed, active, rollover), off-page window backgrounds, and on-page colours. Switching to a different colour scheme instantly updates all elements that use scheme colours!

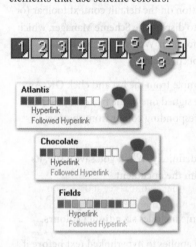

Colour schemes in WebPlus work much like a paint-by-numbers system, where various regions of a layout are coded with numbers, and a specific colour is assigned (by number) to each region (see the flower opposite, using the "Nursery" scheme). Swapping different colours into the "paint jars" numbered 1 to 5, while keeping the numbers on the flower the same, would automatically produce quite a different colouration.

The example above shows how the scheme "Atlantis" could be applied to the site to replace the "Nursery" scheme, the "Chocolate" scheme could then replace the "Atlantis" scheme, etc.

In WebPlus, the "paint jars" are known as "Scheme Colour 1," "Scheme Colour 2," and so on. When you apply Scheme Colour 1 to an object, it's like saying, "Put the colour from jar number 1 here."

Each site can have just one colour scheme at a time; the current scheme is indicated in the Swatches tab. You can easily switch schemes, modify scheme colours, apply schemes to any site, even create your own custom schemes. Colour schemes are saved globally, so the full set of schemes is always available.

To select a colour scheme:

1. Display the **Swatches** tab. The five colours in the current scheme appear as numbered samples, from 1 to 5, at the bottom of the tab. (You'll also see additional samples labelled **H** (Hyperlink), **F** (Followed Hyperlink), **A** (Active Hyperlink), **R** (Rollover Hyperlink), **B** (Background) and **O** (On-page colour.)

2. Click the ◇ Colour Scheme button on the default context toolbar (or choose **Tools>Scheme Manager...**) to display the **Scheme Manager**, which lists the various available schemes for your Web site, each with a different set of colours in their respective "jars."

3. Select a different colour scheme sample from the list and click **OK**. Any regions in the site that have been assigned one of the five colour scheme numbers are updated with the corresponding colour from the new scheme.

You can repeat this selection process indefinitely. When you save a site, its current colour scheme is saved along with the document.

Adjunct colours

Besides the five basic colours, each scheme includes six **adjunct colours**.

*   The **Hyperlink** colour (labelled **H**) applies to hyperlinked text **before** it's been clicked on.

*   The **Followed Hyperlink** colour (labelled **F**), applies to hyperlinked text after a visitor has clicked to "follow" the link.

*   The **Active Hyperlink** colour (labelled **A**), applies to hyperlinked text when a visitor's mouse button is depressed. Typically this is the colour shown after clicking and before the hyperlink's page is displayed.

*   The **Rollover** colour (labelled **R**), applies to hyperlinked text when a visitor's mouse button rolls over it.

- The **Background** colour (labelled **B**) applies to the off-page background outside your Web page dimensions if the user resizes the browser's window to be larger than the Web page dimensions. This can be either a solid colour or picture.

- The **On-page** colour (labelled **O**), is used to fill the page's background. If you make this transparent, the currently set underlying background shows, making the page boundaries invisible (content is still constrained to page dimensions).

- If you use a picture background with transparent regions, the Background colour is still active and will show through; otherwise the picture will cover the background colour.

The adjunct colours defined in the Scheme Manager normally apply throughout the site, with several important exceptions:

- Individual hyperlinks can specify their own colour. In the Hyperlinks dialog, uncheck **Use scheme hyperlink colours**. This will allow the underlying object's colour to show through on both the original and Followed hyperlink.

- Using the Master Page Manager (Background tab), you can override the Scheme Manager's background colour/picture and on-page colour settings for a particular **master page**, which affects all pages that share that master page. **Pages** that don't use a master page default to the Scheme Manager setting, but you can also override this via the Page Properties dialog (Background tab) in a similar way. In both cases, uncheck **Use Scheme Manager settings** and set the options **Background colour**, **Use picture**, and/or **On-page colour** independently.

Applying scheme colours to objects

If you create new elements in a Web template site, or start a site from scratch, how can you extend a colour scheme to the new objects? Although you'll need to spend some time working out which colour combinations look best, the mechanics of the process are simple. Recalling the paint-by-numbers example above, all you need to do is assign one of the five scheme colour numbers to an object's line and/or fill.

To assign a scheme colour to an object:

1. Select the object and choose a ⬜ **Fill**, ▬ **Line**, or **A** **Text** button at the top of the Swatches tab depending on the desired effect.

2. From the bottom of the Swatches tab, click on a scheme colour (numbered 1 to 5) that you want to apply to the fill, line and text (or you can drag the colour instead).

If an object's fill uses a scheme colour, the corresponding sample in Swatches tab will be highlighted whenever the object is selected.

Modifying and creating colour schemes

If you've tried various colour schemes but haven't found one that's quite right, you can modify any of the colours in an existing scheme and update the scheme, or create your own separately named scheme based on the existing scheme.

To modify a colour scheme:

1. Click the ◇ **Colour Scheme** button on the default context toolbar (or choose **Tools>Scheme Manager...**) to display the **Scheme Manager.**

2. Pick a colour scheme from the list on which to base your new scheme, and jump to the Edit tab at the top of the same dialog.

3. On the Edit tab, each of the five scheme colour numbers (plus the adjunct colours Hyperlink, Followed Hyperlink, Active Hyperlink, Rollover Hyperlink, Background Colour, On-page colour) has its own drop-down list, showing available colours in the WebPlus palette.

4. To set or change a scheme colour or adjunct colour, simply click the adjacent button and select a new colour. Click **More Colours...** to display the Colour Selector.

5. For a "schemed" picture for use as the off-page browser window background, check **Use picture** and pick an image (click **Browse...** to swap an existing picture). Set **Export Options...** to dictate how images are to be exported.

6. For an on-page colour, i.e. a schemed page background, select from the **On-page colour** drop-down menu.

7. To store the modified scheme in the Schemes Manager, click **Save Scheme....** Leave the name unaltered to overwrite the existing scheme.

8. To apply the scheme to the current Web site, click **OK**.

To create a new scheme, you can follow the above procedure but, at Step 7, enter a new scheme name instead of overwriting the existing scheme.

Working with gradient and bitmap fills

Gradient fills (linear, elliptical, or conical) provide a gradation or spectrum of colours spreading between two or more colours. A gradient fill has an editable path with nodes that mark the origin of each of these key colours. A bitmap fill uses a named bitmap—often a material, pattern, or background image—to fill an object.

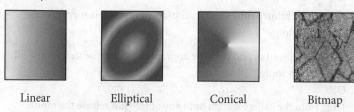

Linear   Elliptical   Conical   Bitmap

You can apply preset gradient and bitmap fills from the Swatches tab to shapes, text frames, table cells, and to any artistic, creative frame, and creative table text (but not to HTML frame text or HTML table text) . Using the **Fill Tool** from the Tools toolbar's Fill flyout (or from **Format>Fill**), you can vary the fill's path on an object for different effects (see online Help).

Applying different transparency effects (using the Transparency tab) won't alter the object's fill settings as such, but may significantly alter a fill's actual appearance.

Applying a gradient or bitmap fill

The easiest way to apply a gradient or bitmap fill is to use one of a range of pre-supplied swatch thumbnails in the Swatches tab's **Gradient** or **Bitmap** palettes. The Fill Tool and a Fill dialog are alternative methods for creating gradient fills (these are covered in online Help).

To apply a gradient or bitmap fill using the Swatches tab:

1. Click the Swatches tab and ensure the ⬜ **Fill** button is selected.
    NOTE: The colour of the underline reflects the colour of your selected object (or selected node).

2. ◣ ▾ For gradient fills, select Linear, Elliptical or Conical as the gradient type from the **Gradient** button's drop-down menu.
    OR
    ▨ ▾ For bitmap fills, select a drop-down menu category from the **Bitmap** button.

3. Select the object(s), and click the appropriate gallery swatch for the fill you want to apply.
    OR
    Drag from the gallery swatch onto any object and release the mouse button.

4. If needed, adjust the fill's **Tint** at the bottom of the tab with the tab slider or set a percentage value in the input box.

Setting transparency

Transparency effects are great for highlights, shading and shadows, and simulating "rendered" realism. They can make the critical difference between flat-looking illustrations and images with depth and snap.

Transparency may seem a bit tricky because by definition, you can't "see" it the way you can see a colour fill applied to an object. In fact, it's there all the time in WebPlus. Each new object has a transparency property: the default just happens to be "None"—that is, no transparency (opaque).

Transparencies work rather like fills that use "disappearing ink" instead of colour. The more transparency in a particular spot, the more "disappearing" takes place there, and the more the object(s) underneath show through. Just as a gradient fill can vary from light to dark, a transparency can vary from more to less, i.e. from clear to opaque, as in the illustration:

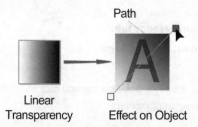

Path

Linear
Transparency

Effect on Object

Here, the hexagonal shape has had a Linear transparency applied, with more transparency at the lower end of the path and less at the upper end. It makes a difference which object is in front (here, the pentagon); where there's more transparency, more of the object(s) behind will show through.

In WebPlus, transparency effects work very much like greyscale fills. Just like fills...

- Transparency effects are applied from the Studio—in this case, using the Transparency tab.

- The Transparency tab's gallery has thumbnails in shades of grey, where the lighter portions represent more transparency. To apply transparency, you click thumbnails or drag them onto objects.

- Most transparency effects have a path you can edit—in this case, with the Transparency Tool (see WebPlus help).

As for the effects available on the Swatches tab, all are comparable to the fills of the same name:

- **Solid** transparency distributes the transparency equally across the object.

- **Gradient** transparencies include linear, elliptical, and conical effects.

- The **Bitmap** gallery includes texture maps based on the Swatches tab's selection of bitmaps.

You can apply gradient and bitmap transparency from the Transparency tab to shapes, text frames, table cells, and to any artistic, creative frame text, and creative table text (but not to HTML frame text or HTML table text). Alternatively, using the Transparency Tool from the Tools toolbar's Fill flyout (or from **Format>Transparency**), you can vary the transparency's path on an object for different effects.

To apply transparency with Transparency tab:

1. With your object selected, go to the Transparency tab.

2. For solid transparency, select the [ ] **Solid** button and pick a thumbnail from the solid transparency gallery.
   OR

   For gradient transparency, choose the [ ] **Gradient** button and pick your thumbnail.
   OR

   For bitmap transparency, choose the [▾] **Bitmap** button and pick a thumbnail from a range of categories.

3. The transparency is applied to the object(s).

Alternatively, drag the desired thumbnail from the gallery to an object.

To apply gradient transparency with Transparency Tool:

1. Select an object.

2. Click [ ] **Transparency Tool** on the Tools toolbar's Transparency flyout.

3. Drag on the object to define a transparency path. The object takes a simple Linear transparency, grading from 100% to 0% opacity.

The process of editing gradient transparencies is the same as that for editing gradient fills (see online Help).

Adding Hyperlinks and Interactivity

Adding hyperlinks and anchors

Hyperlinking an object such as a box, some text, or a picture means that a visitor to your Web site can click on the object to trigger an event. The event is most commonly a jump to one of the following:

- Web page (either on your site or somewhere else on the Web)

- Smart object (specifically a forum or blog in Serif Web Resources)

- Email composition window

- Graphic, text, audio, or video file on your local disk or network

- Anchor (a designated target within a Web page)

- RSS feed or podcast

- Shopping cart

- Navigation element

- User Data

- Picture

Well-designed hyperlinks are an important aspect of site structure. They help visitors navigate through your site and serve as an important adjunct to logical page relationships as shown in the Site Structure tree. (But don't overlook the time-saving advantages of using theme graphics for navigation elements such as navbars and Previous/Next buttons.)

You can manage all hyperlinks and anchors throughout your site by using the **Site Manager**, accessible from the Hintline or via **Site Manager>Hyperlink Manager...** on the Tools menu.

To add a hyperlink:

1. Use the Pointer Tool to select the single or grouped object or highlight the region of text to be hyperlinked.

> You can also simply click for an insertion point in text. If you select in—or immediately before/after—a word, then the whole word will be hyperlinked. If your selection point has a space on both sides, WebPlus inserts helpful text (for example, the name of the target page).

2. Click the 🖲 **Hyperlink** button on the Tools toolbar.

   The Hyperlinks dialog appears.

3. Click to select the link destination type, and enter the specific hyperlink target, i.e. a page, Uniform Resource Locator (URL), Smart object, email address, etc.

4. Depending on the link type, choose type-specific options.

5. A range of target windows or frames can be chosen depending on how you want the link destination to be displayed. The types (along with expected results) are:

   - **Same Window**: the link destination is shown in the same window from which the hyperlink was clicked.

   - **New Window**: A new window is used to display the link destination whose properties (dimensions, position, or navigation bar usage) can be defined via the **Settings...** button. The original window will remain open.

   - **Top of Current Window**: the link destination is shown in the top level window. Use for hyperlinks created within a frame on a page (or for frames within frames).

   - **Parent Frame**: the link destination is shown in the Parent Frame or Parent Window of the frame from which the hyperlink was clicked. Use for hyperlinks created within a frame on a page (or for frames within frames). (See Working in frames on p. 41).

- **Named Window**: A custom window can be defined by entering a new window name in the right-most drop-down menu. Its properties (dimensions, position, and navigation bar usage) can be defined via the **Settings...** button (check **Use JavaScript popup code** first). You can also adopt an existing named window from the same drop-down menu.

- **Document Frame**: The link destination is shown in a previously created frame (using the Framed Document Tool). The HTML ID (e.g., ifrm_1) of any existing frame is selected from the right-most drop-down menu.

  If you're targeting an active document frame, select the active frame from the **Open in active document frame** drop-down list. If it doesn't show in the list you'll need to set the frame to be "active" by double-clicking the frame and checking **Active Document Frame**.

6. Choose other properties such as Title name (text displayed on-screen on hover over) and a shortcut access key.
   Note: As a visual cue, hyperlinked words are normally underlined and appear in the colour you've specified for Hyperlinks in the Scheme Manager or elsewhere (see Using colour schemes on p. 215).

7. Click **OK**.

To modify or remove a hyperlink:

1. Use the Pointer Tool to select the object, or click for an insertion point inside the linked text. (It's not necessary to drag over a hyperlinked region of text.)

2. Click the 🔗 **Hyperlink** button on the Tools toolbar's Hyperlink flyout.

The Hyperlinks dialog appears with the current link target shown. If the link is in text, the whole text link highlights.

- To modify the hyperlink, select a new link destination type, target, and/or options.

- To remove the hyperlink, click the **No Hyperlink** button.

To view or edit existing hyperlinks:

- Choose **Site Manager>Hyperlink Manager...** on the Tools menu to view and manage site-wide hyperlinks.

Inserting an anchor

An anchor is a specific location on a page that can serve as the target for a hyperlink. Invisible to the Web page visitor, it typically marks a point within some text (such as the start of a particular section) or an image at some point down the page. Anchors are useful if your page has enough content to be divided into sections, but not enough to require carving up into separate pages. These let the reader jump to related content without leaving the current page. In the same way, keeping Web visitors on the same page makes it less likely they'll get "lost' while perusing the information on your site.

To insert an anchor:

1. Use the Pointer Tool to select the target object, or click for an insertion point inside the target text.

2. Click the ⚓ **Anchor** button on the Tools toolbar's Hyperlink flyout.
   OR
   Choose **Anchor...** from the Insert or right-click menu.

3. In the dialog, type a name for the anchor.

4. (Optional) Check **Include Anchor in Navigation** to allow the anchor (typically a selected object) to be accessed via a navbar instead of a hyperlink. You'll need to check **Include anchors** on your navbar first. Give the anchor a title.

5. Click **Remove** to delete the anchor intelligently, i.e. you can control what happens to any referencing hyperlinks (i.e, ignore, delete, or redirect).

6. Click **OK**.

To view or edit existing anchors:

- Choose **Site Manager>Anchor Manager...** on the Tools menu to view, rename, or remove an anchor attached to a particular object. You can also include the anchor in page navigation.

Adding hotspots to a page

A hotspot is a transparent hyperlink region on a Web page. Usually placed on top of graphics, hotspots act like "buttons" that respond when clicked in a Web browser. They are especially useful if you want the visitor to be able to click on different parts of a picture (such as a graphic "menu" or map of your site). You can draw and edit hotspots by hand, or create them to match an existing shape.

To draw a hotspot:

1. Click the ▦ **Insert Hotspot** button on the Web Objects toolbar.

2. Click and drag to draw a rectangular hotspot region. The Hyperlinks dialog appears.

3. Click to select the link destination type, and enter the specific hyperlink target.

4. Click **OK**.

To match a hotspot to an existing shape:

1. Draw the hotspot as described above, and create the shape as described in Drawing and editing shapes on p. 165.

2. Select both objects and choose **Fit Hotspot to Shape** from the Tools menu.

> The two objects will still be separate, so you can easily delete the shape if it's no longer needed once you've used it as a template to produce a hotspot of a desired shape.

To modify a hotspot hyperlink:

*   Using the Pointer Tool, double-click the hotspot.
    OR

*   Click to select the hotspot and click the 🔗 **Hyperlink** button on the Tools toolbar's Hyperlink flyout (or choose **Hyperlink...** from the Insert menu).

The Hyperlinks dialog appears with the current hotspot link target shown.

- To modify the hyperlink, select a new link destination type and/or target.

- To remove the hyperlink, change the link destination to **No Hyperlink**.

Editing hotspots

You can move and resize hotspots on the page, just like other objects. A selected hotspot has both an outer bounding box and an inner outline, which serve different purposes.

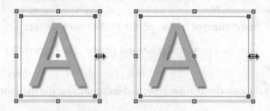

To move or resize a hotspot:

- Click to select the hotspot, then:

    - To move, click and drag from the centre, or from the hotspot's bounding box. To constrain the hotspot to vertical or horizontal movement, hold down the **Shift** key while dragging.

    - To resize, click and drag on its outer (bounding box) handles.

By editing the inner outline, you can convert rectangular hotspots into freeform shapes that closely match the parts of the underlying graphic you want to be "hot." To edit the outline, first move the mouse pointer over the hotspot's inner outline until the cursor changes to indicate whether you're over a node or a line.

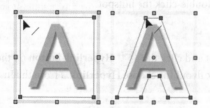

To create an extra node on a hotspot:

- Click anywhere along the hotspot's outline when you see the cursor.

To change the shape of a hotspot's outline:

- Click and drag a node when you see the $^{-}_{\mid}^{-}$ cursor.

Adding rollovers

The term **rollover** refers to an interaction between a mouse and a screen object. For example, you can point your mouse at a graphic (such as a navigation bar button) on a Web page, and see it instantly change colour or become a different picture. When you point to a Web page object, your mouse pointer physically enters the screen region occupied by the object. This triggers an event called a "mouseover" and, if the underlying code is there to "trap" this event, it can trigger some other event—such as swapping another image into the same location. An object whose appearance changes through image-swapping in response to mouse events is called a **rollover graphic.**

As a prerequisite to creating a rollover graphic in WebPlus, you'll need to prepare a picture for each distinct rollover state, using a separate graphics program. The necessary event-trapping code is generated for you automatically. WebPlus also lets you directly import rollover graphics created in Serif DrawPlus (see below).

Rollover options

Adding rollovers is basically a matter of deciding which rollover state(s) you'll want to define for a layered graphic, then specifying an image for each state. WebPlus provides four basic choices:

- **Normal** is the "resting" state of the graphic before any rollover, and is always defined.

- **Over** is the state triggered by a mouseover— when the mouse pointer is directly over the object. For example, a button's text might change colour, or an outline appear, to show the button is "alive." Prior to a mouse click (see Down), moving the pointer in and out of the graphic's area will alternate between Over and Normal.

- **Down** is triggered by a mousedown on the graphic. The term derives from a typical button's behaviour: its "up" state changes to "down" once it's been clicked.

- **Down+Over** (only available if Down is activated) implies a mouseover that occurs when the graphic is already Down, i.e. after it's been clicked. If you don't activate Down+Over, then the button just stays in its Down state after a mousedown event, which can cause unresponsiveness (see the above Note). For a more responsive button, set the Normal and Down states to graphic A, and the Over and Down+Over states to graphic B. In this case the Down state effectively means "Down+Not Over" and the button will revert to its Normal appearance if the user moves the mouse outside the button, even after a mousedown. It sounds complex, but it works!

You'll also have the option of specifying a **hyperlink** event—for example, a jump to a targeted Web page—that will trigger if the user clicks on the object. And you can even group buttons on a page so they work together and only one at a time can be down.

To create a rollover graphic:

1. In a suitable image-editing program, create the variant source images for each state you'll be defining. (See "Creating variant graphics" below.)

2. Click the **Insert Rollover** button on the Web Objects toolbar's Navigation flyout.
    OR
    Choose **Web Object** from the Insert menu and select **Rollover...** from the submenu.

3.   Specify which rollover states (see above) you want to activate for each graphic by checking boxes in the Rollover Graphic dialog. For each one, use the **Browse** button to locate the corresponding source image and specify Export Options for that image (see Setting image export options on p. 189).

4.   Check **Embed files in site** if you want to incorporate the image(s) in the WebPlus file. (For details, see Embedding vs. linking on p. 184.)

5.   Check either **Normal** or **Down** as the button's initial rollover state. For example, common sense dictates that on a site's actual Home page you should initially show the "Home" button itself as down, and/or unresponsive to mouse actions—after all, the viewer is already on that page—whereas buttons that link to other pages should be in their normal "up" state and responsive.

6.   Click **Set...** to define a hyperlink target for the button. (For details, see Adding hyperlinks and anchors on p. 225.)

7.   Check **Radio button** if you want to link all the buttons (on a given page) that have this option checked, so that only one of them at a time can be down.
     If you use this technique, make sure all rollover graphics you want to link have the option checked. Although it doesn't matter how the buttons are distributed on the page, typically they'll constitute a visible unit like a navigation bar. Any buttons with the option unchecked are independent.

8.   Click **OK**. The first time you define a rollover state, you'll see rollover layers established in the document (see below).

WebPlus displays the image assigned to the Normal state. It's a good idea to preview the page and test each rollover object, then return to WebPlus and revise as needed. When you preview or publish the Web site, WebPlus takes care of exporting one image file for each rollover state, and the HTML file for the published page incorporates the JavaScript code for the rollover event trapping.

To revise a rollover graphic:

1.   Right-click the graphic and choose **Edit Rollover...**.

2.   Make new selections as needed and click **OK**.

Creating variant source images

For each object with at least one activated rollover state, you'll need to provide a source image. It's the often subtle differences between the Normal image and the "variants" that make the object appear to switch from one state to another. For example, if you've checked the "Over" state for an object, you need to include a variant image that the Web page can display when the button is moused over. In the following example, two variants of a Home button are shown—one showing the button highlighted (on mouse over), and a second image in its default Normal state.

You'll need to create these source images in a separate image-editing program. Here are some things to consider:

- Variant images will stretch to fit into the region occupied by the Normal image, so all the source images should have the same dimensions.

- Make sure the variants are all in precise registration with the Normal image, so there's no unintended movement when images are swapped on rollover. To simplify matters, use an image editor with layering capability and create each variant on a separate layer directly above the Normal image.

- WebPlus displays only the Normal image, so preview the effect of swapping graphics by hiding and showing layers in the image editor.

- You only need to provide variant source images for the rollover states you've activated.

- Once you're satisfied with the source images, export each layer to a separate file, and then return to WebPlus to define the rollovers.

- When assigning the source images, you'll need to choose between linking and embedding. As long as a source image is linked (not embedded), WebPlus will always use the latest version of a file. So as a rule, until you're truly sure your source images are final, you may wish to uncheck the "Embed files" box so that linked images will be used. You can easily repeat the assignment process, using embedding instead, once the source images are final. If you do find yourself needing to update an image that's already been embedded, the best way is to save the revised file under a different name, then repeat the assignment process and specify the new file instead of the old.

Adding popup rollovers

The most common use for popup rollovers in WebPlus is to hover over a picture thumbnail to show its larger representation, usually offset next to the thumbnail. The feature is simple to use and works in a similar way to the more advanced Flash Photo Gallery. One exception is that the WebPlus rollovers can have several states and only work with identically sized different "variant" images, whereas popup rollovers has two states (normal and hover over) and shows the same or a different image (normally resized to be larger).

WebPlus lets you choose the position and size of the popup in relation to the thumbnail; even the thumbnail can be selected and resized at any time.

With respect to states, WebPlus provides two basic choices:

- **Normal** is the "resting" state of the image before any rollover, and is always defined. A thumbnail can be used but numbered or bullet icons could also be used, perhaps identifying pictures as part of a catalogue, quiz, etc.

- **Over** is the state triggered by a mouseover—when the mouse pointer is directly over the thumbnail the popup "Over" image will appear, disappearing when the mouse pointer moves off the thumbnail.

If captioning is required on popup rollovers this can be made to popup next to your Over image. Caption text can adopt various attributes such as font, bold/italic, size, colour.

To create a popup rollover:

1. Click the **Popup Rollover** button on the Web Objects toolbar's Navigation flyout.

2. From the dialog, for the Normal rollover image click the **Browse...** button, and navigate to and select the image. Click **Open....**

3. For the Over image, the previously chosen Normal image is used by default (typically for photo thumbnails). However, you can **Browse...** to use a completely different image.

4. (Optional) To hyperlink from the Normal image, click the **Set...** button and enter a URL. The user jumps to the hyperlink destination by clicking the image.

5. (Optional) For either image, specify **Export Options...** for that image (see Setting image export options on p. 189).

6. (Optional) Check **Embed image files in site** if you want to incorporate the image(s) in the WebPlus file. (For details, see Embedding vs. linking on p. 184) .

At this stage you've defined normal and over images to use. However, for popup rollovers to work effectively you'll need to position the Normal and Over images on your page.

Positioning is carried out from a dedicated dialog, where each state image can be moved and resized by dragging (or by setting absolute pixel values). Each image adopts a coloured border—green for Normal state, blue for Over state.

The dialog additionally shows any previous popup rollovers in its preview window, and offers previously used Left, Top, Width, and Height values for easy alignment with the existing popup rollovers.

To position rollover images:

1. In the Rollover Graphic dialog, click the **Set Rollover Position...** button at the bottom of the dialog.

2. From the dialog, select an image. The drop-down list indicates the current selection status, i.e.

   - **Normal Selection**: a Normal image is selected and shows a green border.

   - **Over Selection**: an Over image is selected showing a blue border.

   - **Caption Selection**: caption text is selected showing a red border (only shown with captioning enabled).

   If you deselect an image, the drop-down list shows **No Selection**.

3. Reposition either image by dragging corner handles (aspect ratio is always maintained when dragging). Alternatively, enter exact **Left**, **Top**, **Width**, and **Height** values in the input boxes for fine positioning. The box down arrows offer a drop-down list showing the last three values used for Normal, Over, and Captions (from top to bottom)—this lets you align images exactly.

4. (Optional) Check **Position relative to Normal image** to maintain the Over image's position in relation to the Normal image (when the Normal image is resized).

5. (Optional) Uncheck **Maintain aspect ratio** to allow your Normal or Over image resizing to be unconstrained. You have to then use the input boxes (not dragging) to affect unconstrained resizing.

6. Click **OK**. The Normal image will show on your page, but the Over image will only popup after previewing or publishing.

By building up additional Normal images as separate popup rollovers on your Web page you can create a stylish popup gallery of images, with each Normal image being part of a sequence of clickable thumbnails.

To edit a popup rollover:

- Double-click the Normal image on the page, to display the Rollover Graphic dialog. Modify settings as appropriate.

To add captioning to Over images:

1. In the Rollover Graphic dialog, check **Display caption with Over image**.

2. Enter your caption text in the **Caption** input box.

3. Set the text attributes for the caption text using the **Font** and **Size** drop-down lists, and the **Bold** and **Italic** check boxes. For applying text colour, use the **Text Colour** drop-down gallery.

4. Check **Apply Background Colour** to enable a colour to be selected from the adjacent drop-down gallery.

5. Click **OK**.

The caption text only shows on the Over image, so to position the text on your Over image you'll need to double-click the Normal image on your page. From the dialog, click the **Set Rollover Position...** button and reposition the text (as you would for Normal and Over images). All selected caption text shows with a red border during preview.

Adding navigation elements

In WebPlus, certain types of theme graphic called **navigation elements** are programmed to understand your site structure, making it easy to design a site that's simple to navigate. You just select a navigation element—such as a **Navbar** (navigation bar), or a **Previous** or **Next** button—from the Studio's Theme Graphics tab (or a dialog) and WebPlus does the rest!

Previous/Next buttons automatically link laterally, to adjacent pages on the same level. Navbars combine buttons with popup menus to facilitate movement between the various sections and levels of a site. For example, in this navbar the buttons provide links to the Home page and various top-level section pages, while popup menus link to child pages within each section.

You can easily install navigation elements at any level of your site, reconfigure them to link to a particular part of the site, change the appearance of the popup menu, and exclude particular pages from navigation as needed.

When you define a navigation element, you use standard terminology like "Parent Level" or "Previous/Next" to specify which part of the site should be linked to, relative to the starting page—i.e. which buttons should be included.

Because navigation elements "understand" your site structure, they update dynamically if you alter page names or relationships, or cut/paste the navigation element to another page! The links are always relative to the page where the element is located. For example, if a navbar links to child-level pages, it will continue to do so—even if that means linking to different pages—if you move it, or the page it's on, to a different place in the structure.

You can place navigation elements on master pages, too—which saves you the trouble of pasting the same element to multiple pages. A navigation element on a master page behaves *as if it's on each page*—consistent with the notion that its buttons and menus are relative to where each page sits in the overall site structure.

Navigation elements can also be set to include any anchors that you have defined. This opens up possibilities for navigating to various sections of long pages or to repeating areas.

To add a navigation element:

1. From the **Web Objects** toolbar, click the ![button] **Insert Theme Graphic** button.
2. From the **Theme Set** dialog, choose the element type and the theme set that you want to use.

To add a navigation bar:

1. Click the Insert Navigation Bar button on the Web Objects toolbar's Navigation flyout , or choose **Navigation Bar...** from the Insert menu.

2. On the dialog's **Theme Set** tab, choose a Horizontal or Vertical orientation and select a theme for the navbar.

3. Customize the **Navigation Type** and **Popup Menu Properties** (see steps 2 and 3 of To configure a navigation bar).

4. Click **OK**.

All navigation elements can also be added from the Studio's **Theme Graphics tab**. To add any element, expand your chosen gallery for the element's Set or Type, and simply drag and drop onto the page.

Because navigation elements are theme graphics, you can use the Theme Graphics tab to select coordinated design elements (buttons, etc.) for a consistent look, and change the overall appearance with a single click. To edit theme graphic properties such as font, text colour, and mouseover fill colour, select the object and click its ☐T☐ **Edit** button. (You can also right-click it and choose **Edit Theme Graphic...**.) For details, see Incorporating theme graphics on p. 50.

Navigation bars have their own special dialog for reconfiguring navigation properties.

To configure a navigation bar:

1. Double-click it, or right-click it and choose **Edit Navigation Bar...**.

2. On the dialog's **Theme Set** tab:
   • Select the type of navigation bar—**Theme Graphic** (Horizontal/Vertical), **Text Only** (Horizontal/Vertical) or **Combo**.
   • If a **Theme Graphic** type is used, select the Theme type.

3.   On the dialog's **Navigation Type** tab:
     • Select which buttons should be included in the navbar: **Top Level**,
     Parent Level, **Same Level**, **Child Level**, **Home**, **Previous and Next**, **Previous**,
     Next, **Up**, **Breadcrumb**, **Anchors**, **Back** or **Custom**.
     • Depending on the main selection, you can opt to include the **Home**
     page, **parent page**, **anchors** and/or **Hide current page**.
     • As a design choice, you may elect to **Make all buttons the same size**
     (otherwise buttons will autofit to their text) and/or **Use page names**
     (otherwise buttons will have functional names like "Previous" or
     "Home").

     • Set the **Anchor Point** for the navbar. By default, the bar will be
     anchored at the top left. This means that any pages added will grow the
     navbar to the right.
     • Set **Target Frame/Window** to change where the new page will open.
     Choose from **Same Window** (most common), **New Window** (useful for
     off-site pages), **Top of Current Window**, **Parent Frame**, **Named Window**
     and **Document Frame**.

4.   On the dialog's **Text Only Properties** tab:
     • Set the text and menu colour using the controls (only available if Text
     Only navigation is selected).

5.   On the dialog's **Popup Menu Properties** tab:
     • To prevent the popup menu from appearing, uncheck **This navigation**
     object has menus.
     • To change settings for the text and appearance of the popup menu, use
     the controls at the right.

By default, all pages in the tree are **included in navigation**—that is, they can
be linked to by navigation elements. You can **exclude** certain pages (any but
the Home page) so they'll be ignored by navigation elements. For example,
suppose you had a section of reference or archival pages that you didn't want
visitors to explore top-down. Excluding the parent page for that section would
remove it from the navbar. Note that excluding the page from navigation
doesn't remove it from the site—the page will still appear in the Site Structure
tree and you can still install hyperlinks to it; it just won't show up in a navbar.

Included pages show a ✓ mark in their page entry in the Site tab's Site Structure tree, while excluded pages lack the mark.

To exclude a page from navigation:

- On the Studio's **Site** tab, right-click the page in the Site Structure tree and choose **Page Properties...**. Below the tree, uncheck **Include in Navigation**.

> 📝 The setting is also available in the Page Properties dialog (Page tab).

If you're looking to rearrange the order or hierarchy of your navigation bar items to be different from you Site Structure, WebPlus will allow you to customize any navigation bars—you can also add, edit, or delete elements which will access a range of link destination types (see Adding hyperlinks and anchors on p. 225) just as in Site tab's Site Structure.

To customize a navigation bar:

1. Double-click the navigation bar.

2. Jump to the Navigation Type tab, and select the "Custom" option. The Customize tab is automatically displayed.

3. Rearrange the order of the navigation bar items by drag and drop (or use the **Move Up**, **Move Down**, **Make Child** or **Make Parent** buttons.

4. Click the **Add Element** button to add a new element to the end of your navigation bar list. The element is assigned a link destination, a target frame or window and a title in the displayed dialog. Click **OK**.

5. Click **OK** again.

Any selected element in the customize window can be edited or deleted.

Adding navigation site maps

WebPlus lets you add a navigation site map to your Web site. This useful feature enhances Web site accessibility by providing clickable links to all sections of your site.

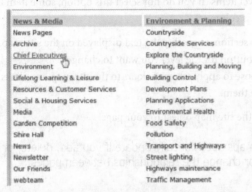

> You may like to create your site map on a Web page which is included in your Web site's Navigation Bar. This allows site map access from all Web pages.

To add a navigation site map:

1. Click the ⊞ **Site Map Tool** on the Web Objects toolbar's Navigation flyout.

2. From the Site Map dialog, in the **Navigation** section:

   - If you have used anchors in your site and want to list them in the site map, check the **Include anchors** check box.

   - Select the **Target frame / Window** from the drop-down list, i.e. the window/frame in which you want the site map to open. For example, you may want the site map to open in a new window so that the user can view the site map independently of the current page.

3. In the **Columns** section, select the number of columns you want your site map to display.

    If you select a multi-column site map, you can also set the column margin width, and choose to keep second and third-level items with their respective top-level items (if you do not select this option, some item lists may be split across columns).

4. In the **Text Styles** section, to modify the text displayed on the site map, click the **Modify** button for the level you want to change.
    You can also choose to apply scheme colours to the site map hyperlinks and/or underline them.

5. Click **OK** to add the site map object to your page.

> Navigation site maps automatically update if you add, delete, or rename pages, or change the relationships between pages.

Adding Java applets

Java is a cross-platform, object-oriented programming language used to create mini-applications called **applets** that can be attached to Web pages and that run when the page is viewed in a Web browser.

You can add add a Java applet to your page by click the 🍵 **Insert Java Applet** button on the Web Objects toolbar's Media flyout. See online Help for more information.

Adding Dynamic Content

Creating HTML pages

HTML code is the underlying tagged code which your Web site visitor's Internet browser reads, interprets and formats your page according to the tags used. The code and tags used are the instructions to which a page will be formatted, and as such it is vital that the code is correctly structured and conforms to HTML convention.

WebPlus supports the development of web pages in HTML. You can add pages within the Site tab's Site Structure window—a distinct HTML page icon is shown.

HTML pages in the Site tab can be controlled in a similar way to standard pages, i.e. you can drag/drop, rename, preview, insert offline links to, estimate download time, or include the page in navigation. However, HTML pages do not have master pages associated with them. In addition, a double-click of the HTML page icon will launch the HTML's Source window for HTML editing (rather than the WYSIWYG display of a standard page). In the Source window you'll see some basic HTML tags which, if you're an experienced HTML developer, will be very familiar to you!

```
<!DOCTYPE HTML PUBLIC "-//W3C//DTD HTML 4.01
<html>
<head>
<meta http-equiv="Content-Type" content="text
<meta name="Generator" content="Serif WebPlu
<title>%thistitle%</title>
</head>
<style type="text/css">
<!--
a:link {color: %hyperlink%;}
a:visited {color: %followed%;}
a:hover {color: %rollover%;}
a:active {color: %active%;}
-->
</style>
<body style="background: %background%;">
<p><a href="%home%">%homename%</a>
</body>
</html>
```

> There is no WYSIWYG view when you work with HTML source code directly.

From this point, editing of the "template" HTML structure is required. Typically, text is inserted (by typing or pasting) between the opening <body...> and closing </body> tags; each paragraph starts and ends with the <p> and </p> tags, respectively. You can also insert annotation tokens into your HTML code (see Attaching HTML code on p. 249) via right-click (pick **Insert Token**). The remainder of the HTML code outside of the opening/closing body tags does not need to be altered.

> ⚠ Editing HTML code requires prior understanding of HTML language and its convention. Poor editing may result in corruption of your code on the page or site level.

If you're new to HTML and need to start with the basics, it's best to search for "HTML tutorials" in your favourite Internet search engine before tackling HTML editing in earnest.

To create an HTML page:

1. In the Pages Window (Site Structure tree) of the Studio's Site tab, select a page after which you want to add the new page. A click on the page's entry suffices to select the page (its page name will become bold); double-clicking also displays the page in the workspace.

2. ⊞ ▾ To add one page after the original page, click the down arrow on the **Add** button directly above the Pages window. From the drop-down menu, choose **New HTML Page**.

To edit an HTML page's source:

- Double-click the HTML page (see above) in the Site tab's Site Structure and edit the displayed code.

- ⚞ Clear Changes If you want to discard all changes to the HTML code, select the **Clear Changes** button on the context toolbar above the HTML window.

To return to Design View:

- Select the ✕ Design View button on the context toolbar above the HTML window.

Attaching HTML code

In WebPlus, you can create pages in HTML (see Creating HTML pages on p. 247). However, WebPlus also lets you attach code to your WebPlus objects (e.g., in frames or table cells) and pages, primarily to expand the capabilities of the objects (or the page), making them more intelligent and interactive. The object or page can either dynamically generate content or can have its appearance altered within its area as a result of embedded script content.

It's not possible to edit the HTML code itself (there's no real benefit in doing so), but specific areas of the displayed code are editable for additional code to be added, i.e. clearly identifiable placeholders (text surrounded by a white highlight) will appear in your source tab's window.

```
__AddCode="here"
```

```
<!--Header code for
```

```
<!--Preamble-->
```

```
<!--MainDivStart-->
```

```
<!--MainDivEnd-->
```

```
<!--Postamble-->
```

```
<!--Body-->
```

```
<!--Page Body Start-->
```

These are just a few of the **editable** placeholders present in the source of an HTML fragment, object or page (in fact differently named placeholders exist depending on the type of element). For example, the last placeholder shown in the list above is unique to a page's source and won't appear for an object or HTML fragment.

Any code can be inserted by cut and paste into any of the placeholder positions but typically you can include tokens, HTML code or specific scripts, e.g. JavaScript. This could be used to affect rollover behaviour on an object not otherwise possible without scripting support, e.g. an image "on-click" handler.

Adding HTML

WebPlus also allows you to "view source" on a page—allowing extra **HTML code** to be added to the page. Using this approach, you can include fragments either copied from another Web page, or perhaps written by yourself.

You can also import formatted HTML text from a browser or email program via the Clipboard (for example with a browser's **Select All** and **Copy** commands), using WebPlus's **File>Paste Special...** command. Using the Import Web Pages option, you can import one or more HTML pages into your new or existing WebPlus site, with control over which additional elements are imported.

Before you import your HTML code, WebPlus lets you position an HTML Code Fragment window on your page. Since you won't be able to see the effect of the HTML until you preview the site, be careful to place the window correctly. You'll definitely want to check your Web page in a browser! If there's a problem, double-check the code you entered and its position on the WebPlus page (resizing if necessary). If you have some grasp of HTML, examine the page source in a text editor such as Notepad or use your browser's "View Source" mode.

To add an HTML code fragment to a page:

1. Click the ⌨ **Insert HTML Code** button on the Web Objects toolbar.
   OR
   Choose **Web Object...** from the Insert menu and select **HTML...** from the submenu.

2. Click on the page or pasteboard to create a new HTML Code Fragment window at a default size or drag to create a sized window.

3. In the dialog, use the **Paste to Head** or **Paste to Body** button to insert the clipboard text into the header of the file or into its body.
   OR
   Use the scrollable code window. Enter one or more HTML code fragments into the appropriate field.

4. If the code calls for external files, use the **Add** button to locate them. Click the **Embed** button if you want to keep the file(s) separate from your project file.

5. Click **OK** to close the dialog. The code will appear on your page in the HTML Code Fragment window.

Adding JavaScript

To source a vast array of JavaScript code, try searching for "javascript snippets" in your favourite search engine. You should find many thousands of sites hosting freely available code snippets. Most of these sites will clearly indicate what the JavaScript will do for you—they'll also normally let you select the JavaScript code and copy it for pasting into an HTML fragment's, object's or page's Source window, HTML table cell or directly onto the page.

Here are some typical uses when applying code to your web pages:

*   Disable right-mouse click on page objects

*   Add a Print current page button

*   Add a date and time to your page

*   Change an object's colour when selected

Let's look at how to add some of JavaScript (sourced or written by yourself if you've experience of JavaScript programming).

To illustrate, compare the two pieces of example code below. A very simple JavaScript code snippet is added to the Source window which will display the current date on your web page. The first section of code uses the last placeholder in the above list (*<!--Page Body Start-->*), the second how the code looks after a script has replaced the placeholder.

```
-->
</style>
<script><!--
var blankSrc = "_wp_scripts/blank.gif";
--></script><script src="_wp_scripts/jspngfix.js" ty
</script>
</head>


<body link="#000080" vlink="#000080" alink="#000080"
<!--Page Body Start-->
<center><div style="position:relative;width:750px;">
<!--Page Start-->


<!-- Quick Rectangle qs_2 -->

<!--Preamble-->
```

Code showing placeholder

```
-->
</style>
<script><!--
var blankSrc = "_wp_scripts/blank.gif";
--></script><script src="_wp_scripts/jspngfix.js" ty
</script>
</head>


<body link="#000080" vlink="#000080" alink="#000080"
<script type="text/javascript">

document.write(Date())

</script>
<center><div style="position:relative;width:750px;">
<!--Page Start-->
```

Code after added JavaScript

This example illustrates where simple code is placed in a source window.

To attach code to an HTML fragment or object:

1. Select an existing HTML fragment or object.

2. From the Format menu, select **Attach HTML...**.
    OR
    Right-click on the object and choose the same option.

3. In the dialog, scroll the source window to locate editable placeholders. Which placeholder you choose depends on what you want to achieve.

4. Select all of the placeholder and paste HTML, script or any other text string to overwrite the placeholder text.
OR
Select all of the placeholder and type directly in the placeholder's location (again overwriting the placeholder text).

5. Click the **OK** button to return to your normal page view.

> You can make use of tokens to add a range of variables to your HTML. Use for breadcrumb navigation that will update dynamically if you add, remove or change pages within the site.

For more complex scripting, it may be necessary to add supporting files (graphics, text files, etc.) that the inserted script may use—these can be either embedded or linked. This means the files are either kept with the WPP project (embedded) or are referenced externally via a link (much like a hyperlink). Consider your final project file size when embedding several images.

To add supporting files:

1. Click the **Add...** button.

2. From the Open dialog, navigate to then select one or more files (use **Ctrl**-click and **Shift**-click for non-contiguous or contiguous selection, respectively). Click **Open**.

3. The files are listed in the **Files** list and will be embedded in your project by default. If you choose not to embed files (making your project smaller), then select each file and click the **Make Linked** button.

4. Click **OK**.

At any point, you can **Add**, **Delete**, and change **Export Options** for any file.

To attach code to a page:

1. Right-click on the page and choose **Attach HTML**.
    OR
    Choose the **Attach HTML** button on the Standard toolbar.

2. In the dialog, scroll the window to locate editable placeholders. Which placeholder you choose depends on what you want to achieve.

3. Select all of the placeholder and paste HTML, script or any other text string to overwrite the placeholder text.
    OR
    Select all of the placeholder and type directly in the placeholder's location (again overwriting the placeholder text).

4. To switch back to your normal page view, click the project tab at the top of the source window.

Using IDs

All objects in WebPlus are given unique alphanumeric IDs for referencing by scripting languages. By default, ID generation is automatic for each object, text column, table row and table cell. For example, a newly drawn QuickShape will automatically be assigned an ID of "qs_1", a second QuickShape will be "qs_2", pictures could be "pic_1", "pic_2", etc.

It may be perfectly acceptable to utilize these automatic IDs in your scripts but if you need to assign your own IDs, it's possible to turn off the site-wide automatic generation of IDs in the **Options** tab of the Site Properties dialog (select **Site Properties...** from the File menu). Uncheck the option specific for object, text column, table row and/or table cell and press **OK**. Your own replacement IDs can instead be added in the available placeholder, i.e.

```
___AddCode="here"
```

> If the object is copied on the same page or to another Web site, the ID number will be replaced by a new ID number.

Any object ID can be edited once the object is on the web page. A different name can be used or, if you don't want to show an object's ID (but want to keep site-wide ID generation), you can prevent the ID from being shown in source code.

To edit an object ID:

1. Right-click an object and select **ID**.
   OR
   Select the object and choose **HTML ID...** from the Format menu.

2. In the dialog, modify the HTML ID value.

3. (Optional) Choose whether to **Write ID for this object**. Selecting "Use Site default" means that the setting in the **Options** tab of the Site Properties dialog is honoured—"Yes" or "No" means that the object's ID is always shown or never shown irrespective of the site default setting.

Tokens

WebPlus provides a range of grouped HTML annotation tokens which can be attached to HTML fragments, objects or pages. They get replaced by appropriate "real" values when you export to a file or preview your page.

Adding tokens is a simple case of inserting a token string, by copy and paste or typing directly, into one of the placeholder positions in any HTML source.

A full list of such tokens is provided in the WebPlus Help (search for tokens in the Index)

Adding forms

Web-based forms allow information to be collected from visitors to your Web site in an efficient and modern manner. In much the same way as traditional paper forms are used to collect information, Web-based forms offer the same form completion concepts, but take advantage of the Internet as a powerful information conduit. Some common form types include request forms, feedback forms, and guest books.

Form data can be collected in a variety of ways—by email, to a local/remote script file, or via Serif Web Resources.

Form Structure

The building blocks of a form comprise a mixture of text, graphics and form controls. Form controls are intelligent as they collect web visitor data and can be added, moved and modified in a similar way to familiar objects in WebPlus such as graphics and table elements. A control can be a button, edit box, text area, combo box, check box, radio button, File browser, or CAPTCHA object. A typical form, perhaps a email feedback form, is made up of a combination of some of these controls, i.e.

- From the web visitor's perspective, information is typed into text boxes or selected from check boxes, radio buttons, or drop-down boxes. The information entered can be numeric, textual, or a mixture of both, depending on the type of field. The tab order by which fields are to be completed is configurable, as is validation of input data (see WebPlus help for more about tab order and validation).

- Each field has its own set of properties relating to its appearance, its value(s), validation, or the action expected of the field.

In WebPlus, the form should be integrated into your site design as you develop your site. Of course, a whole page could occupy a single form, and the page could be a part of the site-wide navigation bar (check **Include in Navigation** in Page Properties).

A form's functionality only becomes active when your Web site is published (of course you can still preview your forms from within WebPlus, see Previewing your Web site on p. 321). When a web visitor enters data into, or selects a form option, the data will be sent back to a chosen destination when the form is submitted.

JavaScript can be used to allow interactivity in your Web forms. It drives formatting, validation, calculations, and actions—all key functions in Web-based form development.

Where is data sent?

After submission, form data can be sent to one of the following:

- an email address (of the Web developer).

- a script file (stored locally or remotely); this could write text to a text file or into a server database.

- Serif Web Resources; for transit of form data to your email (via Serif).

As is standard in Web form management, it is possible to set the encoding type, target window/frames, submission methods (POST or GET) can be used.

Creating forms

Several methods exist for creating forms dependent on whether you wish to be helped with a Form Wizard, use standard forms (i.e. pre-defined ready-to-go forms supplied with WebPlus), or create a form from scratch. Whichever method is chosen will depend on the level of customization you want to go to—as a rule of thumb, it's always best to familiarize yourself with WebPlus's standard forms that could be used first. This may save you time, and allow you to create your form more easily.

To create a form (via Form Wizard):

1. Click the ▨ **Form Wizard** on the Web Objects toolbar's Form flyout.

2. In the dialog, click the **Create a new form with the wizard** icon and then **Next>**.

3. In the next screen, you need to add form controls that will make up your form. In the Add box, either:

    *   For a ready-to-go form control, click the **Pre-defined** button, and pick your chosen form control. You'll need to double-click the new control in the window to name the control.
        OR

    1. Click on one of the other form controls to create from scratch. See Form controls on p. 260 for a description of each control.

    2. In the dialog, use the internal name for the control (to uniquely identify it), or edit it and enter a label to accompany the control (this is shown on-screen). You can also edit the control by using the **Edit Control** button. Editing a control allows validation, control of form length, and other control attributes to be set. See Editing form controls on p. 263 for more information. If you've edited a value, click **OK**.

4. Repeat the above for each chosen form control as needed. They will be listed (in order of creation) in the upper window.

   Before continuing, you have to add a Submit form control to your form. This is vital to pass data to its destination. Click the **Submit Button** to automatically add the button to your form. It is normal practice to accompany this with a **Reset Button**, used to clear out form fields of data not yet submitted.

   Click **Next>**.

5. From the next dialog, choose a destination for your form data by clicking a destination button for email, script file (local or remote) or Serif Web Resources and a name to define the whole form. (See Submission of forms on p. 265). Select **Finish** to complete the wizard.

6. ⊞ To insert the form at a default size, position the form place cursor where you want the form to appear on the page, then simply click the mouse.

If you prefer a different approach, you can add a Standard form. Standard forms are pre-defined forms for Contact information, User comments, CV submission, Opinion, and Address forms to name a few.

To create a standard form:

1. Click the ▨ **Form Wizard** on the Web Objects toolbar's Form flyout.

2. In the dialog, click the **Use and adapt a standard form** icon and then **Next>**.

3. From the list of forms, select a form type while using the lower Preview pane.

4. Click **Next>**.

5. In the next screen, choose to add, modify or delete controls.

   - To add, click a button in the **Add** box.

   - To modify a standard object, select an existing control in the window and choose **Edit Control....** See Editing form controls on p. 263 for more information.

- To delete a standard object, select an existing control in the window and choose **Delete** (or press the **Delete** key).

- To rearrange the control order, use the 🔲 **Move Up** and 🔲 **Move Down** buttons.

6. After clicking **Next>**, choose a destination for your form data by clicking a destination button. Select **Finish** to complete the wizard.

7. 🔲 To insert the form at a default size, position the form place cursor and click the mouse.

If you're looking for design freedom, WebPlus provides a blank form and form objects from which you can design your form from scratch. You can add form controls or standard form objects, or both. See WebPlus help for more details.

Form controls

Each form control is an "intelligent" object which differs from other WebPlus objects. They are intelligent because they can store user input and pass it on to a central location during form submission. Controls can be moved as for other objects but cannot have colours or transparency applied, borders adjusted, or resized.

A range of form controls are available from within the Form Wizard or directly from the Web Objects toolbar's Form flyout (or via the **Form** option on the Insert menu). You assign an internal unique name to each field and then set a variety of properties—each form control has its own set which can be modified.

Form Control Icon	Form Control Name	When to use?
`OK`	Form Button	Use when specifying an action that can be triggered by a button click. A whole range of buttons of varying design and function can be created. Some uses include:

- Advanced - Displays menu options that are only applicable for advanced uses.

- Show All - Displays all menu options.

- Next page - Jumps the form recipient to the next page.

- Open - Opens a file or Web link.

- Import - Imports form data.

> Submit and Reset buttons are available in the Form wizard. They perform form submission and clear all form data, respectively.

Edit Box		Use for entering single-line text, numbers, or a mixture of both. Someone's surname or insurance number would be a good example.
Text Area		Use for adding multi-line text, numbers or a mixture of both. Generally used for entering input, either textual or numerical, e.g. an enquiry, recipe, or list of figures.
Combo Box		For selection from a list of items in a drop-down menu where only one item can be selected by default, e.g. a gender combo.

Combo boxes also allow for a scrollable list of items; with optional support for multiple selection. For example, to select Afghanistan, Algeria, and Andorra, use **Ctrl**-click on each item:

You can use **Shift**-click to group select a range of items.

> When designing multiple selection combo boxes, drag the top or bottom of the Combo box to allow several items to be displayed by default.

Check Box

Ideal when you want to select multiple items displayed side by side. A good alternative to a Combo Box if space allows. The web visitor clicks once to select or deselect the box, e.g.

Would you like to be notified of any upcoming events in the near future?

Radio Button

Good for selection of a single mutually exclusive item from a grouped subset of choices. For example, a set of radio buttons can be used to obtain gender information from the web visitor.

Male
Female

| | File Browser | Use the File browser to have your web visitors upload any file from their computers. The visitor simply navigates via a **Browse...** button and selects a local file of their choice. Some examples include uploading pictures, CVs, drawings and instructions. |
| | CAPTCHA | Use as a security check for protecting against spamming. The form control offers a random text string for the Web visitor to reproduce in an text box. Passing the check initiates form submission. |

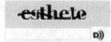

TIP: If you don't want the security check placed on your form you can enable the check during form submission instead (see Submission of forms on p. 265).

Hidden objects can be added as a form control if you use the Form Wizard. Although the web visitor does not see the field it is typically used by the Web developer to ensure the data collected has an identifiable string stored with the user's data. An example could be a publish date relating to the web page—useful for identifying incorrectly working pages.

In addition, hidden fields can be added by right-clicking on the entire form and selecting **Edit Form Properties...**. The dialog's **Hidden Fields** tab allows for input of any number of hidden fields.

Editing form controls

Each form control type (buttons, text field, etc.) has different characteristics and therefore different values for editing. Values can be changed as you create the form or at a later time after the control has been added to the form. Typically you may want to:

- change the internally stored control **Name** and its **Initial Value** (what gets displayed on-screen by default).

- treat the control's value as script (check to preserve initial value's script content instead of converting it to HTML).

- set a **Maximum length** for the field (use as a type of validation).

- set the field to **Disabled**. Check to make the control inactive unless activated by script.

- set an **Access** key. Jump to the form control with a keyboard shortcut (use with Alt key and keyboard letter).

- make a control **Read only** (check to make control non-editable unless changed by script). Could be conditional on other fields being completed.

- create a control suitable for a **Password** (web visitor input is masked).

The Form Wizard's **Edit Control...** button lets you modify the control during form creation. Alternatively, the control can be edited later by right-clicking on the form control on the web page and choosing the Edit option, e.g. Edit Text Box.

Combo Box editing

Editing a combo box is a little more complicated than other fields. The combo box needs to be populated with multiple entries to create selection choices within the box. In the Form Combo Box dialog, use **Add Option...** to sequentially build up your menu entries—this involves adding name and value pairs one-by-one (use the **Add Another** button to speed up the process).

Any Combo Box will also support **Groups**. This means you can categorize entries into common groupings for easier navigation. While the group itself is not selectable you can make more sense of a long list of entries by creating the group name (click **Add Group...**) and moving entries under the group with the **Make Child** button (position entry under the chosen group). For example, a country combo box could be categorized by continent.

Radio Box editing

Radio box from controls operate slightly differently to other form controls. To operate correctly, Radio buttons which are intended to be grouped, must both be configured to be a part of the same configurable **Group Name**. Simply create a group name for the first radio button and adopt that name for any other radio buttons intended for that group.

Submission of forms

All forms have one thing in common—they must be submitted to allow data to be collected. To do this you can either create a **Submit Button** unaided or more usually use the ready-made button in the Form Wizard. The button needs to be present on the form and is typically used with a Reset button to clear all form controls of data.

No action

Form data is not submitted. This option is useful if you want to temporarily disable data collection or if you haven't yet set up scripting or Serif Web Resources. At a later time you can edit the form (right-click then choose **Edit Form Properties...**) and select a valid submission method.

email address

Use this option to bypass the usual POST/GET submission methods. When the Submit button is pressed the web visitor's default email program is launched. The form data (passed in a single string) is added to the email body and is ready to be sent to the configured email destination. Especially useful if there is no local or remote scripting in place.

> This is an unsecure submission method—any private or confidential information will be not be encrypted.

To set up email directly:

1. With the icon enabled, add a Form name.

2. Enter the destination email address in the drop-down menu.

Serif Web Resources

Not everyone will have access to or even want to operate their own Web server so, as an alternative to this, you can use Serif Web Resources (see p. 306). This is a free Web to email gateway service which will transit your valued form data via Serif and send it to your personal email address—the service does require that you firstly have a Serif Web resources login (for security reasons), which will allow you to create, edit and delete your own email destinations; these are called Form Email Targets.

To set up Serif Web Resources:

1. Select **Serif Web Resources** and add a Form name.

2. Click the **Select** button and login to Serif Web Resources.

3. From the dialog, enter your destination email in the **New Target** box and click **Add New Target**. The email entry is created and added to the available email address list—with the email address selected, click **OK**. You'll notice that the entry is classed as "*Not Confirmed*". Before the service commences, you'll get a email confirmation message sent to your email address. By clicking the link, the service will be activated and the entry will change to "*Confirmed*".

4. Check **Use CAPTCHA Gateway** to enable a security check as the Web visitor submits the form. This protects against spamming. A dialog offers a random text string for the Web visitor to reproduce in an text box. Passing the check initiates form submission.

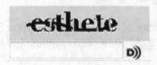

5. Choose a submission method, encoding type, and target window/frame.

You may be wondering what typical form data might look like once sent through Serif Web Resources. Here's an example of data collected from a simple form.

Time Submitted: Thu, 23 Jan 2008 17:45:10 BST
Referrer:
From IP: 80.6.91.225
firstname = Doug
lastname = Walker
gender = Male
info = Social Events

Incidentally, the web visitor will receive a basic confirmation page generated by Serif Web Resources to acknowledge successful receipt of form data. As a useful tip you can create and assign your very own acknowledgement web page to be used instead of this basic page. Your own page is just like any other web page so you can add your own information, and design the page in the same style and appearance as the rest of your Web site.

To add your own acknowledgement page:

1. Right-click on the form (must submit data via Serif Web Resources) and choose **Edit Form Properties...**.

2. Switch to the Hidden Fields tab, click the **Add...** button and add the word "redirect" to the **Name** field and your intended target URL with http:// prefix (i.e., the web address of your own acknowledgement page) in the **Value** field.

3. Click **OK**. The new web page will display on the next form submission.

> No personal data will be stored on Serif Web servers. All form data is redirected in real time.

Script file from my hard drive

This option is for experienced Web developers with scripting expertise.

Typically a script file is written and stored along with WebPlus's other web pages and is uploaded during the Publish to the Web operation. If uploading to an ISP, it's essential to check with your ISP in advance if scripting is allowed on your web space. If not, you will have to adopt another solution, perhaps choosing another ISP that allow scripting or choose a script file hosted on your ISP (most provide a simple script; you would use the **Remote script** option below for this). If in doubt, contact your ISP if you're not sure.

To set up a local script file:

1. With the **Script file** icon enabled, add a Form name.

2. Navigate to your local script file, typically a .CGI, .PL, .DLL, or .EXE file with the **Browse...** button.

3. Check **Embed** to include the script within the WebPlus project. If unchecked, the script file will be unconnected to the project (any updates to the script will be invisible to the project).

4. Optionally, the **Export Options...** button lets you define a web file name and folder for the script.

5. Choose a submission method, encoding type, target window/frame, and Character set.

A Remote script

Use if your ISP will not allow you to run your own scripts on your ISP web space. Instead, your ISP may supply a basic script file that can be linked to from your web page. Typically, the script will send the form data back to your email address (already setup with your ISP).

To set up a remote script file:

1. With the **Remote script** icon enabled, add a Form name.

2. Enter a URL pointing directly to a script file, typically a .CGI, .PL, .DLL, or .EXE file.

3. Choose a submission method, encoding type, target window/frame, and Character set.

RSS feeds and podcasts

Really Simple Syndication (RSS) feeds are streams of constantly changing news and information which are very popular on fast-paced Web sites. The popularity of RSS feeds is evident if you use Internet-based news services regularly. You'll see RSS feeds indicated on Web sites by a 🔲 symbol—by clicking the symbol the user may be able to manually or automatically subscribe to that RSS feed via a RSS Reader.

Podcasts are syndication feeds just like RSS feeds but offer slightly different options that reflect a podcast's use of digital media such as audio and video files. Put simply, RSS feeds will publish articles, while podcasts will broadcast information as episodes.

In WebPlus, you can create your own RSS feeds or podcasts that you can frequently publish and update. In essence, you become the publisher (rather than the reader) of one or more information services containing headlines, Web site summaries or your very own articles. For podcasts, you broadcast media clips as episodes. Web visitors can subscribe to these feeds via manual or one-click subscription. For the latter, the visitor simply clicks on a diagnostic symbol which indicates the type of feed, i.e.

 For RSS Feeds.

 For podcasts.

One-click subscriptions are set up to subscribe the visitor to a chosen reader, i.e. Google Reader, My Yahoo!, or Apple iTunes®. For manual subscription (e.g., to Internet Explorer or Mozilla Firefox) your published RSS feed or podcast offers a clickable subscription button, i.e.

 Subscribe to this feed

Using podcasts as an example, the Web visitor sees a podcast in their chosen reader once subscribed. The examples below show a constantly updating fictitious school's podcast with clickable links to media (both audio and video).

Bluewood School PodCast

Start of term - Welcome back!

07 January 2008, 11:39:49

A simple message to welcome all pupils back to school. We're all raring to go!

🎧 NewTerm.mp3

Major's Visit (video)

04 January 2008, 11:56:37

Find out how Bigwood welcomed the Major to the school. A big focus was put

📹 Major_visit.wmv

WW2 soldier Interview (audio)

04 January 2008, 11:56:00

Our history group got the chance to spend some time with Arthur Peel, a WWII Desert Rats) in North Africa against Field Marshall Rommel.

🎧 Interview_soldier.mp3

Podcast	Category	Release Date ▼	Description
▼ Bluewood School PodCast	Training	07/01/2008	A school Podcasting
☑ Start of term - Welcome back!		07/01/2008	A simple message to
☑ WW2 soldier Interview (audio) `CLEAN`	Interviews	04/01/2008	Our history group go
☑ Yorkminster trip (video) `CLEAN`	school trips	04/01/2008	Year 10's trip to York

RSS feeds and podcasts can be configured in a very similar way in WebPlus. In fact, the process for creating your own RSS feed or podcast utilizes the same **RSS Feed Tool** within WebPlus.

If you want to reuse a third party RSS feeds/podcasts and add it to your own Web page, a reader can be embedded into your Web page by using the **RSS Reader Tool**.

Browser support for feeds

As an emergent technology, feeds will only be viewable in the latest versions of Internet browsers. Here is a simple list outlining browsers and their versions which can read a feed within its own browser (with no third-party plug-ins required).

- Internet Explorer 7.0 (or later)

- Mozilla Firefox (all versions)

- Opera 8.0 (or later)

- Netscape Browser 8.1 (or later)

If you are using a previous version of the above don't worry! There are a range of feed readers available via the Internet (type "RSS reader" into your favourite search engine) which will work equally well. Notable readers include Newz Crawler, FeedDemon and Awasu.

Creating RSS feeds or podcasts

The **RSS Feed Tool** enables you to create one or more RSS feeds/podcasts from which web visitors can subscribe via their standalone feed reader, Web browsers or Apple iTunes®. As you create a feed a series of settings can be applied to the feed which relate to feed title/descriptions, associated images, copyright information, categories, keywords, etc.

To insert an RSS feed or podcast:

1. Click the 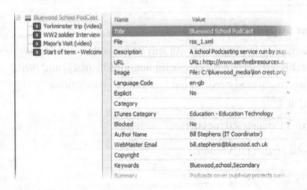 **RSS Feed Tool** button on the Web Objects toolbar's RSS flyout.

2. Click the **Add RSS Feed** or **Add Podcast** button to create a new RSS feed or podcast entry. A new feed name called **New RSS Feed** or **New Podcast** appears in the left-hand menu. With the entry selected, you'll see a list of settings for the new entry which can be modified by clicking in the Value column. Drop-down lists, dialog boxes or text input boxes let you add, select or modify values for the feed.

   For example, a podcast feed for a school's podcasting service (shown above) would look as follows:

Name	Value
Bluewood School PodCast	
Yorkminster trip (video)	
WW2 soldier Interview	
Major's Visit (video)	
Start of term - Welcome	
Title	Bluewood School PodCast
File	rss_1.xml
Description	A school Podcasting service run by pup...
URL	URL: http://www.serifwebresources.c...
Image	File: C:\bluewood_media\lion crest.png
Language Code	en-gb
Explicit	No
Category	
ITunes Category	Education - Education Technology
Blocked	No
Author Name	Bill Stephens (IT Coordinator)
WebMaster Email	bill.stephens@bluewood.sch.uk
Copyright	-
Keywords	Bluewood,school,Secondary
Summary	Podcasts cover pupil-run projects cam...

You'll notice a series of episodes associated with the podcast feed. We'll look at how to add these later.

3. Click **OK**.

4. For Podcasts, the **RSS Feed** dialog can automatically subscribe the podcast within the visitor's Google Reader, My Yahoo!, or iTunes application. Pick from the **Open Podcast with** drop-down list. Otherwise, for manual subscription of RSS feeds or podcasts, the RSS Standard option is used.

5. Click **OK**.

6. To place the feed on the page, position the ⊕ cursor and simply click the mouse.

A ░ or ● button appears at the cursor position (for an RSS feed or podcast, respectively).

> For one-click automatic subscription of podcasts, label your podcast symbol indicating which application the subscription will be made to.

To swap the feed for another:

*   Once an RSS feed or podcast exists, clicking the ░ **RSS Feed Tool** button again will display an interim dialog that lets you redirect the button to another feed. Simply select a different entry and click OK.

Once the RSS feed or podcast is created, articles or episodes (respectively) can be added to the feed and then published just as in the printing industry (newspapers and magazines) and broadcasting (BBC, CNN, ITV, Sky, etc.), respectively. Once updated, you'll need to republish your Web site (see Publishing to the Web on p. 322).

To add or update articles:

1. Click the [ ] **RSS Feed Tool** button on the WebPlus's Web Objects toolbar.

2. From the RSS Feed dialog, ensure the correct feed is selected, then click the **Edit...** button.

3. At the right of the dialog, click the **Add Article** button. This creates a new article, provisionally titled New Article (for an RSS feed) or New Episode (for podcast) under the selected feed.

4. Edit your article/episode and its settings. Drop-down lists, dialog boxes or text input boxes let you add, select or modify values for the feed.

   Again, using the above school podcast example, the associated first episode could have been added with the following settings.

Name	Value
Item Title	Yorkminster trip (video)
Description	Year 10's trip to York to learn about th...
Media file	File: C:\bluewood_media\2007\Yorkmin.
Duration	00:58:00
Publication Date	04/01/2008 11:13:41
Explicit	No
Category	school trips
Blocked	No
Author E-mail	cassy@bluewood.sch.uk
Author Name	Cassy McDonald (Y10 head teacher)
Keywords	Yorkminster, cathedrals, history, religion
Summary	The trip was arranged to purils can un...

5. Click **OK**, then click **OK** again.

> If you're broadcasting media files stored locally, you'll be prompted to define a Site Base URL (see p. 63) during publishing. This makes local files accessible to visitors.

Submission of podcast feeds

For podcasts via iTunes, as a broadcaster you'll need to have your podcast submitted to iTunes. The podcast feed has to be reviewed by iTunes staff to check for technical problems, an acceptable login, inappropriate use of explicit language, offensive material, and misuse of copyright material. This step means that if your feed is approved, iTunes users will then be able to subscribe to your podcast feed.

To submit a podcast feed to iTunes 7:

1. Launch iTunes.

2. Click on **Podcasts** in the LIBRARY section.

3. Select the **Podcast Directory** button at the bottom of the iTunes workspace.

4. Scroll down to the bottom of the window and in the FOR PODCASTERS box, click **Submit a Podcast**.

5. In the next screen, paste your Feed URL into the **Podcast Feed URL** box. Your Feed URL will be a URL with an xml file name (e.g., rss_1.xml) at its end.

6. Click **Continue**.

Subscribing

Subscription to RSS feeds or podcasts differs depending on whether automatic or manual subscription is to be offered, and which Web browser/feed reader is to be used. When a web visitor visits a Web page which hosts a feed, they should be able to spot the diagnostic feed button for subscription.

Instead of a direct button, a hyperlink (see p. 225) can be created from anywhere in your site which links directly to your new feed. A special link destination type called **RSS Feed** is used.

Automatic subscription to podcasts

An 🎙 icon (or associated hyperlink) is clicked according to the visitor's preferred chosen subscription. The podcast and reader is defined explicitly, so subscription is automatic. An example could be as follows:

Google Reader
(One-click subscription)

My Yahoo!
(One-click subscription)

ITunes
(One-click subscription)

Manual subscription via Web browsers

1. Navigate to the Web page, then click the button. The feed page is displayed.

2. Click the available "subscribe" link whose appearance may differ depending on browser, i.e.

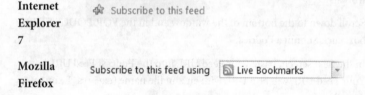

Internet
Explorer
7

Mozilla
Firefox

The feed is added to the visitor's browser Feeds tab within the Favorites Center (Internet Explorer) or as a Live Bookmark (Mozilla Firefox). See your Web browser documentation for more details on these "bookmarking" processes. To unsubscribe, simply delete from the Feeds pane or delete the Live Bookmark in Bookmarks, respectively.

Including third-party feeds

Instead of creating you own RSS feed or podcast you may wish to include an RSS feed from another Web site on your own Web page—a web page's content can be boosted by inclusion of a feed from any popular news service (Reuters, BBC News, sport, etc.) or other information service (e.g., financial). Many major news and information services host lists of RSS feeds relating to specific areas of interest (geographical, entertainment, political, music, etc.) so it's just a case of copying the link for the Web site's RSS feed and pasting it into a dialog shown when clicking the WebPlus's **RSS Reader Tool**.

Please bear in mind any terms and conditions in using a third-party RSS feed—these should be clearly indicated on the originating Web site.

The addition of the RSS feed reader to your page automatically subscribes yourself to the chosen RSS feed or podcast. There are other ways of subscribing to RSS feeds or podcasts via Web browsers and iTunes, but here we'll focus on how to include the feed on your page and have it automatically receive articles or episodes.

Here's an example of a BBC News podcast added to a WebPlus Web page:

> 01/03/2008 05:15 PM
> **NewsPod: 03 Jan 08**
> Iowa caucuses / Kenyan election
> probe / Radiohead on free music
> downloads / Frog extinction fears.
>
> 01/02/2008 05:16 PM
> **NewsPod: 02 Jan 08**
> Crisis in Kenya / Pakistan elections
> postponed / Britain and USA
> 'addicted' to fast food / Should the
> size of your car dictate how much it
> costs to park?

To include an RSS feed or podcast on your page:

1. Locate an RSS feed available on Web pages of popular news and information services. Look for one of the following distinctive buttons, e.g.

2. Copy and paste the Feed URL from a Web page to the clipboard. For Internet Explorer, you can right-click on a subscribe button/link and choose **Copy Shortcut**. For Mozilla Firefox, choose **Copy Link Location** via right-click.

3. Click the **RSS Reader Tool** button on the Web Objects toolbar's RSS flyout.

4. In the dialog, paste the Feed URL into the **RSS Feed URL** field.

5. Optionally, select a different colour, font, font size, or font style for the feed's Title, Headline, or Summary Colour.

6. Set the local time zone for your site in the **Time Zone** drop-down list.

7. Click **OK**.

8. A ⊹▨ cursor is displayed. To insert the feed in a window of default size, simply click the mouse.

   OR

   More typically, to set the size of the feed window, drag out a region and release the mouse button.

The feed window will be filled with a peach colour with the URL shown— you'll need to publish the page to view the current new feed. Remember that the content will update automatically as the feed is updated on the original Web site. A typical published podcast feed could look as follows (but will update frequently):

NewsPod: 03 Jan 08

03 January 2008, 17:15:00 →

Iowa caucuses / Kenyan election probe / Radiohead downloads / Frog extinction fears.

Ω   newspod_20080103-1715.mp3

NewsPod: 02 Jan 08

02 January 2008, 17:16:00 →

Crisis in Kenya / Pakistan elections postponed / Brit fast food / Should the size of your car dictate how

Ω   newspod_20080102-1716.mp3

When the Web visitor views the feed each episode can be played by clicking on the audio link, typically pointing to an MP3 file. Once downloaded and saved, the file can be played on a currently set default player (e.g., Windows Media Player).

E-Commerce

Understanding e-commerce

E-commerce entails the buying and selling of goods on the Internet. It's difficult to escape online retailing in any Internet session these days—you've more than likely used some form of Internet shopping at some point, when buying online CDs, books, holidays, etc. Any Web site that supports this kind of e-commerce activity will typically make use of a shopping cart provider and a payment processing system. A shopping cart is a virtual basket (think of a supermarket basket) which stores your chosen items and is used in conjunction with a payment processing system (taking the place of the supermarket's checkout).

For major companies, the shopping cart technology is developed in-house (maybe the payment processing is carried out by a third party company). For smaller companies or organizations, the shopping cart is normally a brought-in third-party solution due to the cost/resource limitations. There are many third-party shopping cart providers that can be used—all account-based and equipped to accept credit cards instead of using a traditional payment gateway (e.g., by phone).

So where does WebPlus fit into all this? Firstly, WebPlus allows you to choose one of several specially chosen shopping cart providers (depending on WebPlus version) and, secondly, it allows you to connect to the shopping cart provider via a form or link on the WebPlus page. Forms allow for buying options (colours, quantity) to be set, as well as calculate tax rates, shipping, bulk items, etc. Links offer simple one-click purchasing without buying options. The features are provider-specific and as a result vary widely.

Configuring your shopping cart provider

A number of different shopping cart providers can be configured within WebPlus. These are the most commonly used and some, like PayPal©, you may have come across directly as an eBay© customer. The configuration process directs you to the provider's own Web site from where you can sign-up as a registered user.

> Use the provider's Web site to find out more about unique shopping cart features.

To setup a shopping cart provider:

1. Click the **Configure E-Commerce** button on the Web Objects toolbar's E-Commerce flyout.

2. From the **E-Commerce Configuration** dialog, you have two options depending on if you are an existing or new user of one of the shopping cart providers, i.e.

   - If you're a new user, choose a shopping cart provider by enabling its radio button, then click the **Sign Up Now** button. The provider's web site is shown in a new browser window from where you can register with the shopping cart provider.

   - If you're an existing user, enable the button next to your chosen provider, and click **Next>**. This option simply sets the default provider for your Web site (rather than set up a provider account).

3. The subsequent dialog is provider-specific and may show offline testing options, window selection, store IDs, currency options and/or tax choices.

4. Click the **Finish** button to complete shopping cart configuration.

As an example, choosing PayPal lets you define a email address to receive payments, or use a "Sandbox", a test tool, for trying out your shopping cart before going live (otherwise you may start making money before you're ready!). Click the **Find Out More** button to setup a separate Sandbox login in addition to your "live" PayPal login.

Inserting an e-commerce object (PayPal)

The creation of e-commerce objects within WebPlus takes a Wizard-based approach. An e-commerce object can be added to the web page as a form or link (i.e., a simple button or any object's hyperlink) by completion of a series of dialogs. Whether you choose to use forms or links depends on the characteristics of the items you are planning to sell, and how you want to sell your goods.

For example, if you are a trader wishing to sell a quantity of bricks you could create an **E-Commerce button** (as a Buy Now link). This option would make an assumption about the potential transaction, i.e. that all the bricks are the same style/colour and that the buyer would wish to purchase a fixed amount.

This is because a link is only a button and cannot host any "interactive" buying options that would be need for more complex purchases. One buyer's click will buy a standard product offering—nothing more. Useful in some situations but in others completely inadequate.

More complex purchases using **E-Commerce Forms** offer user interactivity coupled with flexibility. If we take the brick trader as an example again, a form can be used to host quantity and brick style/colour options so that the customer has control and can get what he/she wants!

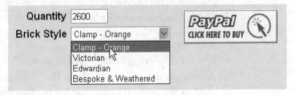

Here the web visitor has chosen to buy 2600 bricks of style "Clamp - Orange."

For e-commerce scenarios, where many items are to be offered for sale, it's possible to store items for sale in a Serif database (SDB) specially structured for use with e-commerce. By adding repeating forms (or areas) on your page, the database items can be listed after database merging, and offered for sale. See Using database merge with e-commerce on p. 297.

Form And Link Options

Forms	When to use?
Buy Now	When directing the shopper straight to the checkout. Up to two buying options can be defined. Form validation is supported.
Add to Shopping Cart	When the shopper is likely to buy more than one different item over the duration of a web session (and pay at the end). Up to two buying options can be defined. Form validation is supported.
Donation	For charitable donation being made via the shopping cart. Form validation is supported.
Subscription	For subscriptions with configurable trial periods and billing intervals. Form validation is supported.
Repeating Buy Now Form	As for Buy Now form but when you want to retrieve items from an e-commerce database and list them repeatedly in merged Web pages.
Repeating Add to Shopping Cart Form	As for Add to Shopping Cart form but use to retrieve items from an e-commerce database and list them repeatedly in merged Web pages.
Repeating Area	Use for displaying items stored in an e-commerce database but without Buy Now or Add to Shopping Cart options for the items.

Links	When to use?
Buy Now Link	When directing the shopper straight to the checkout (no buying options or validation) via e-commerce button or object hyperlink.
Add to Shopping Cart Link	When the shopper is likely to buy more than one different item over the duration of a web session (and pay at the end) via e-commerce button or object hyperlink. (No buying options or validation).
View Shopping Cart Link	Use to check on your shopping cart from any point in your web pages via e-commerce button or object hyperlink.
Donation Link	For charitable donations being made via the shopping cart via e-commerce button or object hyperlink. (No buying options or validation).
Subscription Link	Subscribe to chargeable services or products via e-commerce button or object hyperlink. Single or repeating subscriptions are configurable. (no buying options or validation).
Cancel Subscription Link	For adding a Cancel Subscription button or object hyperlink.

Forms or links can be selected as radio buttons from a single dialog. Remember that the term "Links" is used because an e-commerce hyperlink can be made from a vector object, image, shape or text by use of this dialog (right-click on the object and select **Hyperlink...**). This would be instead of a standard PayPal button. See Adding hyperlinks and anchors on p. 225 for more information.

The dialog that is displayed when you add an e-commerce object will entirely depend on the currently enabled shopping cart provider (see Configuring your Shopping Cart provider on p. 280).

The following procedures assume that PayPal is configured as your shopping cart.

To insert an e-commerce object:

1. Click the $ **Insert an E-Commerce object** button on the Web Objects toolbar's E-Commerce flyout.

2. In the **Add PayPal Object** dialog, pick the email address which is to receive the payment information. WebPlus will already assume that the email address set during shopping cart configuration is used. Alternatively, uncheck the **Use the site default address** box and set a different email address to override the site default.

3. Pick an object type from the PayPal Form box. Select a "Form" radio button if you want to create an **E-Commerce Form** which will contain buying options (e.g., colour or quantity). If the product for sale has no buying options then you can use a "Link" object (i.e., to create a clickable **E-Commerce Button**). Repeating form and area options let you add items from a database rather than defining them explicitly in an Item Details dialog (see Using database merge with e-commerce on p. 297).

4. (Optional). If a Form or Button is not what you are looking for, enable the last option instead to paste code in a subsequent dialog. This would be code generated from PayPal's Web site (look under Merchant Tools). Click **Next>**.

5. In the next dialog, define a button for use. It's possible to enable a standard text button (when enabled, enter any text string), a standard image button (when enabled, pick from an attractive selection of presets in the scrollable window), or load an image button (when enabled, use the **Browse...** button to navigate and select your image). Images are embedded in your site by default; otherwise uncheck the last option. Click **Next>**.

6. Item identification, pricing and tax information can be defined in the Item Details dialog. Options to be selected are:

- **Item Name**: The item name for sale. Shown on the form and shopping cart.

- **Allow customer to specify the item name**: Check to swap the above Item Name for a box in which the web visitor can enter their own item name (also good for specifying donation details).

- **Show the item name on the form**: Uncheck to hide the above item name so it only appears in email confirmations and the shopping cart.

- **Item ID**: Add an easily identifiable string to track the item through PayPal.

- **Currency**: Set the currency in which the transaction will be made in.

- **Price**: The price for the item. Shown on-screen by default.

- **Allow customer to specify the amount**: Check to swap the above Price for a box in which the web visitor can enter their own price. Use with donation forms, where the customer sets the amount.

- **Show the price on the form**: Uncheck to hide the above item price.

- **Override the tax settings..**: Check to override provider's profile's tax setting for the item. If checked, specify a flat tax rate for the item, e.g. 0% for tax-free charitable donations.

  Choose from the above settings and click **Next>**.

  If you're using e-commerce database merging, this Item Details dialog will instead let you choose an e-commerce database for use with your chosen provider. Remember to set the currency you wish to trade in.

7. For e-commerce forms only, the next step can be used to define user-selectable options (only two options can be selected per form in PayPal) if required. Check the **Add an options field** box and create a fixed name, an edit box, radio buttons, or combo boxes as appropriate—you can design from scratch or use previously saved options fields. Click **Next>**. Not shown for repeating forms.

8. Set a default quantity in the input box, or check the box to let the user specify an amount at checkout (not shown for repeating forms).
   OR
   Set the Add Edit box option to let the customer define the quantity to be ordered.

9. For shipping and handling associated with the order, enter a set amount for the handling of the first item, every item or per order.
   If left blank, the default PayPal's profile will be used instead. Not shown for repeating forms. Click **Next>**.

10. In the Extra Customer Information dialog, choose to prompt the customer for an address, don't prompt, or require the customer to enter an address. Optionally, ask a question of the customer in the text box. Click **Next>**.

11. The Payment Pages dialog offers some payment settings, i.e.

    • Enter the name of your Checkout Page Style (if setup in advance via your PayPal login).

    • Set a language for the PayPal login page. Pick for the drop-down list.

    • Change the text for the Continue button on the Successful Payment Page.

    • If needed, define Successful Payment Pages and/or Cancelled Payment Pages. Enter the page's URL or select an entry from the drop-down list.

12. For e-commerce forms only, choose a form layout from the window. Several check box options let you control what gets shown on the form layout. You can disable price, and if repeating area forms are used, hide/show the item image, short/long descriptions, fixed options, and a dummy quantity edit box. Forms can be reformatted with the **Reformat form now** check box.

13. Click **Finish**.

14. 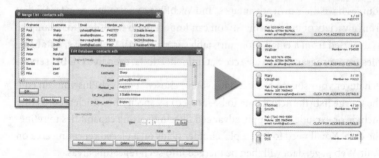 To insert the form or button, position the cursor where you want it to appear on the page, then simply click the mouse.

To edit an e-commerce form or button:

1. Select the form, right-click the form and choose **Edit E-Commerce Form...**.

   OR

   Select the button, right-click the button and choose **Edit E-Commerce Button...**.

2. Modify e-commerce settings screen-by-screen in the displayed dialog.

To convert to a standard form:

- Right-click on the existing e-commerce form and choose **Convert to Form**.

Database merge

Using database merge

Database merge means extracting the data contents of an existing database (Serif databases .SDB, Microsoft Access, dBASE), HTML, Excel file, ODBC, or delimited text file and presenting the information—for example into a repeating area or an HTML fragment. The contents, known as the **data source**, could be a mailing list, personnel list, product list, inventory, sales list. In fact any information which is suitable for storage.

As well as text, it is even possible to merge **picture data** (for example, a digital photo library) into single fields or even auto-create a grid layout of pictures and text suitable for catalogs or photo albums. WebPlus can even create a photo database automatically—a simple database using the .SDB (Serif Database) format—for a set of images in a folder. You can merge images into single fields or even auto-generate a repeating layout with a grid arrangement suitable for catalogs or photo albums.

Overview

For your basic database merge needs, WebPlus provides its own **Serif Database** file format. "SDB files" as they're called (since they use the *.SDB extension) are ideal for storing unformatted, plain text data typically used for product lists, but are suitable for other tasks as well. You can build a list by creating a new SDB file and then "fill in the blanks." One advantage of using the Serif Database format is that you can edit your data (even add new fields and information) directly within WebPlus. Of course, more complex data sources have their own advantages, and WebPlus can also merge external data from a variety of other formats. You can import **plain text files** (for example, as exported from a email program), tables from **HTML** Web pages, **database files** from programs such as Access, Outlook, Excel... even live **ODBC servers**!

Whatever your source of data, once you've chosen it in WebPlus you can edit the **merge list** (the actual data to be merged) by specifying which records to include or exclude, and apply advanced filtering/sorting capabilities to refine the data. You'll need to Insert placeholder fields on a placed repeating area on your Web page; data will then be merged into such repeating areas.

In no time, you'll be ready to Merge such that each repeating area is "regenerated" multiply within a new Web site with data from each record appearing in turn.

As more advanced merging features, you can use merge anchors to hyperlink between summary and main pages for each record. Additionally, merge fields can be inserted into generated page titles to allow navigation between summary lists/main pages. See Database merge additional features on p. 303.

In e-commerce, it's possible to use database merging using an e-commerce Serif database and repeating Buy Now forms or repeating Add to Shopping Cart forms. Repeating areas can also be used but e-commerce forms offer transactions directly with your shopping cart provider (e.g., PayPal, Mal's, etc.) in the form of Buy Now/Add to Shopping Cart buttons. (See Using database merge with e-commerce on p. 297).

Creating a data source

You can create a new Serif Database (*.SDB) file easily within WebPlus. This database, once populated, can be used as your data source which can be merged into your Web page.

To create a new Serif Database (*.SDB) file:

1. Select **Create Database** from the Database Merge toolbar (switch on first).

2. With "Serif Databases (*.SDB)" shown in the **Save as type** list, navigate to a folder and enter a file name for the new file, and click **Save**.

3. From the Customize Database dialog, click the **Insert...** button.

4. In the dialog, create each field that makes up your new database by providing a Field Name, clicking **OK** in turn.

5. The Edit Database dialog appears, displaying the first record with six fields in view. Scroll down to view additional fields if created. Since it's a new database, the fields will be blank; you can start entering information now (i.e., add a record), or wait until later. To enter information, simply type into a field. To create a new record, click **Add** then repeat for each record then once finished, click **OK**.

6. Click **OK** to close the Merge List dialog and return to the Web site.

WebPlus lets you create your own photo databases for showcasing digital art—EXIF data is also stored. See WebPlus help for more details.

Inserting repeating areas for your data

For merging to work correctly you'll need to include the contents of your data source on a Web page. WebPlus assists by allowing you to quickly create a **repeating layout** that arranges placeholder fields, generating a new document with as many pages as needed and populating the fields with text or images from a specified data source. You can create any number of data sources, but can only have one open at a time per repeating area.

Each repeating area has its own data source; only one repeating area can occupy each Web page.

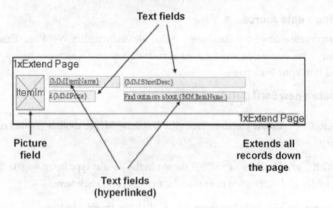

A repeating layout starts with a **repeating area**—basically a single cell whose unit size determines how many database records can tile across and down on a page. Within the repeating area, you can place any elements, such as:

- One or more **text fields** with data drawn from the same record.

- One or more **picture fields** where you want merged picture(s) from a particular data record to appear.

- Other objects such as artistic text, QuickShapes... anything you want!

You take care of creating the repeating area and placing the fields (or other elements), while WebPlus takes care of replicating them into a repeating grid layout and merging text or pictures from your data source into a new Web site. Each repeating area is "regenerated" multiply within the new Web site, with data from a different record appearing in turn.

To create a repeating layout:

1. Choose any suitable data source.

2. Click the ⬚ **Insert Repeating Area** button on the Database Merge toolbar (switch on first).

3. From the Choose Merge Database dialog, click **Browse...** to select a data source, click **Open**, then click **OK**. You can also create a new database at this point by clicking **New...** (see Creating a data source above).

4. The Tile Setup dialog appears, showing a page layout that initially consists of a 1x4 tiling grid: one repeating area across the page, and four down. The preview region at the left reflects the current dialog settings.

5. You can either set precise properties for the repeating area (the basic unit) in the dialog, or close the dialog and use direct dragging to establish the area's size and shape. Or you can use a combined approach, reopening the dialog as often as needed.

- Using the dialog, specify the grid **Layout** as the number of repeating areas you want to appear **Across** and **Down**. Other settings you can change include the **Left** and **Top Position** on the page, the repeating area's **Width** and **Height**, and optional horizontal or vertical **Gaps** between repeating areas. Check **Extend page to fit all tiles** to have all records shown on a single page (especially recommended for single-line summary lists)—the Down layout option is ignored.

- On the page, you can drag the repeating area object to move it, or drag a handle to resize it.

When you save a Web site, WebPlus "remembers" the current data source and reopens it "behind the scenes" automatically the next time you open the Web page—so as long as you're using the same source, you won't need to reopen it yourself.

To edit an existing repeating layout:

1. With repeating area selected, click the 🔡 Edit Layout button on the context toolbar.

2. The Tile Setup dialog appears, which lets you modify the repeating area layout.

Opening a different data source

As well as creating a Serif database file, WebPlus will also let you open a different already existing Serif database file or other external data source such as plain text file (comma-delimited or fixed-width), other database, spreadsheet, and more. You can edit, select, filter, and/or sort the actual data to be merged.

To open a different data source:

1. With repeating area selected, click the 🗄 Choose database button on the context toolbar.

2. In the dialog, click the **Browse...** button and from the down arrow on the file format drop-down list adjacent to the **File name** drop-down list, select the type of data source you want to open, and click **Open**.

3. Locate the file and click **Open**. Depending on the type of data source, follow any additional instructions provided by WebPlus. For example:

- **If the data source includes more than one table**: You'll be prompted to specify which table to import.

- **If you selected a text file** (.TXT, .CSV, .TAB, .ASC) with source data in delimited or fixed-width format: WebPlus displays a Data Format dialog, with a preview of the selected file's data.

- On the first screen, specify either **Delimited** or **Fixed Width**. If the first data record lists the titles of the various columns, check **First Line Contains Column Headers**. If your source file uses a **Text Qualifier** (for example, a quote mark to surround text fields like "Apt 3, 14 Hopalong Crescent" that might contain commas or otherwise be read as multiple fields), select the appropriate character in the list.

- Click **Next**. The appearance of the next screen depends on whether you've specified a delimited or fixed-width file. You can either specify the delimiter OR check (and correct, if necessary) the breaks used to separate the data fields. Double-check that the data preview appears correct, then click **Finish**.
  Note: Should you need to reformat the data once you've closed the wizard, simply reopen the source file and run through the Data Format dialog again, changing settings as needed.

4. Once you've completed any intermediate steps, the Choose Merge database dialog appears. If you click the **Edit...** button, the Merge List dialog appears, presenting the data in row/column format and allowing you to select, filter, and/or sort the actual data to be merged. You can make any necessary changes now or later.

5. Click **OK** to close the Merge List dialog and return to the Web page. The data source you've just opened remains the active data source.

Editing Serif Database files

Each record in a Serif Database (*.SDB) file contains 20 standard fields. For data stored in .SDB format, you can use the Edit Database dialog to create or delete records, enter information, find occurrences of specific text, or revise the field order—even add new fields and data.

Other database files are not editable.

To edit a Serif Database (*.SDB) file:

1. With repeating area selected, click the ⬚🗐 Choose database button on the context toolbar.

2. In the dialog, click the **Edit...** button. (If the button is disabled, the current data source is not an SDB file.)

3. The Merge List dialog appears, presenting the data in row/column format and allows you to edit, select, filter, and/or sort the actual data to be merged. You can make any necessary changes now or later.

4. The first record of the current database appears, with six fields in view (scroll down to view additional fields). Use the Edit Database dialog to edit the data.

- To enter information, simply type into a field. Each field is limited to a maximum of 255 characters.

- To create a new record, click **Add**.

- Use the arrow buttons to navigate between records, or type in a record number and press **Enter**.

- To delete the current record, click **Delete**. If you click **Delete** on the first record, its information is cleared, but the record form remains.

- To find occurrences of specific text, click **Find...** and specify the **Field** to be searched. The Record list displays any text appearing in that field throughout the database. Double-click an entry (or select it and click **OK**), to view that particular record.

- To customize the database fields, click **Customize....** In the dialog, click **Insert...** to create a new field, or select a field and click **Delete** to remove one. To rename a field, select it and click **Rename....** You can also click **Move Up** or **Move Down** to change the order of fields within the list.

5.   To update the list and dismiss the dialog, click **OK**.

Closing the Edit Database dialog does not close the database file; it remains the active data source for database merge purposes. However, any changes you've made are saved to disk at this time.

Inserting placeholders for your data

In order to merge information from a structured data source into a Web page, you need to insert **placeholder fields** into your created repeating area (see above) so WebPlus knows which fields' data to use. There are actually two kinds of placeholders. **Text fields** obviously handle text-based information like address list data; picture fields will add images retrieved from stored file path names in your database.

To insert a text or picture field placeholder:

1. With repeating area selected, click the 🖺 **Insert Text Field** or 🖼 **Insert Picture Field** button on the context toolbar.

   A dialog appears, displaying a list of fields (text or picture) in the currently selected data source.

2. From the scrolling list in the dialog, double-click the field to insert (or select it and click **Insert**).

3. The field appears on your Web page. The dialog remains open so you can insert additional fields if needed.

4. Drag each field so that it is placed exactly within your repeating area— resize if necessary. There's a subtle "locking moment" (with Snapping either on or off) when the field attaches to the repeat area. The field's contents turn shaded and subsequently, dragging the repeating area object also drags its contents.

   For picture fields, set display properties such as picture size and alignment within the picture field, right-click the field and choose **Frame Properties....** Typically, the **Scale to Minimum Fit** option works best for Picture fields. You can also resize the frame itself by dragging its handles.

5. To dismiss the dialog, click **Close**.

Selecting, filtering, and sorting the merge list

Whatever kind of data source you're using, at any time you can view the current data in row/column format, with the option of customizing the **merge list** (the actual data to be merged) by including or excluding specific records. You can do this "by hand" or preferably by applying powerful filtering and sorting options that let you include just certain records, or arrange records in order, based on the contents of specific fields. For example, with an address list or contact database you could sort by postal code and then by last name.

To edit the current merge list:

1. With repeating area selected, click the 🔲 Choose database button on the context toolbar.

2. Use the **Edit...** button to access the Merge List dialog.

3. Specify which records to include or exclude (by checking/unchecking), and apply advanced filtering/sorting capabilities (via **Filter...** button) to refine the data.

4. Click **OK**.

Merging and publishing

Once you've selected which records to merge (your **merge list**) and inserted all necessary placeholders as detailed above, you're ready to merge your database content to a temporary Web site, and then publish.

To merge to a new Web site:

1. Click the 🔲 Merge to New Site button on the context toolbar.

2. WebPlus now generates a new Web site in a separate window, replicating the basic repeating area as many times as there are records in the data. The layout uses the grid arrangement you specified, with each unique cell including data from a single record, following the order of records in the merge list. WebPlus inserts new pages as needed to include all the records. Note that the repeating area is no longer present; it's been converted to a grid layout using merged data rather than placeholder fields.

> Should you need to adjust display properties such as picture size and alignment for any individual picture frame, right-click the frame and choose **Frame Properties...**.

The original Web site remains open in its own window. Don't forget to save it in case you need to repeat the merge process with another data set! If you're not happy with the resulting Web site, simply return to the original, make adjustments, and repeat the merge process.

To publish your Web site:

With your merged site currently active, choose **Publish Site>** on the File menu and select Publish to Web (see p. 322).

> By default, merging will take place automatically before you publish; if you don't want to merge each time, uncheck Merge before publishing in the Publish to Web dialog.

Using database merge with e-commerce

Basic database merges can be used for presenting text, images or a combination of both as display-only data, e.g. lists, galleries, etc. However, when used in conjunction with a more interactive feature such as repeating e-commerce forms, it is possible to create e-commerce solutions that are driven by e-commerce data sources containing saleable items. The database, which must be a Serif database file (.SDB), must adopt a field structure specific to your chosen shopping cart provider (e.g., PayPal) and can store item name, description, item image, price, quantities, shipping costs, and other buying options (colour, size, etc).

Typically, a specific type of e-commerce form can be added to the page which will allow e-commerce transactions to be performed. For single item purchases, a **Repeating Buy Now Form** takes the user straight to checkout, while multi-item purchases use a **Repeating Add to Shopping Cart Form**. As both forms are repeating, the form is "regenerated" multiply within a new merged Web site with data from each item record appearing in turn. See Inserting an e-commerce object (PAYPAL) on p. 281 for more information.

Instead of a repeating form, a **Repeating E-Commerce Area** can be placed on the Web page. This is essentially a display-only version of the above forms without the Buy Now or Add to Shopping Cart buttons, i.e. you can view items but not buy them.

As with basic database merges, e-commerce database merging can make use of merge lists to select, filter, and/or sort the actual data to be merged. Once a merge list is defined, merging and publishing can be performed. (See Merging and publishing on p. 296).

Creating an e-commerce data source

You can create an e-commerce database within WebPlus by choosing a shopping cart provider and choosing provider-specific database fields. This database, once populated with item records (i.e. the things you want to sell), can be used as your e-commerce data source which can be merged to a new Web site.

To create a new e-commerce database:

1. Select ⁺▤ **Create E-Commerce Database** from the Database Merge toolbar (switch on first).

2. From the dialog, select your shopping cart provider (PayPal, etc.) that you're already signed up to by clicking the appropriate radio button. If you're not signed up to a provider use the **Sign Up Now** button.

3. From the dialog, with "Serif Databases (*.SDB)" shown in the **Save as type** list, navigate to a folder and enter a file name for the new file, and click **Save**.

4. In the Customize Database dialog, you'll be presented with a list of pre-defined fields that will make up the database; these fields are specific to your provider. You can modify this database structure by adding, removing, renaming or reordering fields to suit your purpose.

   - To add a new field, click the **Insert...** button.

   - To remove a field, select it and click the **Delete** button.

   - To rename a field, select it and click the **Rename...** button. Enter the new name in the dialog.

   - To rearrange the field order, use the **Move Up** or **Move Down** button on a field to be moved.

5. Click **OK** to finish field selection.

6. From the E-Commerce Merge List dialog, click the **Add...** button.

7. From the Item Details dialog, add e-commerce database records as described in Inserting an e-commerce object on p. 281.

8. Click **OK** to close the dialog.

To edit your e-commerce database, see Editing Serif database files on p. 293.

Inserting e-commerce forms and repeating areas

If you plan to work with e-commerce, you can choose to work in two ways. Either using repeating e-commerce forms or repeating e-commerce areas. The former offers interactivity with your shopping cart provider, i.e. the user can access PayPal to perform the transaction. The latter does not interact with the provider so can be used only for displaying items.

To insert a repeating e-commerce form:

1. Click the ![icon] **Insert an E-Commerce object** button on the Web Objects toolbar's E-Commerce flyout.

    OR

    Select ![icon] **Insert Repeating E-Commerce Form** from the Database Merge toolbar (switch on first).

2. From the dialog, select your shopping cart provider (PayPal, etc.) that you're already signed up to by clicking the appropriate radio button. If you're not signed up to a provider use the **Sign Up Now** button. Click **Next>**.

3. (Optional; for new sites only) In the dialog, enter the email address which is to receive the payment information. Click **Next>**.

4. (Optional) In the next dialog, uncheck the **Use the site default address** box and set a different email address to override the site default.

5. Pick a repeating form object type from the PayPal Form box. Enable either:

    - **Repeating Buy Now Form**: For single item purchases. This form offers Buy Now buttons to direct the shopper straight to checkout. Items are retrieved from a provider-specific e-commerce database and are listed repeatedly in merged Web pages.

      OR

      Repeating Add to Shopping Cart Form: For multi-item purchases. As above but shopper is directed to a shopping cart.

      OR

      Repeating Area: For displaying items only. No Buy Now or Add to Shopping Cart buttons are defined.

6. In the next dialog, choose how the Buy Now or Add to Shopping Cart buttons are to appear (first two options only).

7. From the Item Details dialog, browse to an existing e-commerce data source or create a new one. Set a currency for pricing fields in your database.

8. In the Extra Customer Information dialog, choose to prompt the customer for an address, don't prompt, or require the customer to enter an address. Optionally, ask a question of the customer in the text box. Click **Next>**.

9. The Payment Pages dialog offers some payment settings, i.e.

   • Enter the name of your Checkout Page Style (if setup in advance via your PayPal login).

   • Set a language for the PayPal login page. Pick for the drop-down list.

   • Change the text for the Continue button on the Successful Payment Page.

   • If needed, define Successful Payment Pages and/or Cancelled Payment Pages. Enter the page's URL or select an entry from the drop-down list.

10. Choose a form layout from the window. Several check box options let you control what gets shown on the form layout. You can disable price, and if repeating area forms are used, hide/show the item image, short/long descriptions, fixed options, and a dummy quantity edit box. Forms can be reformatted with the **Reformat form now** or **Reformat form after merge** check boxes.

11. Click **Finish**.

12. To insert the form or button, position the cursor where you want it to appear on the page, then simply click the mouse. The form is placed on the page with fields positioned in their default location (according to the chosen form layout above).

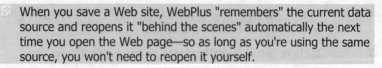

When you save a Web site, WebPlus "remembers" the current data source and reopens it "behind the scenes" automatically the next time you open the Web page—so as long as you're using the same source, you won't need to reopen it yourself.

To edit a repeating e-commerce form:

1. Double-click the body of the form.
   OR
   Right-click on the form and choose **Edit Repeating E-Commerce Form**.

2. Run through each dialog, modifying settings, then click **Finish**. The form is reformatted.

Optionally, you can modify the look and feel of your form object in the page. Each form field can be moved, resized or deleted according to requirements.

Avoid dragging a form field away from its form object. Doing so will prevent the field from repeating.

To create a repeating e-commerce area:

1. Choose any suitable e-commerce data source.

2. Click the ⊞ **Insert Repeating E-Commerce Area** button on the Database Merge toolbar (switch on first).

3. From the dialog, select your shopping cart provider (PayPal, etc.) that you're already signed up to by clicking the appropriate radio button. If you're not signed up to a provider use the **Sign Up Now** button.

4. From the Choose E-Commerce Merge Database dialog, click **Browse...** to select a data source, click **Open**, then click **OK**. You can also create a new database at this point by clicking **New....** Set the currency you wish to sell in.

5. The Repeating Area Tile Setup dialog appears which lets you position and/or resize the area (See Inserting e-commerce repeating areas for your data on p. 290 for more details).

6. Click **OK**.

Database merge additional features

The use of database merging, whether using e-commerce or not, is enhanced by using some additional features. These features may offer differing ways of presenting record data or improve the navigability of merged pages, especially between summary/full description pages.

Adding repeating HTML fragments

Repeating areas can be used to create simple drop-down menus, perhaps listing products, options, or email addresses (below) derived from a database. You can apply scripting to each option to initiate some action.

Remember that for combo boxes with a limited set of options you can use WebPlus forms instead (see p. 255).

To add a repeating HTML fragment:

1. Select **Insert Repeating HTML Fragment** from the Database Merge toolbar (switch on first).

2. You'll see the Paste cursor. What you do next determines the initial size and placement of the HTML fragment.

    To insert the HTML fragment area at a default size, simply click the mouse.
    OR
    To set the size of the area, drag out a region and release the mouse button.

3. With repeating fragment selected, click the ⊞ **Choose database** button on the context toolbar to link to a database.

4. Double-click on the fragment to view and edit the underlying HTML code.
   OR
   Select **Attach HTML** from the context toolbar.

5. Specific HTML tags and database fields need to be inserted (by typing) within the Body Preamble tags—SELECT to create the object, OPTION to allow the database field name to be placed as a repeating area, and the database field within the OPTION tags. Use the illustration below as a guide. Of course, you'll need to replace the example ItemName field with your own database field name(s).

```
<!--Body Preamble--><SELECT>
{{FOR}}
  <!--Repeating Body-->
            <OPTION>
            {MM:ItemName}
            </OPTION>
{{ENDFOR}}
  <!--Body Postamble--></SELECT>
```

6. Merge your site and then preview your Web page.

See Attaching HTML code on p. 249 if you need to brush up on HTML editing.

Adding merge anchors

Merge anchors can be used when hyperlinking between an item name in a simple summary list to its associated full description page. The named anchor is created on the repeating area/form on the full description page which allows a hyperlink (created in the Hyperlinks dialog; below) to be made. See Adding hyperlinks and anchors on p. 225.

Once the database is merged to a new Web site, the merged pages maintain the summary/full description links for each record stored in the database. To do this, the **Same record as origin of link** option has to be selected for the hyperlink's anchor (e.g., FullDesc).

For page navigation between next or previous records, the **Next record after origin of link** or **Previous record after origin of link** option can be selected with the anchor when defining the hyperlink (e.g., a Next link) between full description Web pages.

Adding merge fields

In the example above, you may have noticed an unusual looking field {MM:ItemName} as the Page name. This is a merge field which can be inserted into full description Page names to correctly reference the item name in the page title. The field can also be used to declare fields in repeating HTML fragments.

To add a merge field:

1. Right-click on a page, and select **Page Properties....**

2. In the Page name box, click the ▤ **Insert merge field** button at your chosen insertion point.

3. From the Insert Text Field dialog, pick a field for insertion from the field list, then click the **Insert** button.

4. Click **OK**.

After merging, each merged full description page will be correctly titled with the currently viewable item.

Smart objects

Using Smart objects

It's quite common for Web developers to "inherit" content from existing web sites to save time and effort, while bearing in mind any legal implications in doing so. This is fine for simple graphic or text copying, but this process is not possible for more complex, interactive objects such as counters, shout boxes, blogs, etc, which collect information with the object. The power of, for example, a hit counter lies in its ability to keep a count of the number of users that have visited a page at all times. The count needs to be stored somewhere and herein lies the problem. Storing object data (counts, chat text, blog text, is not always encouraged or even supported on ISP web space—due to potential security breaches and disk usage demands. So where can the data be stored?

To resolve the problem for Serif WebPlus users, WebPlus can place such server-sided objects, called **Smart objects**, on the page and also store associated object data on Serif's own secure server space. These objects are available from **Serif Web Resources**, a secure online service for obtaining objects and storing data at the same time. All Smart objects operate with a range of languages.

An advantage of using Serif's Smart objects is that they are optimized and fully tested for use in your current WebPlus project. In addition, the objects are hosted online so new updates may be added over time without having to load WebPlus and republish parts of your site.

Let's look at each Smart object you'll find in Web Resources and what you can do with them.

Name	Use
Access Control	Control site accessibility by using user lists or user groups.

Access Control

- Enable CAPTCHA anti-spam protection.

- Create user groups (with optional user sign-up, auto-login, and connection to Smart objects).

- Add, remove, suspend, or ban users from user groups.

See Access Control on p. 70 for more details.

Active Viewers

Use to show how many people are currently viewing the web page.

Blog

A blog (short for weblog) acts as a personal journal on your web page which hosts your own published articles in an easy-to-use RTF editor. Articles can be commented on by visitors to the Web page. With blogs you can:

- Add your own personal **profile**

- Add **social bookmarking links**

- Use article **trackbacks** for inter-blog cross-referencing; use receive trackbacks.

- Use **tagging** to categorize articles for easier user access.

- Enable users to subscribe to articles (most recent articles/comments) via RSS feed readers.

- Enable CAPTCHA anti-spam protection.

- Apply a **Visual Styles** (theme) to your blog

- Use **Editor groups** for multi-author article publishing

Forum	Add a thread-based discussion forum to your Web site, optionally in a full-sized window. With forums you can:

- Under different **categories** (e.g., Motoring) add multiple **subforums** (Classics, Convertibles, Custom, etc.)

- Establish user **access control**

- Add **moderator groups**

- Set forum **privacy** as publicly readable or private

- Apply a **theme** (style) to the overall forum object

- Create, edit, and assign **user ranks**

- Set **user permissions**

Users can view number of topics, posts, and last post submitted, and obviously post to the forum.

For an in-depth look at forums, follow the *Adding a Forum to your Site* tutorial on the WebPlus Resource CD (if purchased).

Hit Counter	A straightforward count of the number of hits on the current page (reset as needed). Different styles can be adopted.
Mailing List	Have web site visitors sign up to newsletters, party confirmations, information request, and many more. After the visitor confirms addition to the mailing list by return email, the email address is stored with other subscribers for future correspondence.
News	Add a news window onto your page. The object supports RTF editing as well as paragraph styles, hyperlinks, inserted media, and even HTML source editing.
Poll	Set up an online poll to canvass web visitor's opinions.

Shout Box   Acts as an interactive chat window similar to Windows Messenger. Let your web visitors chat amongst themselves.

Analytics   Collect and display Web usage statistics via the Web Analytics. This is enabled via Site Properties (see p. 55) and cannot be added to the page.

For security reasons, the objects are only available via a Serif **Web Resources** login accessible from within WebPlus. If you don't have a valid username and password you must create a Web Resources account first.

- If your email address is already known to Serif (maybe you've just registered or have registered previously) you'll be asked for a limited number of questions to completed account registration.

- If you're new to Serif and unregistered you'll have to complete full security as required. Full instructions are provided on login screens.

To create a Serif Web Resources account:

1. Click the   **Smart Object Tool** button on the Web Objects toolbar.

2. In the login dialog, click the **Create Account** link under the login boxes.

3. In the next dialog, enter your current email address and a password twice. You'll need to review and agree to Serif's terms and conditions of use (via a check box).

4. Click the **Signup** button.

5. An additional dialog, will ask for personal details, plus a few check boxes if you would like to receive the Serif Community newsletter, Serif offers, and/or other third-party offers.

6. A confirmation email will be sent to your email address. Click the link in the email and you're ready to login to Serif Web Resources (by clicking the Smart Object Tool again).

To clear Account details:

- Go to **Tools>Options** and click **Clear Account Details** shown from the General menu option. This will clear the stored login details for Serif Web Resources so that automatic login will no longer work. Details will need to be entered next time so be sure you've remembered your password.

To access Web Resources:

1. Click the [icon] **Smart Object Tool** button on the Web Objects toolbar.

2. At the login prompt enter your username and your password. Check **Remember account details** to access Web Resources directly in future (bypassing the login screen).

3. Click the **Login** button. The Smart objects dialog is displayed.

Creating Smart objects

Think of a Smart object as being a general term for elements that you'll use on your page—as discussed previously. Smart objects are not added directly to the page from Serif Web Resources, but are first added to your own object library (the library lets you manage and edit each object)—objects can then be added to the web page immediately or at a later date.

> Some Smart objects are conditional on another Smart Object being created first. An example is the Forum Smart Object which requires the Access Control object to be created first.

To add an object to the library:

1. Select the **New...** button at the bottom of the My Smart Objects Library pane.

2. In the **Create Smart Object** dialog, use the scroll bar to navigate the list of Smart objects, hover over an object of interest and click.

3. (Optional) For your Smart Object to operate in a language other than English, select from the **Language** drop-down menu.

4. Select **OK**. Depending on the type of object selected, a different Create dialog will be displayed showing options specific to the Smart object.

For detailed help on the options available for each Smart object, use the context-sensitive Help button in the Create dialog.

5. From the dialog, change the **Name** of the object and optionally a **Filter Offsite** string (this prevents the URL from being copied). Optionally, change the object specific settings, e.g. for some objects you can also set the titling, colours (for body, text and border), and border thickness if appropriate.

6. Click **OK**.

The named object will be shown in a list in the My Smart Objects left-hand pane. Here's an example of all Smart objects , i.e.

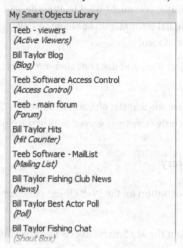

All Smart objects can be added to the page, but sometimes it makes sense for some Smart objects (i.e., forums and blogs) to not be added to a Web page and instead access Serif Web Resources directly (via offsite links or hyperlinks; see p. 38 or p. 225, respectively). The main advantage is that there is no constraint by having the forum or blog contained within your page dimensions (avoiding window scrolling).

To add a Smart object to your web page:

1. From the Smart Objects dialog, select the chosen object from the left-hand pane and click the **Insert** button.

2. ⊞ To insert the object at a default size, position the cursor where you want the object to appear on the page, then simply click the mouse.

The Smart Object will automatically preview on the page so you'll get a good feel for how your published Smart object will look.

Editing Smart objects

Once an object is created it can be edited either in the My Smart Object Library or directly on the page. Typically, you might want to alter the appearance of the object from its original settings, maybe change a Poll question, or reset a Hit Counter back to zero.

Editing an object only affects the object itself and does not alter any collected data.

The dialog options for editing and creating a Smart object are the same, except that the object's Name is read only (shown as greyed out) in the object edit dialogs.

To edit a Smart object in your library:

1. Click the 🗿 **Smart Object Tool** button on the Web Objects toolbar (and login if necessary).

2. Select a Smart object for edit from the My Smart Objects Library pane.

3. In the adjacent window, select the Edit... button under the object preview.

The selected object's edit dialog is displayed. For detailed help on the editing options available on each Smart object, use the context-sensitive Help button in the Edit dialog.

To edit a Smart object on your page:

- Double-click the object to reveal the object's Edit dialog.

If you edit an object on the web page the change is also reflected in the Objects library and vice versa.

Managing Smart objects

While editing Smart objects affects how the object operates, managing Smart objects can be used to manage the object's "gathered" data when the Web page is published. Some Smart objects such as Hit Counters don't need to be managed as they just increment on each web visit (you can reset the counters though). However, other more complex Smart objects, such as forums/blogs, mailing lists, polls, and shout boxes will store articles, email addresses, poll results, and a chat messaging log, respectively.

For detailed help on the management options available, use the context-sensitive Help button next to the Smart object.

To manage a Smart object from your library:

1. Click the **Smart Object Tool** button on the Web Objects toolbar (and login if necessary).

2. Select the object from the My Smart Objects Library pane.

3. In the adjacent window, select the Manage... button under the object preview. The next step depends on the object type, i.e.

Object type	Reason for object management	How?
Access Control	Control site accessibility by using user lists or user groups. <ul><li>Enable CAPTCHA anti-spam protection.</li><li>Create user groups (with optional user sign-up, auto-login, and connection to Smart objects).</li></ul>	• See Access Control on p. 70.

	• Add, remove, suspend, or ban users from user groups.	
Blog	Add, edit, or delete articles. Add and manage comments associated with articles. Pick an **Editor group** for multi-author article publishing.	• Click the **New** button to add an article.
	For new article (or ones for edit) you can create/edit your article in RTF, add tags, pick article poster, allow trackbacks, and make comments	• Click the **Edit** button to edit an existing article in your blog.
		• Click the **Delete** button to delete an existing article in your blog.
		• Click the **Comments** button to access a Manage Blog dialog. To remove a comment, select it and click the **Delete** button.
		• Select an **Editors group** from the drop-down list. This lets you select a previously created multi-author user group where logged-in authors can each create articles.

Forum	Manage forum with respect to privacy, category/subforum control, moderation, theme, and user ranking (most posts, special rank such as Site Supporter).	• Set permissions for non-registered visitors from the **Forum Privacy** drop-down list.

• In the **Forum Management** section, use **Add Category** and **Add Forum** buttons to create a new category or subforum. Once created, edit Category/forum names and click **Update Category** or **Update Forum.**

• Set a different look and feel from the **Forum Themes** drop-down list.

• In User Rank Management, create a new rank title from **Add New Rank** (by minimum posts or special status such as Site Supporter), and then assign a user to that rank in the **Rank User** drop-down list. Edit ranks via the Edit Ranks section.

Mailing List	Remove a web visitor's email address (or all email addresses), save to a delimited text file (CSV), or synchronize gathered email addresses with an Access Control Smart object.	• To delete an email address, select an entry and press the **Delete** key, or for all addresses, press the **Clear All** key.
		• To save the mailing list to a file, choose the format from the **Save As** drop-down list and click the **Save** button.
		• To sync to an Access Control Smart object, click the **Sync To Access Control** button.
News	To update the news article.	• Edit the text as for any RTF word processor, then click the **Save** button.
Poll	Zero the votes for a specific voting option or reset entire poll.	• Click the **Click here to zero the votes for this option** link or click the **Reset All** button.
Shout Box	Removal of unwanted text lines.	• Select an entry and press the **Delete** key, or for entries, press the **Clear All** key.
Analytics	View Web page statistics such as number of visits, browsing environments, referrers, and most submitted search terms.	• Select a statistics category from the drop-down menu.
		• Select a time period for which the statistics are presented.

- Some of the Smart objects such as forums and blogs take more time to set up correctly. As a result, advanced help is available for each Smart Object from within Serif Web Resources. A help button is located next to each Smart Object in your Smart Objects Library.

To manage Smart objects directly over the Internet:

- Login to serifwebresources.com to control all your Smart objects independently of your WebPlus project. Use your usual Web Resources login as before.

Deleting Smart objects

To delete an object from the library:

- Select the object's entry in the My Smart Objects Library pane and click the **Delete** button. A confirmation message is displayed.

This will cause any uploaded web page which includes the object to display an empty space until the object is removed from the corresponding WebPlus's web page and the web site uploaded again.

To delete an object on your page:

- Select the object and press the **Delete** key.

Previewing
and Publishing
to Web

13

Previewing your Web site

Previewing your site in a Web browser is an essential step before publishing it to the Web. It's the only way you can see just how your site will appear to a visitor. You can **preview** a page or site at any time, either within WebPlus (using an internal window based on the Internet Explorer browser) or separately using any browser installed on your system.

To preview your Web site:

1. Click the down arrow on the   **HTML Preview** button on the Standard toolbar.

2. Select an option from the submenu:

    - **Preview in Window** (shortcut **Alt+P**) opens the site in a new internal WebPlus window with its own tab for convenient switching. (For details on using multiple windows, see Working with more than one site or window on p. 24).

    - Choose **Preview Page...** or **Preview Site...** to use an external browser. The names will reflect which browsers are currently installed, e.g. the entry may read "Preview Page in Internet Explorer." If you have more than one browser installed, you can select which browser(s) to display on the submenu. The page or site is exported to a temporary folder and appears in the specified browser.

When previewing in a window, you can use the Preview context toolbar to control the preview window. Click the toolbar buttons to navigate **Back** and **Forward**, **Refresh** or **Close Preview**, and redisplay the page at one of several standard or custom screen resolutions (all from a drop-down menu).

To customize the list of browsers on the submenu:

1. Choose **Preview Site** from the File menu (or from the Preview flyout on the Standard toolbar) and select **Browser Preview List...** from the submenu.

    The dialog displays a list of browsers registered on your system. The WebPlus **Preview** submenu will list these in the order they're shown here.

2. Use the dialog to make changes as needed:

    - Click **Auto Detect** to refresh the list automatically, or click **Add** to display a dialog that lets you locate a particular browser to manually add to the list.

    - To delete an entry from the list, select it and click **Remove**.

    - You can rearrange the list by selecting an entry and clicking **Move Up** or **Move Down**.

    - To change the entry's name on the submenu or its path, select the entry and click **Edit**. For example, you could change "Internet Explorer" to appear as simply "IE7".

3. Click **OK** to confirm any changes.

> It is good practice to install several of the common browsers in order to test how your site will look on an alternative system.

Publishing to the Web

Publishing to the Web involves uploading your completed Web project to your Web host provider, turning your project into a live Web site, viewable by the whole world! You can specify that all Web pages are published or, if updating your site, only pages changed since the last "publish."

Before publishing to the Web, it is worth checking for potential problems by running the Site Checker (**Tools>Site Manager>Site Checker...**).

> Remember that you can publish to disk folder at any time, which lets you test your Web site offline (and locally) before publishing to Web. See online Help for more details.

To publish your site to the Web:

1. Choose **Site Properties...** from the File menu and double-check export settings, particularly those on the Graphics tab.

2. Click the 🖳 **Publish to Web** button on the Standard toolbar (or choose **Publish Site** from the File menu and select **Publish to Web...** from the submenu).

If this is your first time publishing to the Web, you'll see a Publish to Web dialog without any account information present (you'll see your local Web site ready to upload). You'll need to set up at least one account before you can proceed. See the **Accessing your free Web space** tutorial for more information on ISP hosting.

3. Click the **Accounts...** button to display the **Account Details** dialog.

4. In the dialog, enter:

   - The **Account name**. This can be any name of your choice. You'll use it to identify this account in WebPlus (in case you have more than one).

   - The **FTP address** of your Web host will be a specific URL starting with "ftp://" as supplied by your service provider.

   - **Port number**: Unless directed by your provider, you can leave this set at "21."

   - Leave the **Folder** box blank unless directed by your provider, or if you want to publish to a specific subfolder of your root directory.

   - You'll also need a **Username** and **Password** as pre-assigned by the provider. Most likely these will correspond to email login settings. Be sure to enter the password exactly as given to you, using correct upper- and lower-case spelling, or the host server may not recognize it. Check **Save password** to record the password on your computer, if you don't want to re-enter it with each upload.

   - **Passive mode**: Leave checked unless you have FTP connection problems (check with your ISP). ISPs can operate passive or active FTP modes of operation.

- **Web site URL**: Set your site's URL. This allows you to view the web site from a dialog after FTP upload.

- Click **OK** to close Account Details.

You can also use the dialog at this point to **Add...** another account, and **Copy...**, **Edit** or **Delete** an account selected from the drop-down menu. It's a good idea to test your new or modified account by clicking the **Test** button—a dialog showing Web site details is displayed if the test is successful.

5. If you've set up at least one account and clicked the **Upload...** button, the **Publish to Web** dialog appears with the last used account name shown in the drop-down menu and its settings in subsequent boxes. The drop-down menu lets you swap to another account. Select the account you want to use (if you've more than one).

6. If your Web site is using a database, the **Merge before publishing** option is checked. Clear this option only if you do not wish to merge changes (the option will be greyed out if no database/changes are detected). For more on databases, see Using database merge.

7. For the greatest control over the publishing, ensure that the **Unattended upload** check box is cleared. This will allow you to review the changes that will take place to your published Web site before they are made. It will also give you the option to cancel the upload if you discover a problem. (See Automatic Operation on p . 325 for more details on this feature.)

8. Choose which pages you want to upload—check specific page(s) in the window or **Publish All Pages**. Use the **Toggle Select**, **Toggle Branch** and **Select All** buttons to aid page selection.

9. To safeguard your WebPlus project, check the **Backup the document to the remote server** option. If the project is unsaved you'll be prompted to save it.

10. Click **OK**. WebPlus seeks an Internet connection, then:

11. If uploading for the first time, selected files will be uploaded directly.
    OR
    If uploading to an existing site, an Uploading Files dialog is displayed showing local file action (whether files will be added (Add), will replace the live file (Replace) or not updated (Leave)).

    In the dialog, check the option to Delete unused remote files if you want WebPlus to automatically remove any unused graphic and page files.

    Select either the **Incremental Update** or **Full upload** Button. Choose the former to upload only files that have altered since the last upload. When doing an incremental update, you can get WebPlus to **Check for missing files** by checking the option box. However, as this can dramatically slow the upload, this option is unchecked by default.

    You'll see a message when all files have been successfully copied. Click **OK**.

12. You'll be able to see your page(s) "live" on the Web following upload. Use the displayed Web Site Publishing dialog to view the site in your Web browser to the URL of your live site.

If you rename/delete files and then republish one or a few pages to the Web, the old files are not deleted automatically so you'll need to delete these manually by using **Publish Web Site>Maintain Web Site...** on the File Menu. However, if you republish the whole site to the Web automatically (using Automatic Operation), you can choose to delete any unused files; check the **Delete unused files** check box.

Automatic Operation

If you have a very large Web site, you may want to use the Automatic Operation feature. The actual process is virtually the same but it allows you to upload the site without having to "OK" each dialog that may appear. This is especially useful if you are updating a site containing a large database with images.

1. If you do not wish to merge any database changes, clear the **Merge before publishing** option. (This will be greyed out if there is no database linked to the pages being published or if the database has already been merged.)

2. Choose which pages you want to upload—check specific page(s) in the window or **Publish All Pages**. Use the **Toggle Select**, **Toggle Branch** and **Select All** buttons to aid page selection.

3. To safeguard your WebPlus project, check the **Backup the document to the remote server** option. If the project is unsaved you'll be prompted to save it.

4. Click **OK** to begin the upload process. (Now is the time to get that cup of tea...)

5. Once the upload is complete, the Uploading files dialog will remain on screen until you click **Close**. You will now be able to view your live site.

Trouble Shooting

After publishing your Web site, you may find that some changes are missing. Before you attempt to do another upload, try clearing the cache on your browser. To clear the cache, press **Ctrl+F5**. This will often cure any problems relating to the display of images and other objects.

If clearing the cache doesn't resolve the problems, you may need to manually delete old image files or objects. See Maintaining your Web site in online Help.

Viewing your published site

Once your site has been published, you have the option to 🖳 **View Site Online** on the Standard toolbar. This displays your site in its most recently published state in the default web browser. The first time View site online is used, a dialog pops up asking for the default site URL. This can be amended later using the **Site Properties...** dialog.

🔍▾ It is important to remember that any changes made since publishing will not be reflected. To see unpublished changes, use **HTML Preview** button. (See Previewing your Web site on p. 321).

Index

14